FOR SO LONG AS THE SUN AND MOON ENDURE

Indian Records
from the
North Carolina
General Assembly
Sessions &
Other Sources

William L. Byrd, III

HERITAGE BOOKS
2006

HERITAGE BOOKS
AN IMPRINT OF HERITAGE BOOKS, INC.

Books, CDs, and more—Worldwide

For our listing of thousands of titles see our website at
www.HeritageBooks.com

Published 2006 by
HERITAGE BOOKS, INC.
Publishing Division
65 East Main Street
Westminster, Maryland 21157-5026

Copyright © 2005 William L. Byrd, III

All rights reserved. No part of this book may be reproduced or transmitted in any form or by any means, electronic or mechanical, including photocopying, recording or by any information storage and retrieval system without written permission from the author, except for the inclusion of brief quotations in a review.

International Standard Book Number: 978-0-7884-3588-4

For Tina

Contents

CONTENTS V

INTRODUCTION VII

ACKNOWLEDGEMENTS IX

CHAPTER ONE 1
   TUSCARORA RECORDS 1

CHAPTER TWO 163
   GENERAL ASSEMBLY SESSIONS 163

CHAPTER THREE 187
   GOVERNOR'S OFFICE 187

CHAPTER FOUR 259
   NORTH CAROLINA LAWS 259

INDEX 297

Introduction

The records in this book were gleaned from papers found in the North Carolina State Archives, the University of North Carolina, and Duke University.

Chapter one is comprised of records pertaining to the Tuscarora Indians of North Carolina and New York. The plight of the Tuscaroras has long been controversial in the State of North Carolina. As late as 1911, members of the Tuscarora Nation of New York were inquiring about their land. Information and statements made by various parties in this book may shed light on this issue. Any person affiliated [with] or researching the Tuscarora Nation should read this book.

Chapter two of this book contains Indian records from the General Assembly Sessions of the State of North Carolina. Chapter three contains Indian related papers from the Governor's Office, and Chapter Four contains the laws of North Carolina relating to the Indians of North Carolina.

Acknowledgements

All acknowledgements regarding this book belong to the staff of the North Carolina State Archives. Without their help, it would not have been possible. Also, a great deal of the driving force behind the publishing of this book and other books is due to my wife and partner, Tina, who was always there to give me a little nudge when I needed it.

Chapter One
Tuscarora Records

Chapter One

Tuscarora Records

"NORTH CAROLINA HISTORICAL AND GENEALOGICAL REGISTER"
VOLUME 2, PAGES 218-219
J.R.B. HATHAWAY, ED., (EDENTON, 1900-1903)

1. That there be a firm, perpetual and invioble peace to continue so long as Sun and Moon Endure between all and every the Inhabitants and people of North Carolina and all the nation and people of the Tuscaroroe Indians.

2. That iff any occasione of difference should followeth thatt there may be as soon as conveniently can be a meeting of the greatt men appointed to settle itt friendly and peaceably.

3. That iff any Servant, Servants, Slave or Slaves come among the Tuscaroroe Indians That they Forthwith with all Expedition and Diligence apprehend him or them and bring them in and what arms or goods they may have with them to some of the greatt men of the English who shall be obleidged to give them a Matchcoat or the Value for their trouble.

4. Iff any Englishmen of this Government shall injure or wrong any of the Tuscaroroe Indians upon complaint and proofe to the Great Men of this Government the English shall be ordered to make Satisfactione to him or them injured according to law.

Chapter One
Tuscarora Records

5. Iff any Tuscaroroe Indians shall steall, purloine or doe any other injury to the English not exceeding the value of twoe or three skins then the sd Indian being brought before some greatt man of the English and proofe made of itt he shall order the Indian to make present satisfaction to the person injured which if he doe nott he shall order him to have lashes.

6. If any Tuscaroroe Indian shall kill any of the English or Steall a robe more than the Value of the 3 skins above mentioned or doe any injury to any of the English that shall deserve death or Banishment to be broughtt before any great man of the English he shall be secured until notice given unto some of the great men of the Tuscaroroes thatt they may come in iff they please att his Tryall to see that no prejudice may come in to him: But iff the Indian or Indians hath done sutch as above mentioned should make his escape among the Tuscaroroe Indians Thereupon notice given to the greatt men of the Tuscaroroe Indians they shall be obleidged to send him in to the English to have his tryal according to law.

7. Thatt no Tuscaroroe Indian or Indians settle any quarters on the N. West side of Morattuck River.

8. That no Tuscaroroe Indian or Indians have any Cabins or quarters within half a days travell of any English plantation nor burne the woods within the bounds above mentioned & any English plantation itt being a great injury to their stock.

9. Whereas the Tuscaroroe Indians many tymes leave pauns and pledges with the English for the paymentt of skins whitch they promise to bring in so many and doe nott performe may be in many dayes after the tyme appointed which may occasion much difference wherefore itt is agreed that iff any Tuscaroroe Indians who leave pauns doe nott bring in skins to redeem them att the day shall bee, he shall loose his pawne and the English may dispose of them after as they please.

Lastly, That they be always a friendly and amicable correspondence between the said English and Tuscaroroe Indians.

Also itt is agreed that iff the Tuscaroroes have any wars wth any other nation of Indians the English of this Government (on notice being given) shall not assist that other natione wth men, powder or Shott or any other wise and also itt is agreed that iff the English of this Government shall have wars, with any other natione of the Indians, The Greatt men of

Chapter One
Tuscarora Records

the Tuscaroroes (on notice being given them) shall call home all other Indians (iff any be with that natione) and give no manner of assistance to the sd nationes. Butt if required by the Government here shall assist the English against the Indians the Government here giving them reasonable Satisfactione for their tyme.

[Editor's Note: The above paper appears among the items relating to the Assembly. It is without date and not signed. Presume it was a draft of the articles agreed upon between the English and Tuscaroras.]

****

North Carolina State Archives
Colonial Court Records
CCR - 192
Miscellaneous Papers, 1675-1775

File Named: Indians - 1697-1758
Treaties, Petitions, Agreements, and Court Cases

Pamlico in North Carolina ffeby 29th: 1703/4

To ye Honble ye Govr: and Council wee whose names are undr written Doe Hum present to yr Honrs

That wee have great reason to believe ye neighboring towns of ye Tuscororah Indians are of late dissatisfied wth ye Inhabitants of this place and Several actions and discorses of ye Bare River Indians and more than Ordinary familiarity of late yt is between them and ye Tuscorodos: Induses us to believe yt they are Indeavoring to persuade them yt ye English here designs a war against them ye 13th[?] occasions us to [?] yt if yor. Honrs does not speedily take Sum Care in ye mattr; wee may receive Sum preiudice from them the wch wee Suppose might bee prevented[?] and yt Sum of ye Cheifs of ye Indians would come in to yor. Honrs. if you would spedily please to hr. a good Interpreter here wth orders what to doe and Such of us as yr Honrs. Shall appoynt are ready to gve wth Such Interpreter wee pray yr. Honrs. will take Sum Speedy Care in ye [?] for our preservation as to yor. wisdom Shall serve much and remain yr. hum. Svtts.

Chapter One
Tuscarora Records

Lyonell Reading
Richard Smith
Nicholas Tylor
Tho. Dereham
Levi Truewhitt

Wm. Britt
Hum: Legge
Wm. Powell
Edward (E) Gatlin
Tho. Poi[?]

Mr. Reading Sayes yt the Indians of late are more Impudent in Killing their Calves than formerly and openly **[Faded]** of it Mr. [?] Sayes the like.

****

North Carolina State Archives
Colonial Court Records
CCR - 192
Miscellaneous Papers, 1675-1775
File Named: Indians - 1697-1758
Treaties, Petitions, Agreements, and Court Cases
Papers: 1695-1705

Mr Brice
his
Petition

To ye honorable Governor & Counsell

The Petition of William Brice most humbly Sheweth

Thatt wherof your honor Petitioner upon ye twenty fifth day of June last past recovered an order at A Counsell held at Mr. Tho. Blountt in Chowan against one Thomas Blount an Indian for ye Returning of a mare within ye tirm of three months after ye Sd. Date, or to pay fifty doe Skins, & whereas Sd. order he humbly Craves yr honors would be pleased to grant an Order for an Execution versus ye Sd. Indian or other Sattisfaction & Shall Pray

****

University of North Carolina
Southern Historical Collection
Preston Davie Papers
Collection # 3406
Box #1, Folder #13

Chapter One
Tuscarora Records

My Lord   Virginia Septembr the 20th 1708

Haveing on the 24th of June last given my self the Honour of writing to your Lordship by her Majestys Ship the Garland and at the same time sent a duplicate by a Merchant Ship of that ffleet, I humbly beg Leave to be referred to that letter and the papers therewith sent without giveing your Lordship the Trouble of repeating anything. I then laid before your Lordship.

    I herewith send your Lordship the Journals of Council from the 15th of October 1706 to the 30th of April last an abstract of which I sent your Lordship in my last. There have been four meetings of the Council since cheifly intended for giveing the necessary orders for hastning the Merchants Ships in their joining Capt. Stewart in June and Commodore Huntington now, but the severe and extraordinary fevers and other sicknesses with which all parts of the Country have been afflicted for almost two months past & under which severall of the members of the Council at this time labour hath hindred the reading the last proceedings of the Council so as to prepare them for your Lordship's view.

    After the departure of her Majestys Ship the Garland, Commodore Huntington ordered out one of her Majestys Ships under his command to cruise, but that Ship did not proceed on the Service for severall days after haveing been obliged to go round to York River to take in bread and provisions dureing which time we had daily advices of the appearance of Privateers on our Coast, and after the man of War was out cruiseing One Capt. Tarleton of Liverpole was chased from his anchors at the mouth of York River by a Privateer Sloop, Whereupon at the Council held the 29th of July, upon Consideration of our danger It was the unanimous opinion of the Council that for the secureing this Coast and Trade against the Privateers it was necessary to have a fourth Rate man of war and a Brigantine or Sloop of about 8 or 10 Guns and Proportionably maned, the latter to give Chase to the Privateer Sloop in the Shoal water, where, by the Report of all the Captains of the men of war that had been discoursed on that Subject. It appeared very early for such Sloops to pass without comeing within Gun shott of a large Ship. I have by this Conveyance laid this matter before his Royal Highness the Lord high Admiral, And I humbly beg your Lordships favourable Recommendation thereof, for it is demonstrable from the boldness of those Privateers in comeing within our Capes even in sight of her Majestys Ships of war, that they place their cheif Confidence in the lightness of their Vessells and the impossibility of

Chapter One
Tuscarora Records

a large Ships following them among the Shoals. I must on this beg Leave further to observe to your Lordship that the Sloops which have been occasionally hyred here for the assistance of the men of war in that Service have never answered the end proposed, for besides the almost impossibility of procureing a good Sloop fitt for such a design, the difficultys the Captains of her Majties. Ships have pretended of divideing their men and of sending out the Sloop, without their Ships going in Company have made all services intended by them fruitless, so that the hyreing of them has been only a Charge to the Queens Revenue without any real advantage, and this consideration obliged the Council to advise the discharging of the sloop impressed last Summer, after she had been employed and paid out of the Queens Revenue for six weeks and yet in all that time not above five days out a Cruising.

Inform'd Your Lords in my last that we were under some apprehensions from the Tuscarora Indians, who had not complyed in delivering up some of their Nation suspected of a murther committed in this Colony last year, and in order to make them more yielding in that particular, it hath been thought fitt to prohibit all trade and commerce with them. This hath had some affect on them already, for they have made Overture for an Accomodation, and I'm inform'd their coming in to compleat it, hath been only obstructed by the raging of a violent distemper among them for several weeks past.

I thought it necessary to advise with the Council concerning calling an Assembly, the cheif occasion for which at this time is the raising an additional ffund for finishing the Governors house, the whole Sum appropriated by Act of Assembly for that use being already expended and yet the rooff not raised nor any inside work done. I should have been very glad to have had an Assembly for this purpose, but the majority of the Council thought it too great a charge to the Country to have an Assembly now, and another on the arrival of the Govnr. (he being daily expected &) by whom they thought it was very probable her Majesty would send such directions as might make the calling an Assembly of absolute necessity, nor were they of opinion that either the danger of the Country from Privateers, nor the apprehension we were under from the Tuscarora Indians were sufficient grounds for calling an Assembly at this time, the presenting of the first being a work too great for this Country to undertake, and the danger of the latter not so apparent, since there was hopes of an Accomodation with those Indians.

A nation of Indians called the Saponies who were formerly Tributarys to this Governmt. and removed Westward about 20 or 25 years

Chapter One
Tuscarora Records

ago, have lately returned and prayed the protection of this Government, and Land to be assyn'd them for a Settlement, which by advice of the Council, I have granted them in consideration of their being one of those Nations included in the articles of peace made with the Indians in 1677. Their number is not considerable being only about 30 Bowman, but the character they have of being stout fellows and with all very friendly to our inhabitants, makes me hope their Settlement well be a kind of Barrier against the Tuscaroras or any other Indians that might be suspected to annoy us on that side since they'l be able to advise us of their motions soon enough to present both their and our dangers.

I have lately reserved her Majestys commands for paying unto Collo. Hunter £1418,,S. out of the Quitrents as a Compensation for the loss of his Equipage, & £500 Per annum out of the same Fund from the first of July 1707 till his arrival in this Government, and pursuant to her Majtys. commands I have passed a Warrant for the money Ordered for his assessage, and also for one years allowance to the first of July last, both which Sums will be remitted him by this Conveyance, But there's so all the less in the bag, that I am afraid the accruing allowance (which is ordered to be paid quarterly) cannot be paid till the next year if he stays out so long. I hop'd to have sent your Lords copys of the accounts of her Majestys revenues of Quitrents and two shillings per hogshead, but the unfortunate absence of the Council has hindered their being audited, so that I must beg Your Lords patience till after our General Court when I hope to have the opportunity of sending by some of the Latter Ships.

I am informed from North Carolina that there are very great Commotions in that Governmt. occasioned chiefly by the Quakers, who after they had prevailed with the Proprietors to send out the Deputy Governor, and give [?] the Council (who were most of their persuasion) a power to chuse their own President, first made an Election, and because they did not find that Gentleman for their own turn, voted him out again. They have had the cunning to set all that Country in a flame, and all but themselves in arms agt. one another. It would be tedious to to trouble yr Lords with an account of the proceedings of both partys wch look like the freaks of madmen than the actions of men of reason, there has been one man already unfortunately killed in the fray, and tho tis said they are coming to some accomodation yet by the best information I have it is not like to end so. I thought it my duty to acquaint tour Lords of this, as it happens so nigh this her Majestys Colony, tho I hope it will have no ill consequences on us. I am with the greatest respect
My Lord

Chapter One
Tuscarora Records

Your Lordships
Most Oblidged & Most Obedient
Servt.

E. Jenings

****

North Carolina State Archives
Private Manuscript Collection
Alexander Spottswood Papers, 1676-1740
Call Number: P.C.24.1

Page 14
24th Dec 1710
On receipt of a letter from Col. Carter.
Reporting encroachments against the Meherrin Indians.

Page 18-19
"... I am credibly informed the Indians have more reason to complain of injustice from the people of Carolina who are daily trespassing upon them ... I have received private advertisement of some in your Government intending to fall upon the Indians and to compel them by force to yield to their unreasonable pretentions..."

Page 34-35
1711
Speaking of Miles Cary states he "... is since retired to a remote part of that Country whether it is impracticable to march the Militia from hence to attack him He is there gathering a greater Force and Threatens to bring down the Tuscarora Indians to his assistance..."

Page 37-38
1711
"Mr. Porter one of Mr. Careys pretended Council was with the Tuscarora Indians endeavoring by promises of great Rewards to enguage them to cut off all the inhabitants of that part of Carolina that adhered to Mr. Hyde..." He convinced the young Indians but not the older ones. The older ones figured it was a trick and refused.

Chapter One
Tuscarora Records

Page 49
"Virginia October 15th 1711
To the Council of Trade
My Lords
"...on the 22nd of the last month some towns of the Tuscarora Indians and nations bordering on Carolina made an incurtion upon the head of the Neuse and Pamplico rivers in that province without any previous declaration of war or show of discontent and having divided themselves in parties at sunrise which was the signal for their bloody design began a barbarous massacre on the Inhabitants of the Frontier plantations killing without distinction of age or sex about 60 English and upwards of that number of Swiss and Palatines besides a great many left dangerous by wounded."

****

North Carolina State Archives
Source: P.C. (Private Collection) 574
Francis Lister Hawks (1798-1866) Papers,
[1711], 1805, 1850-1851. 13 items
(undated letter to John H. Bryan
containing transcript of letter and
memorial from Christopher Gale
describing Tuscarora, Nov. 2, 1711.
Private Manuscript Collection, North
Carolina State Archives.

Note at beginning of letter:
"Nichol's Literary Illustrations Vol. IV. pp 489-492

Added note concerning Baron de Graffenried:
"This is a Mistake. The Baron was alive in 1726 & then mortgaged his lands to Pollock."

Note concerning Christopher Gale:
"This gentleman was Attorney General, Chief Justice of N. Carolina and married Sarah daughter of John Harvey Esq. Governor of Carolina. He was son of Rev. Miles Gale Rector of Keighley in Yorkshire."

Note from F.L. Hawks:

Chapter One
Tuscarora Records

"My dear sir,
  In the foregoing you have the copy which I promised you of Gales letter. My paper only allows me room to say that I hope it will prove worth the postage of the Sheet, & that I am very truly Yours
  F.L. Hawks"

Nichol's Literary Illustrations
Vol. IV. pp 489-492

A letter from Major Christopher Gale *
from Charles Town in N. Carolina Nov. 2. 1711

My dear,
  I cannot omit by all opportunities to inform my self that you have still living in a brother, the most faithful friend that ever was, though perhaps by as signall or hand of Providence as this age can demonstrate: I could not trouble you with repetitions, but refer you to the after written memorial, which I laid before the government and shall only acquaint you how far I had been concerned on the bloody * if kind Providence had not prevented. About ten days before the fatal day, I was at the Baron's and had agreed with him and Mr. Lawson on a progress to the Indian Country; but before we were prepared to go, a message came from home to inform me that my wife and brother lay dangerously sick; which I may call a happy sickness to me, for on the newes I immediately repaired home, and thereby avoyded the fite which I shall hereafter inform you.

  The Baron with Mr. Lawson and their attendants, proceeding on their journey were on the 22d, of September, (as you will see by the memorials,) both barbarously murdered, the matt on which the Baron used to lye on such like voyages, being since found all daubed with blood, so as we suppose him to have been quickly dispatched. But the fate of Mr. Lawson, (if our Indian information be true), was much more traggicall, for we are informed that they stuck him full of fine small splinters of torchwood like hoggs bristles, and so set them gradually on fire. This, I doubt not, had been my fate, if Providence had not prevented; but I hope God Almighty has assigned me for an instrument in the revenging such innocent Christian blood.

  On Sunday, October 21, I arrived here in the quality of an agent, and in order to procure the assistance of the govt. to destroy our enimies, which I doubt not in a little time to effect. The family which I left in garison at Bathe town, my wife and brothers pritty well recovered, but what has happened since I know not. Two days after I left the town at day

Chapter One
Tuscarora Records

break; (Which is the Indians usual time of attack,) above 100 guns were heard, which must have been an attack made by the Indians upon some of our garisons, which are in all eleven in number; but cannot hear the success of it, though a small vessell came from the out part of our gov't. here the other day, by which I have the following newes: That on my coming away, Capt Brice detached from our out garisons 50 men, and in the woods met with a body of Indians, who fought them three days, and forced them at last to retire into their garisons. The Indians lost in this engagement 15 men, and we two, one of who was killed by one of our own men. During this engagement, another body of the Indians, being advised that the garison was weakened by this detachment, came and attacked the garison, and at the same time a number of Indian prisoners of a certain Nation, which we did not know whether they were friends or enemies, rose in the garison but were soon cut to pieces, as also those on the outside repelled. In the garison were killed 9 Indian men, and soon after 39 women and children sent off for slaves. This is the condition we at present labor under. I shall not trouble you with a particular relation of all their butcheries, but shall relate to you some of them by which you may suppose the rest. The family of our Mr. Nevill was treated after this manner: The old gentleman himself, after being shot, was laid on the house floor with a clean pillow under his head, his wife's head clothes put upon his head, his stockings turned over his shoes, and his body covered all over with new linen. His wife was set upon her knees, and her hands lifted up as if she was at prayers, leaning against a chair in the chimney corner and her clothes turned up over her head. A son of his was laid out in the yard with a pillow under his head, and a bunch of rosemary laid to his nose. A negro had his right hand cut off and left dead. The master of the next house was shot, and his body laid flat upon his wife's grave. Women were laid on their house floors, and great stakes run up through their bodies. Others big with child, the infants were ript out and hung upon trees. In short their manner of butchery has been so various and unaccountable, that it would be beyond credit to relate them. This blow was so hotly followed by the hellish crew, that we could not bury our dead, so that they were left for prey to the dogs and wolves and vultures, whilst our care was to strengthen our garison to secure the living.

The ship by wh: this comes is ready to saile so cannot enlarge, only desire my duty may be presented to my father and mother, my sincere love to yourself and brothers, and service to all friends, hoping for a speedy answer to my last by Madam Hyde is whatt offer from,

Your sincerely affectionate brother Christopher. Gale.

Chapter One
Tuscarora Records

From Charles Town Carolina
The Memorial of Christopher Gale, from the government of N. Carolina, to the honourable Robert Gibs Esq. Gov. & Commander in chief, and to the honourable Council and General Assembly. To lay before your Honour the prospect or representation of as promising a country, as was ever watered with the dew of Heaven, would take up more time than the present exigency of the affair I am now set upon would give me leave; but much more time and a hand more skilfull would be requisite, to give you a view of the calamities and miseries of so fine a country laid waste and desolate, by the most barbarious enemies, I mean the Corees and Tuscarora Indians. Although I shall not use much eloquence to implore your aid and assistance in revenging such being their own best orator, yet I presume I have all the advantages that may be; of making a true representation of that affair to your Honours, being an inhabitant of Beaufort precinct, where a great part of this hellish tragedy was acted. I shall therefore inform your Honours, that on Saturday the 22 of Sept. last was perpetrated the grossest piece of villany that perhaps was ever heard of in English America, - 130 people massacred at the head of the Nuse, and on the south side of Pamplaco rivers, in the space of two hours; butchered after the most barbarous manner that can be expressed, and their dead bodies used with all the scorn and indignity imaginable, their houses plundered of considerable riches, (being generally traders,) then burnt and their growing and hopefull crops destroyed. What spectacle can strike a man with more horror and stir up more to revenge than to see so much barbarity practised in so little a time and so unexpected! and what makes it the more surprising that nefarious villany was committed by such Indians as were esteemed as members of the several families where the mischiefs were done, and that with smiles in their countenances, when their intent was to destroy. I must inform your Honours that the governors of N. Carolina are not in a condition to take a full (I might say any) satisfaction on the enimy, now to prevent their further progress, by reason their neighboring Indians not to be relyed on for any assistance, but rather to be feared they would be prejudicial in any expedition; if not joined with the enemy as we have good reason to judge by their behaviour both before and since the act was committed, therefore a strict and jealous eye is necessarily kept over them by the gov't, and our whole country drawn into garisons to prevent mischiefs that way, which very much hinders the getting men into a body to pursue the enemy, who are at present between 2 & 300 effective men and above 1000 women and children and I believe your Honours will be of

Chapter One
Tuscarora Records

opinion, that it is altogether impracticable to attempt such a body of men, flushed with their first success, without Indians who are acquainted with their manner of warring.

Wherefore, on the behalf of the gov't of N. Carolina by which I am employed, I earnestly entreat your Honours to permit and encourage so many of your tributary Indians as you think proper to fall upon those Indians our enemies, whose families are since fled down to the sea board between Weatuck and Capefare rivers, whilst their men are still ravaging and destroying all before them within sight of our garisons, that by your assistance exemplary justice may be done to such barbarous villains as have laid waste and desolate such a flourishing part of the Lords Proprietors Country, and which without your speedy reliefe will be wholly deserted.

If any Indians are found innocent of that massacre, and will assist in the destruction of those inhumane wretches, ease will be taken to distinguish those from the rest; but I very much fear that upon strict enquiry, it will be found that the whole nation of the Tuskaroras (though some of them may not as yet be actors) is as knowing and consenting to what was done, and that the success of those already in motion, if not put a stop to, will at last induce the rest to join with them in carrying on these bloody designs. Besides the daily expectation of a considerable number of Senekoes, which we are certainly informed are coming to cohabit with the Tuskaroras our enimyes this winter, and become one nation, which in time may affect our neighboring governments as well as us. I firmly persuade myself that so much prejudice as the Lords Proprietors will receive by that fatal blow, the barbarous murders of so many of our fellow subjects, among which number is the Hon. Baron de Graffenried, a Landgrave of Carolina and a member of the Councill, Mr. Lawson the Surveyor General with divers others of note will excite your Honours compassion towards such a country and hasten your assistance and relief.

I am, with all respect,
Your Honours' most obedient humble servant
Christopher Gale.

****

The University of North Carolina
Southern Historical Collection

Chapter One
Tuscarora Records

Manuscripts Department
Preston Davie Collection
Collection # 3406
Box # 1, Folder # 15

Williamsburg
Febru: 27th 1711
Letter from Govr. Spotswood to his Excellency

Sir

By a ship they arrived here some days ago. I received under my cover the inclosed letters for you, which I now dispatch by an express to the President of Maryland to be forwarded to your Parts.

Tho I have several letters from England as late as December, I have yet no advice of the arrival of the bills. I desired the favour of you to draw for the Pork, bought here on the Queens account, which I confess gives me some uneasiness not only in respect to My Lord Orkney who you know doth not bear such disappointments very patiently; but for the sake of the other persons, who begin to fancy they shall suffer for their readiness to promote the Queens Services. The Lords Commissioners for trade have done me the honour to assure me, that had they known how much I had advanced, they would have solicited the Lord Treasurer in my behalf, while at the same time Severe Reflections pass on some Governments for their backwardness in furnishing provisions for the expedition: but if the remitting those bills is delayed, they'l have still the better bargain, since they only suffer in their Reputation, and I shall suffer both in my purse and my Credit among the People.

You have no doubt heard of the Massacre committed last Fall in North Carolina by their neighboring Indians, since which they have very much distressed the Inhabitants of that province by burning their houses and destroying their Corn and stocks, and forcing the people to betake themselves to Garrisons for their own Safety: And all thee news I can send you from hence, is that about the beginning of this month a body of 700 of the South Carolina Indians commanded by one Collo. Barnwell fell upon those Rogues, and cutt off six towns of the Tuscaroras, and are now in Search of the rest: They have taken abundance of prisoners and found among them a considble. Booty of English goods, and by the blow have I

Chapter One
Tuscarora Records

hope disappointed their designs of carrying on a formal War against the Province and us, in conjunction with the Senequas inhabiting your Frontier, who ti said prompted them to this Villany by promises of supplys of Arms and Ammunition from your Governmt., and of the Assistance of thee whole Strength of that Nation. There were about thirty of the Senequas among them, some few days before Collo. Barnwell arrived, who is like to have had the same Fate with the rest. I once expected to have had a share in cutting off those Indians. Our Assembly having voted twenty thousand pound for that service, but after consulting the means here to raise it they found it too large for their purses, and instead of going on as they began thought of nothing more than how to get off that hasty Resolution; In order to which they fell upon raising Funds prejudicial to the service of Great Brittain, which I could not consent to, and so that project dropp'd and I have been obliged to dissolve our Lower house, finding them runing into fruitless Contests with the Upper House about Points which they could not well defend. I am with great Truth & Esteem

Sir   Your Most Obedient
        Humble Servant

              A Spotswood

****

North Carolina State Archives
Papers and Research of Wesley White
Source: George B. Stevenson

"The original to this peace treaty remains in private hands in Raleigh, N.C., according to a note attached to a negative photostat thereof in a box of papers having to do with the Tuscarora Indians, in the N.C. Archives (Raleigh). The following seems as if a more-nearly-accurate transcription of the treaty than do any of the series of definitely-partly-innaccurate transcriptions of the treaty already published:"

"North Carolina ss.
    Preliminary Articles in order to a general peace had, made, and concluded and agreed upon this 25th day of November Anno Domini 1712 between: Tom Blount, Saroonha, Heunthanotineh, Nawoontootsere (Chief Men of several of the Tuskarora towns), for and on behalf of themselves

Chapter One
Tuscarora Records

and the towns of Eukuskuerent, Rarookahee, Tostehant, Rauroota, Tarharota, Kenta, Toherooka, Juninits, and Canookehee, of the one part; and the Honorable Thomas Pollock, Esquire, President, and the rest of the Council, for and on behalf of themselves and this Government of North Carolina, of the other part, WITNESSETH

"Imprimus. The aforesaid Great Men do hereby covenant and agree to (and, with the said President and Council) that they shall (and will, with the utmost expedition and diligence) make war on all the Indians belonging to the towns or nations of Catashny, Core, Nuse, and Bare River, and Pamptico. And, that they shall not (nor will not) give any quarter to any male Indian of those towns or nations above the age of 14 years. And also, that they shall (and will) sell off and dispose of all the males under that age. And that further, after they shall have destroyed those towns (or as soon as this Government shall think proper to require it), the said Great Men do hereby promise to join the English with so many men as may be thought proper to destroy and cut off all the Matchepungo Indians.

"Secondly. The aforesaid Great Men do hereby covenant and agree that if, in this war, they shall take any articles which shall be proved to have been owned by the English (and taken away in the late horrid attacks) ---- such articles shall be delivered to the rightful owners thereof.

"Thirdly. It is hereby further agreed, by the said Great Men, that they shall (and will) well and truly deliver up to the English, all the white captives and horses that they shall find among the said Indians.

"Fourthly. It is hereby agreed by the Great Men aforesaid, that: The several towns of Tostehaut, Rauroota, Tarhuntah, Kentah, Toherooka, Juninits and Canookehee --- nor any of the Indians belonging to them or either of them --- shall not hunt nor range among the English plantations nor stocks without leave; Nor then, above the number of three at one time. Neither shall they claim any property in the land on the south side of Nuse called Chatooka river; nor below Catashny creek on Nuse; nor below Bare creek at No-sha-hum-han-ro on the north side of Pamptico river.

"Fifth. It is mutually agreed by and between all the said parties to these presents that --- If any injury shall hereafter be done on either side; upon complaints made (to such persons as shall hereafter be appointed for that purpose), full satisfaction shall be made.

"Sixth. The aforesaid Great Men do hereby agree that --- From and after the ratification of a general peace, they shall (and will) pay unto this Government such a yearly tribute as hereafter shall be agreed upon.

"Seventh. The aforesaid Great Men do hereby further agree that (for the full and true performance of all and every the above Articles on

Chapter One
Tuscarora Records

their parts to be performed) --- The several towns of Tostehaut, Rauroota, Tarhunta, Kenta, Taherooka, Juninits, Canookehee; shall bring in (and deliver up to this Government at the Honorable Colonel Thomas Pollock's), six of the chiefest women and children for each town, for hostages, by the next full moon (provided that they do not destroy the enemy aforesaid by that time).

"Eighth. The said President and Council do hereby covenant and agree to and with the Great Men aforesaid, that --- Upon the just and true performances of these Articles, the several hostages of aforesaid; shall be well and truly delivered up again. And a free and open trade shall be had with the said Indians as aforesaid formerly.

"Lastly. The aforesaid Great Men do hereby agree that they will endeavor to bring into some of their towns alive Canuneskguoshkene__?__, Enugnerehau, Cannuesk__?__, Neneuhguotkan called John Pagett, Ehehosguos called Lawson, Coresniena called Barber, Colsera called Henry, Lysle Ounskininenee called Squarehookis, Touginanah, Eruntanhyne, and Young Tyler; and send two runners to Mr. Reeding's garrison. (Give these three hoops, then show a white cloth for a signal, in order to pilot such persons as we shall think proper to send, to see execution done upon the aforesaid murderers.)

"In witness whereof, the several parties to these presents have interchangably set their hands and seals the day and year first above written.

Tom Blount
Saroonha
Heuntha-not-neh
Cheunt-haroonthoo
Newoonttootsery
Saroonha Herunt-tocken

Foot Notes By Wesley White

"These correspond to the following names on the list of all fifteen Tuscarora towns (15 separate governments, a single spoken language) published in London in 1709: Oonossoora (?), Conauh-Kare Harooka, Tosneoc, Haruta, Naur-he-ne, Kenta, Anna Ooka, Chunaneets, and Eno. (Underlined: Hocomawananck towns).

This Catashny in 1712 corresponds to Contah-nah six miles up the right-hand bank of Neuse river's Contentnea creek in 1709, one of the

Chapter One
Tuscarora Records

fifteen towns lived in solely by the approximately 3,000 Tuscaroras. "Core" refers to the Connamocksock nation whose main town, Coranine, stood at Cape Look-Out. "Nuse" refers to the Neusiok nation whose main town, Chatooka, stood until 1710 at the present city of New Bern, N.C. "Bare River" means Raudauqua-quank, the village on Bear river (same as Pungo river) recorded as of 1699 and made up of about 5/8ths of the Machapunga nation. "Pamptico" means the Pamlico nation. Defined genocide.

****

North Carolina State Archives
Colonial Court Records
CCR - 192
Miscellaneous Papers, 1675-1775

File Named: Indians - 1697-1758
Treaties, Petitions, Agreements, and Court Cases

North Carolina Ss Charles Eden Esqr Governor etc

To Mr. Robert Hicks powder Receivd. for Albemarle County a Tuskarooroe Indian Named James having in Councill been ordered a reward for some Services done the publick.

These are therefore to require you to deliver to Mr. William Churton three pounds of powder Nine pound of Shote and Twelve Flints who has orders to deliver it to the sd Indian & for so doeing this shall be your Warrant.
      Charles Eden

Aprl. 26 1721
Recd at [?] the Powder Shott & Flints
mentioned in the within Orders

3 Powdr: p Wrt. W.C. Churton
9 Shott
12 Flints

****

Chapter One
Tuscarora Records

North Carolina State Archives
Colonial Court Records
CCR - 192
Miscellaneous Papers, 1677-1775

File Named: Indians - 1697-1758
Treaties, Petitions, Agreements, and Court Cases.

The Deposition of Cullen Pollock about: 24: years Saith That I the SD. Cullen Pollock Living in ye room above my Fathers; On Sunday morning August ye: 5th: at about: 3: a Clock heard a Noise wch seemed to me to be near ye window & ffelt the house shake whereupon geting up & Comeing downe he saw what was the matter heard a Noise in the house where going sawe an Indian Called John Cope sitting on the flore where he seet till two Negroes Carryed him out

North Carolina. George by the Grace of God **[torn]**
        Brittain ffrance & Ireland **[torn]**
        Defender of the faith
        To the Provost Marshall of Albemarle **[torn]**
        or to Philip Waetton Constable
Whereas a Special Court of Oyer & Terminer is to be holden Att Edenton on the **[?]** Day of **[torn]** for the tryal of John Cope an Indian for burglary we therefore Command you to Sumons the persons **[torn]** to appear att the sd Court to Sumon a Grandjury **[torn]** Tryal of the sd John Cope hereof **[faded]**

        Witness Christopher Gale **[torn]**
        Justice of this 9th Day of August
Persons to be Sumd.

Collo Robert West	M = ffrederick [?]
David Henderson	Isaac Still
David Hicks	Lawrence Mague not here
John Herring	
John Williams	
James Castellaw	
John Holbrook	

        (Gale)

Chapter One
Tuscarora Records

North Carolina To the Honble. Christopher Gale Esqr Chief
and the Rest of the Justices for Calling
a Special Court of Oyer & Terminer for this
province

The Jurors for our Sovereigne Lord the King that now is upon their Oaths present that John Cope a Christian Indian belonging to King Blounts Town in this province the fourth day of this Instant August by force and Armes Burglary did comitt by feloniously & burglariously breaking & entring into the Mansion House of the Honorable Colonel Thomas Pollock Esqr. president of this province at Chowan in the County of Albemarle, In the Night, Viz. before Sunrising of the Same Day The Said Colonel Thomas Pollock in the Same House in the peace of God and of our Said Lord the King then being against the peace of our Said Lord the King his Crowne and Dignity
Dan: Richardson &
Jno: Roge

The Deposition of Thomas Pollock Senr. aged about **[torn]** That after Sun Sett Last Fryday night and before Sun Ryse Last Saturday morning the Fourth day of this instant **[torn]** one Indian Man Who cals himself John Cope some **[torn]** day on Saturday morning afsd Broke out a Window **[torn]** Rooms wher I Ly and I believe haveing standed himself **[torn]** fall out of the window upon the Floor of the Roome my Son **[torn]** came downe on the noise he made and so had him **[?]** Secured he made no Excuse only that he said he intended no harm & this is the Truth to the best of my Knowledge

So help me God
Tho Pollock

Capt: & Jurat
8th Dae August
A. Dom: 1722

(Gale) C:J:

1. Edwd. Winget
2. Richd. Wilson
3. Wm Coward

10. Edwd. Howcott
11. Thos. Ashley
12. John Jones

Chapter One
Tuscarora Records

4. Constant Lewton
5. Wm Egerton
6. Jno. White Junr
7. Thos. Jones
8. Thos. Lewton
9. Edwd. Cockerell

Sworne on the Petty Jury

John Coope Dr	
To my Trouble and Hiring Six To Bring you over the Sound	2-5- 0
for impanilling two jurors	0-10-0
To 20 Grand Jures	1-10-0
To Hireing 2 men five Days to gard you 5s pr Day	2-10-0
	6-15-0

by me [?] Spires

The Examination of John Cope a Christian Indian belonging to King Blounts Towne taken before John Lovick and Thomas Pollock Junr Esqrs on Sunday the 5th day of Augt. 1722

The Examinant being asked what he intended by his breaking into the Presidents room the Night before. did not deny the fact. but in his Excuse he was Frank. which was all the Confession he would make

      J Lovick
      Thos. Pollock jr.

[faded] vora	Indictmt
Tho Luton foreman	The King vs
	Cope a
	Christn Indian

Wee of the Jury find John Cope prest at ye bare Gelty of Entering ye house but not with a felonious intent

Chapter One
Tuscarora Records

Edward Wingate formen
Not Guilty
Edward Wingate foreman

****

North Carolina State Archives
Colonial Courts Records
CCR - 192
Miscellaneous Papers, 1675-1775

File Named: Indians - 1697-1758
Treaties, Petitions, Agreements, and Court Cases

Gardener Deposition

The Deposition of John Gardiner being of full Age & Sworn on the holy Evangelist before us Gyles Shute &c Joshua porter Esqrs Two of his Majesties Justices of the peace of the precincts of Beaufort & hyde; Saith; To wit, Lightaea Blount Came upon Mr. Dudley askt him where he was a Goeing And he Said to Catch Beavers and Mr. Dudley Said he Should not hunt here for it was his Lands for his doggs would Scare his Cattle & hoggs & Said Blount made Answer that his Doggs followed, Only, Beaver Racoons & Deer And Said that he would hunt & Mr. Dudley made Answer will you And so Catcht up A board & Struck the Said Blount & the Said Blount took up a Stick to defend & Blount then he Advanced up to Mr. Dudley & they had A Struggle & Mr. Dudley pushed him Against a barril then I halld the Indian away And I told Mr. Dudley to Lett him Alone; And Dudley Bid me then to Keep him of from him; And then the Indian Catcht up the End of a hoop Poll, And made Towards him So I desired the Indian to Stand of So went & Left them and further Saith Not

Juret Corum   John Gardner
Nobis
Gyles Shute
Joshua Porter

Nixon & Gardiners Recogn: to appear at March Cot: 1723

Chapter One
Tuscarora Records

To give Evide: v. Dudley ad Sectr. Dom: Regis

North Carolina
Beauft Prect

Memorandum that on this 16th day of March 1722/3 there Came Before us Gyles Shute & Joshua porter Esqrs two of his majesties Justices of the peace for Beaufort & hyde prects Richard Nixon & John Gardiner Boath of this prect & did acknowlege themselves Indebted to Our Sovereign Lord the King his heirs & Sucessors in the sum of fifty pounds Sterling Each to be leveyd upon their Goods Chattles Lands & tennemts upon Condition following (Viz) that they the Sd Richd Nixon & John Gardiner shall personaly Apear before the Chief Justice & his Assistance at the Court house in Edenton in Albemarle County the twenty Sixth of this Instant then & there to Give Evidence on the Behalf of our Sovereign Lord the King against Christopher Dudley for wounding assaulting hurting & maiming of a Tuskarora Indian And Not to Depart the Said Court without Leave first had & Obtained of the Sd Court then this Recognizance to be void & Null otherwayes to Stand & Remain in full force power & virtue

Capt: & Recogn   Gyles Shute
Corum Nobis   Joshua Porter

Nixon's Deposition

North Carolina Ss:

The Deposition of Richard Nixon being of full Age & Sworne on ye Holy Evangelist before us Gyles Shute & Joshua Porter Esqrs Two of his Magesties of ye peace of ye precinct of Beufort & Hyde Saith that four or five Indians Came to his house & the Mr Dudley was at his house when they Came So when they Came up he asked them where are you a Goeing & the Indians Satt down without Giveing him any Answer; then one Old Indian, Names Sighacka: Blount Came up After ye Rest, & when he Came up he Asked what is ye Matter & Replyed, English men here Allways Scold, then mr Dudley said you shall not hunt here for this Land is all mine, the old Sighacka Said, that he would Goe hunt, & Catch Beavers, with that mr Dudley, Catched up a board, and Said will you Goe, And

Chapter One
Tuscarora Records

Struck him upon ye head, And Caused ye Blood to Run, and then ye Aforsd Sighacka held up his Arm to Defend ye Blow: and Recd ye Blow upon his Arm And Mr John Gardiner; Stept in Between them and parted them And ye Indian Satt down on A block, and Said ye Mr Dudley had broake his Arm And wth; ye Intent to ye Indians and took hold of his arm & felt on it and to ye best of my understanding that there was one bone Broak Bettween ye Elbow & Wrist two dayes after I see ye Indian Again And his hand & Arm was very much Swelld & ye Indian to [?] yt ye Bone was Broak [Torn] & nine or tenn dayes after I See ye Indian Goeing home And his arm was Splintered; And he Said he would Goe and tell King Blount; for King Blount he Said would Goe to Capt. West; & peace make it and further Saith Not

Jurat Corum Nobis   Richd. Nixson
Gyles Shute
Joshua Porter

Warrant for Dudley

No Carolina Sc

Whereas Complaint is made unto me Christopher Gale Esqr Chief Justice of this province that Christopher Dudley of Beaufort precinct in Bath County hath Lately violently assaulted & beaten & broke the Arm of an Indian man belonging to the Tuscarora Nation whereby many ill conveniencys are to be feared to the Tranquilty & peace of this Government

These are Therefore in his majesties name to require & Strictly Charge you Immediately upon receipt hereof to Arrest the body of the Sd. Christopher Dudley & him bring before me to answer the said complaint herein faile Not at ye perill as you will answer the Contrary and for So doeing this Shall be yr. Sufficient warrant

To the Provost marshall   Given under my hand & Seale
of Bath County or to his   this 13th day of March
Deputy Or to mr. Edwd Travise   anno 1722

Chapter One
Tuscarora Records

Summon Mr. Richard Nikson   Gale CJ
and John Gardiner Evidences

Executed in March 1722/3
Edwd Travis

Dudley's Recogn. to appear at March Ct. 1723

North Carolina Ss
Beauft Prect

Memorandum that on the 16th: day of March 1722/3 There came before us Gyles Shute and Joshua Porter Esqr two of his Majesties justices of the peace for Beauft of hide prects: Christopher Dudley of the sd prect. plainter and Did acknowledge himself to Stand Indebted unto our Sovereign Lord the King his heirs & Sucessrs. in the Sum of one hundred pounds Starling to be levied upon his goods Chattles lands & Tenements upon the Condition following viz: that the Sd. Christopher Dudley Shall personally appear before the Cheif Justice & his assistants at the Court house in Edentown in Albemarle county to be held the 26th of this Instant - then & there to answere to Shall be objected against: him on behalf of our Sovereigne Lord the King for hurting & Maiming of a Tuskarora Indian, and not to Depart the Sd. Court without Leave first had & Obtained of the Sd. Court then this recognizance to be void and null Otherwayes to Stand & remaine in full force power & virtue

Capt & Recogn: Gyles Shute
Coram Nobis   Joshua Porter

****

North Carolina State Archives
Colonial Court Records
CCR - 192
Miscellaneous Papers, 1675 - 1775

File Named: Indians - 1697-1758

Chapter One
Tuscarora Records

Treaties, Petitions, Agreements, and Court Cases

William Frys Deposition Relative to the Indians

The deposition of William Fry aged about Eighteen Years on oath Saith

That on the 24th day of May 1757 he was travelling on the Road leading from Bonners Bridge to Cashy after passing Bonner Bridge about one Mile and Some better I saw a woman lying dead on the Road With a great deal of blood lying at the place where She lay being in a Small Branch over which was a pole Caus way I Run with My might till I heard Somebody Call Who Asked me if I saw Ever a woman I told there was one dead a little way of and further Saith not
    Examined before Me Jos. Hardy
    Coroner   William [?]

The Deposition of John Liscomb Matter Concerning the Indian

The Deposition of John Liscomb a man Aged about 36 years on oath Saith

That on the 24th day of May 1757 he was Travilling with Elizabeth Knott to go to Virginia and Between Cashy Bridg and Bonners Bridg They Came to the house of John Wyatts who told them that the Indians Came into his house that day and Behaved Themselves in Very Ill Manner Wyatt told them to Call at the Next house and they would hear a great deal more but when we Come there was nobody at home Mrs: Knott then Missing a handkercheif desired I would goe Back and pick it up she Likewise Said She had it in Sight of the plantation where we then Was She further Said She would walk slowly on till I overtook her again I went and found the Handkercheif in Sight of the plantation as She Said & returning I Mett two Men Near the Spot I parted from her at then I saw the Beast she Rode Coming back full Speed I desired they would assist Me to cetch her then I Taking the beast and went on to look the woman thinking the beast had flung her in Rideing Some better than a Quarter of a mile I called her three times and looking forward I Saw an Indian Rise from the Earth which put me in a Surprise the Indian hallered three times Waugh and stamped I Saw him dart to one side the road Supposing he was going for his gun I turned My horse about and Called to the two men I had left: for to help: one of the

Chapter One
Tuscarora Records

men coming to me I told him I wanted assistance which he refused as having no Arms: we all three turned out of the Road to Gitt Arms: then Seeing a lad Running up the Road I turned about and called to him and he coming to us as Quick as he could I asked him Whether he had Seen any Woman on the road he Replyed for god Sake what Woman is that lyes dead there: I asking where he said there was one dead in a bottom Lying upon Some poles Which Was the place I Saw the Indian Rise from and that it was not Six Minutes from the time I Saw the Indian Rise to the time the lad told Me that he Saw the woman dead and further this deponent Saith not

Taken before Me Jos Hardy Coroner   John Liscomb

North Carolina
At a Supreme Court of Justice Oyer and Terminer and General Goal Delivery began and held at Edenton on the Second Tuesday in October in the thirtieth year of the Reign of our Sovereign Lord George the Second now King of Great Brittain (and so forth) for the Countys of Currituck, Pasquotank, Perquimans, Chowan, Bertie and Tyrell before the Honourable Peter Henly Esquire Cheif Justice of the Province aforsd.

The Jurors for our Lord the King upon their oath present that James Strawberry an Indian late of society parish in the County of Bertie not having the fear of God before his Eyes but being Moved and Seduced by the Instigation of the Devil on the Twenty Fourty day of May in the Thirtieth Year of the Reign of our Sovereign Lord George now King of Great Brittain (and so forth) about the hour of three in the afternoon of the same Day at Society Parish aforesaid in the Province aforesaid with force and Arms made an Assault in and upon Elizabeth Knott then and there being in the Peace of God and of our said Lord the King and that the said James Strawberry at Society Parish aforesaid in the County aforesaid did feloniously wilfully and of his Malice aforethought Strike and Wound the said Elizabeth Knott with a Light Wood Knott which the said James Strawberry had and held then and there in his Right Hand and did feloniously and of his Malice aforethought at Society parish aforesaid in the County aforesaid Give to the said Elizabeth Knott three Mortal Wounds with a Light Wood Knott aforesaid in and upon the Back part of her Head off the length of one Inch and off the Depth of one Inch of which said Mortal Wounds the said Elizabeth Knot at Society Parish aforesaid in

Chapter One
Tuscarora Records

the County aforesaid Instantly Died and so the said Jurors upon their Oath aforesaid Say that the said James Strawberry on the said Twenty fourth day of May in the Year above Mentioned at Society Parish aforesaid in the County aforesaid did feloniously Wilfully and of his Malice forethought, hitt and Murder the said Elizabeth Knott in Manner and form aforesaid against the Peace of our said Lord the King his Crown and Dignity

Ewd [?]   J P Mr. [?]
Thos Kimsey[?]
John Liscomb
Willm. Fry

Dom Rex
Vs.
James Strawberry
Recognizance Concerning the Indian

North Carolina
Bertie County

The Twenty [?] day of May in the year of Our Lord One thousand seven hundred and Fifty seven came before me Joseph Hardy Coroner John Liscomb And william Fry and Acknowledged Each of themselves To be Indebted To our sovereign Lord the King in the sum of Ten Pound sterling Lawful money of Great Brittain the condition of this recognizance is such that if the above bound John Liscomb & William Fry doth Personally appear before our Cheif Justice at the next asize to be holden at Edenton on the second Tuesday of October next For the said County then and there two deliver and set Forth their Knowledge touching the death of Elizabeth Knott and do not Depart thence without License of the said Court. That non effect or else to be and Remain In full Force and Virtue Acknowledged before me the day and year above Written

Jos. Hardy Coroner

****

North Carolina State Archives
Governer' Papers

Chapter One
Tuscarora Records

Petition of the Tuscarora Indians

We the Tuskarora Indians Petition Your Excely. and Council to Grant a Pattent or Some Beter Title for Our Land for the White folks tells this is good for Nothing and they Come and Settle Without leave fall Our Timber and Drive Stocks of All Sorts: We hope Care will be Taken to Protect us in Quiet Possession of Our Land and from the White People Abusing us.

Sept. 5th 1757   {James Blount
                              by order {
                                        {for the Tuskarora Nation

****

North Carolina State Archives
General Assembly Sessions Records
(Colonial - Upper and Lower Houses
1709 - Jan. 1760 (Box 1)
File: Petitions Rejected or not acted on

29 NOVEMBER 1758

To His Excellency Arthur Dobbs Esqr. Captain General and Commander in Chief in and over the Province of North Carolina.

To the Honourable the Members of His Majesty's Council and to the Honourable Speaker and the Members of the Assembly

The Petition of Humphrey Bates humbly Sheweth

That at a Council held at Edenton the seventh Day of November in the Year of Our Lord One thousand seven and twenty three King Thomas Blount Chief Man of the Tuskarora Indians as also some other of their Chieftains appeared before the said Council and prayed that a Tract of Land containing about six hundred Acres lying in Bertie County and known by the Name of Quitsney's Meadow joyning on the Chyahick Swamp which they had made Over unto one William Charlton for some Favours done by him for them might be confirmed by that Board and it was accordingly confirmed by that Board to the said William Charlton and

Chapter One
Tuscarora Records

Ordered that from thenceforth the said Indians should make no sale of any part of their Lands and that no white Person should purchase any of the same from them and it was further Ordered that the said William Charlton should be at Liberty to settle on said Land.

That your Petitioner depending upon the Strength of the above recited Order of Council did purchase of George Charlton Son of the said William Charlton three hundred Acres part of the aforementioned Tract of Land and went and settled on the Same.

That at General Assembly held at Newbern the fifteenth Day of October in the Year of Our Lord one thousand seven hundred and forty eight an Act passed intituled An Act for ascertaining the Bounds of a certain Tract of Land formerly laid out by Treaty to the Use of the Tuskarora Indians so long as they or any of them shall occupy and live upon the same and to prevent any Person or Persons taking up Lands, or settling within the said Bounds, by Pretence of any Purchase or Purchases made or that shall be made from the said Indians. In which it is among other Things enacted that all and every Person or Persons other than the said Indians who then were dwelling on any of the Lands within the Bounds prescribed for the said Indians should on or before the twenty fifth Day of March next ensuing the Ratification of said Act remove him or herself and Family off the said Land under the Penalty of twenty Pounds Proclamation Money and if any other Person or Persons other than the said Indians should neglect or refuse to move him or herself and Family off the said Lands on or before the aforementioned Limmited Time and if any Person or Persons should thenceforth presume to settle inhabit or occupy any of the said Lands by the said Act allotted and assigned for the said Tuskarora Indians such Person or Persons should forfeit the further Penalty of twenty Shillings Proclamation Money for each and every Day he, she or they should inhabit or Occupy and Lands within the said Indian Bounds after the said twenty fifth Day of March.

But Your Petitioner firmly relying on the validity of the aforementioned Order of Council hath and doth still continue in the Possession of the said three hundred Acres he purchased of the above mentioned George Charlton though without some interruption of the said Indians who as Your Petitioner is informed are endeavoring to dispossess him by Virtue of the above recited Act.

Therefore Your Petitioner humbly prays that this Assembly may take the Premises in Consideration and make such an Additional Act to the Act beforementioned to be passed as will quiet Your Petitioner in his

Chapter One
Tuscarora Records

Possession or in some other Manner indemnify him, And Your Petitioner as in Duty bound shall ever Pray &C
                                    Hum: Bate

****

North Carolina State Archives
General Assembly Sessions Records
Nov. 1759 - Jan. 1760
Joint Resolutions

Nov. 29 - Dec. 22
Gent: of His Majestys Honble Council
      This House have resolved that Mr. Cornelius Harnett Provide Necessary Provisions and drink for the Tuscarora Indians now in Town during their stay and that the Public Treasurer repay him such money he shall so advance, and be allowed the same on passing his accounts with the Public
                        Sam Swann speakr
[?] desire your Honrs Concurrence
17 Decr 1759 In the Upper House Concured with
                        Matt. Rowan P.C.
By Order Jno Smith Clk

****

University of North Carolina
Southern Historical Collection
Manuscript Department, Collection # 716
Lewis Thompson Papers

DEED OF LEASE - 12 JULY 1766

This Indenture made the Twelfth day of July in the sixth year of the Reign of our Sovereign Lord George the Third King of Great Britain &c. and in the year of our Lord Christ 1766 Between James Allen John Wiggins Billie George Snip Nose George Billie Cain Charles Cornelious Thomas Blount John Rogers George Blount Wineoak Charles Billie Basket Billie Owin Lewis Tufdick Isaac Miller Harry samuel Bridgers Thomas Senicar Thomas Howett Billie Sockey Billie Cornelious John Senicar

Chapter One
Tuscarora Records

Thomas Basket John Cain Billy Denis William Taylor Owins John Walker Billie Mitchell Billie Netop Billy Blount Tom Jack John Litewood Billy Roberts James Mitchell Capt. Joe & Wm. Pugh Chieftains & principal persons of that part of the Nation of Indians commonly called Tuscarora Indians dwelling in the County of Bertie in the province of North Carolina, of the one part, and Robert Jones junr: his Majesty's Attorney General of the province aforesaid , and William Williams and Thomas Pugh of the said province Gent:, of the other part, witnesseth, That the said James Allen, John Wiggins, Billie George, Snip Nose George, Billie Cain, Charles Cornelious, Thomas Blount John Rogers George Blount Wineoak Charles Billie Basket Billie Owins Lewis Tufdick Isaac Miller Harry Samuel Bridgers Thomas Senicar Thomas Howits Billie Sockey Billie Cornelious John Senicar Thomas Basket John Cain Billy Denis William Taylor Owins John Walker Billie Mitchell Billie Netop Billie Blount Tom Jack John Litewood Billie Roberts James Mitchell Capt. Joe & William Pugh Tuscarora Indians aforesaid as well for & in Consideration of the Sum of fifteen hundred Pounds proclamation Money, to them in hand paid or secured to be paid for their own Use and for the Use of the Rest of that part of the said Nation of Tuscarora Indians dwelling in the County & province aforesaid, as for the yearly Rents & Covenants herein afforementioned; have demised granted & to farm let, by these presents in behalf of themselves and their said Nation, do demise grant & to farm let, untothe said Robert Jones Junr. William Williams & Thomas Pugh all that dividend or parcel of Land situate lying and being on the North Side of Roanoke River, in Bertie County aforesaid, containing about eight thousand Acres, be the same more or less, and bounded as follows, towit, Beginning at the Mouth of deep Creek, otherwise called Falling Run, thence running up the said Creek to the Indian head Line, thence by the said Line South fifty seven degrees East 3200 poles, thence a Course parallel with the general Current of the said Creek to Roanoke River aforesaid, and up the River to the Beginning together with the Trees, Timber [?] Woods, Underwoods, Profits [?] Waters & Appurtenances whatsoever, to the said dividend or parcel of Land above mentioned belonging or in very wise appurtaining: To have and to hold the said dividend or parcel of Land and all & Singular the premises with their & every of their Appurtenances, herein before mentioned, or intended to be hereby demised unto the said Robert Jones William Williams, & Thomas Pugh, their Executors, Administrators & Assigns, to be by the said Robert Jones William Williams & Thomas Pugh, respectively; their Executors Administrators and Assigns, held and

Chapter One
Tuscarora Records

enjoyed in severalty, That is to say, one third Part of the said eight thousand Acres of Land & Premises, the same into three equal parts being divided, unto the said Robert Jones his Executors, Administrators or Assigns, one other third part of the said eight thousand Acres of Land and premises, the same into three equal parts being divided, unto the said William Williams his Executors Administrators & Assigns, and the remaining third part of the said Land & Premises, the same into three equal parts being divided, unto the said Thomas Pugh, his Executors Administrators & Assigns , from the day of the date of the **[Faded]** for & during **[Faded]** full End & Term of One hundred and fifty years from thence next ensuing and fully to be compleated and ended: The said Robert Jones William Williams & Thomas Pugh, respectively, their Executors Administrators and Assigns, yealding & paying therefore yearly and every year, during the said Term; and the said Tuscarora Indians & their Assigns, one pepper corn, if demanded, at or upon the Feast of Saint Michael the Arch Angel. -- And the said James Allen Thomas Blount John Rogers George Blount John Wiggins Wineoak Charles Billie Basket Billie Owins Billie George Lewis Tufdick Isaac Miller Harry Snip Nose George Samuel Bridgers Thos. Senicar Thomas Howett Billie Cain Billie Sockey Billie Cornelious John Senicar Charles Cornelious Thomas Roberts John Cain Billie Denis William Taylor Owins John Walker Billie Mitchell Billie Netop Billie Blount Thomas Jack John Litewood Billie Roberts James Mitchell Capt. Joe & William Pugh for themselves and the Rest of the said Nation of Tuscarora Indians, them, their Heirs & Assigns, do, by these presents, covenant promise grant & agree to & with the said Robert Jones William Williams & Thomas Pugh, respectively, and their Assigns, that it shall & may be lawful for the said Robert Jones William Williams and Thomas Pugh & their Assigns, during all the time aforesaid, to fell take & carry away, sell & dispose of all Trees and Timber being & growing on the said Eight thousand Acres of Land & premises, & the money & profits arising therefrom, to receive take & retain to their own proper Use: And the said Robert Jones William Williams & Thomas Pugh, for themselves, their Executors Administrators and Assigns, and for every of them, so covenant, promise and agree to & with the said James Allen Thomas Blount John Rogers George Blount John Wiggins Wineoak Charles Billie Basket Billie Owins Billie George Lewis Tufdick Isaac Miller Harry Snipnose George Saml Bridgers Tom Senicar Thomas Howett Billie Cain Billie Sockey Billie Cornelious John Senicar Charles Cornelious Thomas Roberts John Cain Billie Denis Wm. Taylor Owins John Walker Billie Mitchell Billie Netop

Chapter One
Tuscarora Records

Billy Blount Tom Jack John Litewood Billie Roberts James Mitchell Capt. Joe & William Pugh and their Assigns, by these presents, that they the said Robert Jones William Williams & Thomas Pugh, their Executors Administrators and Assigns, shall & will from time to time and at all times, during the Continence of this demise, well & truly pay & satisfy the Rents aforesaid, at the days & Times aforesaid appointed for payment thereof: In Witness whereof the Parties to these present have hereunto set their Hand & Seal the day & year above written.

Sealed & delivered
In presence of

David Standley
Saml Grymes
James Bate

Thomas Blount (his mark)

John Rogers (his mark)

Capt. George Blount (his mark)

Wineoak Charles (his mark)

Billie Owins (his mark)

Lewis Tufdick (his mark)

Thomas Basket (his mark)

John Cain (his mark)

Billie Denis (his mark)

William Taylor (his mark)

Billie Basket (his mark)

Owins (his mark)

Billie Blount (his mark)

Thos. Jack (his mark)

34

Chapter One
Tuscarora Records

Isaac his mark Miller

Hary his mark Whealer

Saml. his mark Bridgers

Tho: his mark Senecar

Thos. his mark Howet

Billie his mark Sockey

Billie his mark Cornelious

John his mark Senecar

John his mark Walker

Billie his mark Mitchell

John his mark Litewood

Billie his mark Roberts

James his mark Mitchell

Capt. his mark Joe

William his mark Pugh

James his mark Allen

John his mark Wiggins

Billie his mark George

Snipnose his mark George

Billie his mark Cain

Chapter One
Tuscarora Records

Billie his Netop
    mark

Charles his Cornelious
    mark

****

North Carolina State Archives
General Assembly Sessions Records
Colonial (Upper and Lower Houses)
Nov. 1766 - Dec. 1768, Box 3
File: Nov. - Dec., 1766 Joint Committees
Committee OF Claims

His Excellency the Governor was Allowed his Claim of Sixty four pounds sixteen shillings and six pence for his Disbursements for Fort Johnston & the Chief of the Tuscarora Indians &c as p Account on oath filed

FILE: NOV. - DEC., 1766 LOWER HOUSE PAPERS
MESSAGES FROM GOVERNOR

I am to Acquaint You Gentlemen of an Indian Petition delivered to me last summer by a Sachem from the Tuscarora Tribe settled in the Mohocks Country for the Removal of many of the Tusks, Inhabitants of Bertie County As their Request was made agreeable to the inclination of Sir William Johnson, and with the Approbation of Mr. Stuart Superintendant of Indian Affairs, I granted the Chief Permission to Conduct as many Indians as were willing to Accompany Him to join the six Nations, leaving the Merits of the Petition for the Deliberation of this Assembly. As my correspondence with the Late Attorney General will best Explain My Sentiments on this Business I shall order that Correspondence and the Indian Petition to be laid before you requesting Your Assistance and Concurrence therein.

****

STATE RECORDS OF NORTH CAROLINA, VOLUME XXIX
LAWS, 1715-1776
EDITED BY: WALTER CLARK
NASH BROTHERS BOOK AND JOB PRINTERS

Chapter One
Tuscarora Records

GOLDSBORO, NORTH CAROLINA, 1904

Pages 507-509
1766 Laws
An Act for confirming a lease made by the Tuscarora Indians to Robert Jones, jun., William Williams and Thomas Pugh, Esquires.

I. Whereas, a number of the Tuscarora Indians, being desirous of moving themselves from their lands on Roanoke river, in Bertie county, in this province, and settling and incorporating themselves with the nations of Indians on the River Susquehannah; and whereas, the said Tuscarora Indians, in order to defray the expence of removing themselves and their effects from this province to the settlements on the river Susquehannah, did, on the twelfth day of July, in the year one thousand seven hundred and fifty-six, for the consideration of fifteen hundred pounds, proclamation money, before that time paid and advanced to them, the said Tuscarora Indians, by the said Robert Jones, William Williams and Thomas Pugh, by an indenture under the hands and seals of James Allen, John Wiggins, Billy George, Snip Nose George, Billy Cain, Charles Cornelious, Thomas Blount, John Rogers, George Blount, Wineoak Charles, Billy Basket, Billy Owen, Lewis Tuffdick, Isaac Miller, Harry, Samuel Bridgers, Thomas Seneca, Thomas Howitt, Billy Sockey, Billy Cornelius, John Seneca, Thomas Basket, John Cain, Billy Dennis, William Taylor, Owens, John Walker, Billy Mitchell, Billy Netop, Billy Blount, Tom Jack, John Lightwood, Billy Roberts, James Mitchell, Captain Joe, and William Pugh, chieftains and headmen of the said nation of Tuscarora Indians, for and on behalf of themselves and the rest of the Indians of the said Tuscarora nation, on the one part, and the said Robert Jones, William Williams and Thomas Pugh, of the other part, did demise, grant and farm to let, a certain dividend of land, situate and lying on Roanoke river, in the county aforesaid, containing about eight thousand acres, be the same more or less, and bounded as follows, to-wit: Beginning at the mouth of Deep Creek, otherwise called Falling run, thence running up the said creek to the Indian head line; hence by the said line south fifty seven degrees east one thousand two hundred and eighty poles; thence a course parallel with the general current of the said creek to Roanoke river aforesaid, and up the river to the beginning; together with all trees, timber trees, woods, underwoods, ways, waters and appurtenances whatsoever, to the said dividend, tract or parcel of land belonging or in any wise appertaining; to have and to hold the said dividend, tract or parcel of land, with all and

Chapter One
Tuscarora Records

singular the appurtenances unto the said Robert Jones, William Williams and Thomas Pugh, their executors, administrators or assigns, without impeachment of waste, to be by the said Robert Jones, William Williams and Thomas Pugh, respectively, their executors, administrators and assigns, held and enjoyed in severalty; that is to say, one third part of the said dividend, tract or parcel of land, into three equal parts to be divided, unto the said Robert Jones, his executors, administrators and assigns; one other third part thereof, the same into three equal parts to be divided, unto the said William Williams, his executors, administrators and assigns; the remaining third part thereof, the same into three equal parts to be divided, unto the said Thomas Pugh, his executors, administrators and assigns; from the said twelfth day of July, in the year aforesaid, for and during the term of one hundred and fifty years from thence next ensuing, and fully to be completed and ended, the said Robert Jones, William Williams and Thomas Pugh, their executors, administrators and assigns, yielding and paying therefor yearly, and every year during the said term, to the said Tuscarora Indians and their assigns one pepper corn, if demanded, at or upon feast of St. Michael the archangel.

II. And whereas, the said nation of Tuscarora Indians are desirous that the indenture of the lease made between the said James Allen, John Wiggins, Billy George, Snip Nose George, Billy Cain, Charles Cornelius, Thomas Blount, John Rogers, George Blount, Wineoak Charles, Billy Basket, Billy Owen, Lewis Tuffdick, Isaac Miller, Harry, Samuel Bridgers, Thomas Seneca, Thomas Howett, Billy Socket, Billy Cornelius, John Seneca, Thomas Basket, John Cain, Billy Dennis, William Taylor, Owens, John Walker, Billy Mitchell, Billy Netop, Billy Blount, Tom Jack, John Lightwood, Billy Roberts, James Mitchell, Captain Joe and William Pugh, Chieftains and headmen of the said nation of Tuscarora Indians, and the said Robert Jones, William Williams and Thomas Pugh, should have the force and validity of the Assembly; and that it shall be lawful for the said Robert Jones, William Williams and Thomas Pugh, their executors, administrators and assigns, to enter upon, occupy, possess and enjoy the said dividend, tract or parcel of land, demised as aforesaid, without let, hindrance or molestation of any person or persons whatsoever, and without Incurring any penalties whatsoever by reason of their so entering upon, occupying, possessing and enjoying the said tract or parcel of land, without impeachment for waste.

III. And whereas, the said Robert Jones, since the twelfth day of July, in the year aforesaid, hath departed this life, having first made his last will and testament, and therein and thereby bequeathed his proportion and share

Chapter One
Tuscarora Records

of the said tract or parcel of land, demised as before said, unto his sons Allen Jones and Willie Jones, their executors, administrators, and assigns;

IV. Be it therefore Enacted by the Governor, Council and Assembly, and by the Authority of the same, and it is hereby Enacted, That the said indenture of the demise is hereby ratified and confirmed; and that it shall and may be lawful for the said Allen Jones and Willie Jones, in right of the said Robert Jones, the said William Williams, and Thomas Pugh, their executors, administrators, and assigns, to enter upon, occupy, possess, and enjoy the said dividend, tract or parcel of land, according to the form and effect of the said indenture of the demise; that is to say, that it shall and may be lawful for the said Allen and Willie Jones, their executors, administrators, and assigns, to enter upon, occupy, possess, and enjoy, one third part of the said dividend, tract or parcel of land, the same to be divided into three equal parts, for, and during the term aforesaid; the said William Williams, his executors, administrators and assigns, to enter upon, occupy, possess, and enjoy, one third part thereof, the same into three equal parts to be divided, for and during the term aforesaid; and the said Thomas Pugh, his executors, administrators and assigns to enter upon, occupy, possess, and enjoy, the remaining third part thereof, for and during the term aforesaid.

V. And be it further Enacted, by the Authority aforesaid, that the said Allen Jones, Willie Jones, William Williams, and Thomas Pugh, their executors, administrators, and assigns, are hereby exempted from the penalties of an Act of Assembly, passed at New Bern the fifteenth day of October in the year of our Lord One thousand Seven Hundred and Forty-eight, intituled, An Act for ascertaining the bound of a certain tract of land formerly laid out by treaty for the use of the Tuscarora Indians, so long as they or any of them shall occupy or have the same and to prevent any other person or persons taking up land, or settling within the said bounds by pretence of any purchase or purchases made or that shall be made from the said Indians; and that shall and may be lawful for the said Allen Jones and Willie Jones, William Williams, and Thomas Pugh, their executors, administrators, assigns, to occupy, possess and enjoy, the said dividend, tract or parcel of land demised as aforesaid, during the term aforesaid, without impeachment of waste, and without the let, molestation, or hindrance, of any person or persons whatsoever.

VI. Provided always, and be it Enacted, by the Authority aforesaid, nothing herein contained shall be construed as to invalidate the title or titles of any person or persons who have obtained in a grant or grants for any tract or parcel of land within the limits or boundaries of the lands of

Chapter One
Tuscarora Records

the said Tuscarora Indians, before the fifteenth day of October, one thousand seven hundred and forty eight.

VII. Provided also, and it is hereby Enacted, by the authority aforesaid, That the said Allen Jones, Willie Jones, William Williams, and Thomas Pugh, their executors, administrators, and assigns, shall yearly and each year, during the term aforesaid, on the twenty first day of March pay the right honourable Earle of Granville, his heirs and assigns, a quit rent of four shillings, Proclamation Money, for every hundred acres of land contained within the limits or boundaries of the lands demised as aforesaid: and in case the said quit rents shall be in arrear at any time within the term aforesaid, that then it shall and may be lawful for the Earl of Granville, his heirs and assigns, to sue for and recover all such arrearages of rent, of and from the said Allen Jones, Willie Jones, William Williams, And Thomas Pugh, their executors, administrators and assigns, by all lawful ways and means whatsoever.

****

University of North Carolina
Southern Historical Collection
Manuscript Department
Collection No.: 2145
North Carolina Court of Claims

At a Council held at N: the 18 Decr. 1773

Upon a Comp. of the Chf of the Tuskarora Indians that one Wm. King had entered upon and Committed waste upon the Lands lying on the N: side of Marrattuck which lands were granted to Col. Needham Bryan by the Lds. proprietors upon the failure of that nation of Indians and afterwards confirmed to him by the Legislature of this province it was the opinion of the Board that His Excy. should write a Ltr. to Wm King to remove off the Ld. or to show cause why he held possession of it

****

Universityof North Carolina
Southern Historical Collection
Manuscript Department
Collection No. 716

Chapter One
Tuscarora Records

Lewis Thompson Papers

This Indenture made the second day of December in the year of our Lord one thousand seven hundred & Seventy five Between Whitmel Tufdick Chief of the Tuskarora Indians & Wineoak Charles Senr. Wineoak Charles Junr. Billie Roberts Lewis Tufdick West Tufdick Billie Blount Senr. Billie Blount Junr. Billie Roberts John Rogers John Smith Billie Pugh Billie Basket John Hix Samuel Bridgers John Owins James Mitchel Isaac Cornelius Tom Thomas & Walter Gibson Chieftains of the Tuskarora Indian Nation for our selves & the rest of the Tuskarora Nation of the one part & Thomas Pugh Willie Jones & William Williams of the other part Witnesseth that the sd Whitmell Tufdick Wine Oak Charles Senr. Wine Oak Charles Junr. Billie Roberts Lewis Tufdick West Tufdick Billie Blount Senr. Billie Blount Junr. John Rogers John Smith Billie Pugh John Hix Saml Bridgers John Owin James Mitchell Isaac Cornelious Tom Thomas & Walter Gibson for & in Consideration of the yearly rent or sum of Eighty Duffel Blankets Eighty Oznabrys Shirts Eighty pr boots to be made of half thicks which said Shirts & boots are to be Suitable for the sd. Indians according to their different sizes fifty pounds of powder & one hundred & fifty pounds of Shott to be paid to them Whitmell Tufdick Wineoak Charles Senr. Wineoak Charles Junr. Billie Roberts Lewis Tufdick West Tufdick Billy Blunt Senr. Billy Blunt Junr. John Rodgers John Smith Billy Pugh Billy Baskett John Hix Saml. Bridgers John Owin James Mitchell Isaac Cornelious Tom Thomas & Walter Gibson their heirs & successors have let leased & farmed & by these presents doth let lease & farm unto the sd. Thomas Pugh Willie Jones & William Williams their heirs & assigns a certain Trak or parcel of the Land Lying & being in the county of Bertie being part of the Land none by the name of the Indian Lands Containing by Estimation Two Thousand Acres be the same more or less Meted & bound as follows beginning on the Tacon Swamp at Samuel Williams line there up the sd swamp till it comes [?] to an old path that leads to unacawick Swamp then along that to the sd. swamp then up the sd. [?] to the head then along a bottom till it comes to the swamp where James Wiggins lives caled unrentara[?]ced then along that swamp to the mouth of Quitsna Swamp then up the Quitsna Swamp being the Indian line to the head from thence along the Indian line to a persimon tree on Rocquis then along the Indian line to the line of Jones Williams & Pugh then along that line to the first Station Including all the Lands in sd bounds Except a Track of Land whereon William King now Tends being about three hundred Acres To

Chapter One
Tuscarora Records

have & to hold the sd Piece & parcel of Land Above mentioned unto the sd Thomas Pugh Willie Jones & William Williams their heirs Exeters Admrs and assigns for & during the full end & term of Ninety nine Years from the Twenty fifth day of December in the year of our Lord one thousand Seven hundred & seventy five for yealding & paying therefore Yearly & Every year during the sd. Term unto the sd. Whitmell Tufdick Wineoak Charles Senr. Wine Oak Charles Junr. Billie Roberts Lewis Tufdick West Tufdick Billie Blunt Senr. Billie Blunt Junr. John Rogers John Smith Billy Pugh Billy Baskit John Hix Samuel Bridgers John Owins James Mitchell Isaac Cornelious Tom Thomas & Walter Gibson their heirs or Successors the Yearly rent of Eighty duffile Blankets Eighty Oz Shirts Eighty pair of boots made of half Thicks which sd. Shirts & boots are to be suitable to the Indians According to their different sises fifty pounds of powder & one hundred & fifty pounds of shot as aforesaid & the sd Whitmell Tufdick Wine Oak Charles Senr. Wine Oak Charles Junr. Billie Roberts Lewis Tufdick West Tufdick Billie Blunt Senr. Billie Blunt Junr. John Rogers John Smith Billie Pugh Billy Basket John Hix Samuel Bridgers John Owins James Mitchel Isaac Cornelious Tom Thomas & Walter Gibson as for their selves their heirs & successors promise grant & agree to and with the sd. Thomas Pugh Willie Jones & William Williams their heirs Exors. & Admrs & assigns that the said Thomas Pugh Willie Jones William Williams their heirs or assigns shall peaceably & Quietly have hold Occupy possess & Enjoy the above granted Lands & premises with the Appurtenances there unto belonging or in any way appertaining without threats hindrance & Molestation of us the sd Whitmell Tufdick Wine Oak Charles Senr. Wine Oak Charles Junr. Billy Roberts Lewis Tufdick West Tufdick Billy Blunt Senr. Billy Blunt Junr. John Rogers John Smith Billy Pugh Billy Baskit John Hix Samuel Bridgers John Owin James Mitchel Isaac Cornelious Tom Thomas & Walter Gibson as our heirs & successors in Witness Whereof we the said Whitmel Tufdick Wine Oak Charles &c have hereunto set our hands & Seals the day & year above Written

Billy \ his Cain mark		James Mitchel	(Seal)
	(Seal)	Billy Blunt Junr.	(Seal)
		Tom Roberts Junr.	(Seal)
		Whitmel Tufdick	(Seal)
John Hix	(Seal)	John Smith	(Seal)
John Rogers	(Seal)	Billy Roberts	(Seal)
		Billy Blunt Senr.	(Seal)

Chapter One
Tuscarora Records

John X X Owin	(Seal)	West Whitmel	(Seal)
		Wine Oak Charles Junr	(Seal)
his		Lewis Tufdick	(Seal)
Billy X Smith	(Seal)	Thomas Pugh	(Seal)
mark		Willie Jones	(Seal)
		William Williams	(Seal)

his
James T Hix   (Seal)
   mark

his
Billy - Mitchel   (Seal)
   mark

his
Billy X Pugh   (Seal)
   mark

      his
Wine Oak T Charles (Seal)
       mark

the words for them selves their heirs & successors interlined before signed in the Original was Signed Sealed & Delivered in Presence of us - Henry Bates John Pugh William Williams Junr. William Pugh Junr. Thomas B[?] as to Lewis Tufdick Thomas Pugh Willie Jones & William Williams. Bertie County proved in due form of Law in open Court by the Oath of William Williams Junr. & William Pugh Two of the subscribing Witnesses and ordered to be Registered Test John Johnston

Test True Coppy   John M. Glaukon[?]

Copy of the Indian Lease   1775

****

University of North Carolina
Southern Historical Collection
Manuscript Department
Collection No. 716

Chapter One
Tuscarora Records

Lewis Thompson Papers

PETITION OF 1777

To His Excellency Richard Caswell Esqr. Governor &c the Honorable Senate & House of Commons now sitting at New Bern

The Petition of the Tuskarorah Nation of Indians Living in Bertie County Humbly Sheweth that whereas our Brothers the White people after there Landing in this Country & a Long & Bloody Warr between our fathers & them was Ended, were pleas'd by a Treaty in writing now in our possession on our giving up all pretentions to every other part of this Country to Allow us a Certain tract of Land in this Country mentioned the said Treaty since which the Same Land has been Confirmed to us & our posterity to the Latest Generation by Sundry Acts of your Assembly & we the said Tuskarorah Indians have ever since peaceably & Quietly Possessed & Enjoyed the same under the protection of our good Brothers the White people all but that we have Volenterily & of our own free will when sober & not Intoxicated with Rum or other Spirituous Liquors Spared & Leased out to Sundry of our Good Brothers of this Country for which they have & do fully Satisfy us, after all which we had not more Land than we thought absolutely Necessary for the Support & Maintenance of us our Wives & Children in provisions, as the Rents of Lands that we have Leased out are not more than Sufficient to Suply us with Blankets Clothing and with Powder & Shott for the young men to Hunt with.

Not Withstanding all which one William King of this County having before obtained a Lease for a large Tract of our said Land being not yet Satisfyed did on the [Blank] Day of [Blank] in this present year most wickedly & perfidiously contrive & intend into an agreement With one William Cane an Indian of the said Nation to Cheat & defraud the Rest of the Tuskarorah Indians of another Large Tract of Land more Valuable than the first by calling them the said Indians together under pretence of Giving them a treat did after he had got them all Quite Drunk & Intoxicated with Strong Liquor cause & prevail by that means upon them to Subscribe a Ready Drawn Lease for that purpose for a Long Term unto him the Said Tract of Land mentioned in the Said Lease to Contain but two Hundred Acres when in fact there is within the Limits & Bounds mentioned in the Said Lease as your Petitioners are informed by many of our white Brothers not less than one thousand Acres By means whereof if the Said Lease should be Confirmed your Petitioners will not have Land Sufficient left for

Chapter One
Tuscarora Records

Cultivation or to Subsist themselves and their wives & Children with all but will be Reduced to Great Necessity & want in so much that they will be under the Necessity of becoming Burthensome to their Good Brothers the White people which they would willingly by every means in their power indeavor to avoid as much as possible. Wherefore your petitioners do most Humbly pray that after Duly Considering the premises you Wou'd be pleased to pass Some publick Act of your Assembly to disallow Disannull and totally make Void the above mentioned Lease so fraudulently obtained from us by the said William King or otherwise Relieve your poor Distressed & unhappy petitioners as in your Great Wisdom you shall think fit.

Whitmell Tufdick

his
William X Roberts
mark

his
Lewis X Tufdick
mark

his
Thomas X Roberts
mark

his
Molley X Roberts
mark

W. X Whitmell
his
mark
a Tuskarora

his
John IR Randel
mark

his
Wm X Pugh
mark

his
James X Mitchell
mark

his
Wm X Blount
mark

his
Wineoak X Charles
mark

his
William X Baskitt
mark

his
John + Smith
mark

Chapter One
Tuscarora Records

his
Walter X Gibson
mark

her
Molley X Pugh
mark

****

Duke University Library
Perkins Library, Manuscript Room
Manuscript Reading Room
Special Collections Department
Richard Caswell Papers 1777-1790

To the Honble. the General Assembly

Gentlemen.

    I herewith lay before you the Petition of Whitmill Tuffdick and other Chiefs of the Tuskarorah Indian Nation, which came to my hands only this day; And although tis late in the Session, I persuade myself, the distresses these people Complain of will be an enducement to you to take the same into Consideration them that Releif the Nature of their Case Requires

R Caswell

New Bern
13th. decr. 1777.

Editors Note: The Petition was not included in this collection. It can be found in "Lewis Thompson's Papers", at the University of North Carolina. Collection No.: 716.

****

LAWS OF THE STATE OF NORTH CAROLINA
PUBLISHED ACCORDING TO ACT OF ASSEMBLY

Chapter One
Tuscarora Records

BY JAMES IREDELL
EDENTON, PRINTED BY HODGE & WILLIS, 1791

Page 402
CHAP. XXIII. 1778 LAWS

An Act to amend an Act, entitled, An Act for quieting and securing the Tuscarora Indians, and others claiming under the Tuscaroras, in the possession of their Lands.

I. Whereas by the said Act there is no Penalty imposed on Jurors or Witnesses, duly summoned, and failing to attend;

II. Be it enacted by the General Assembly of the State of North Carolina, and it is hereby enacted by the Authority of the same, That the Commissioners by the said Act appointed, or any three of them, assembled for the Purpose of holding a Court, shall and may inflict Fines on Jurors or Witnesses so failing to attend, not exceeding one hundred Pounds, at their Discretion; and unless sufficient Excuse be to them afterwards shewn, cause the same to be levied and applied towards defraying the County Charges of Bertie: And the Witnesses and Jurors who shall attend on the Trial of any Dispute between the said Tuscaroras and others, shall have and receive ten Dollars per Day for their Attendance, to be paid by the Party cast, with all other Costs; and such Trials may hereafter be had on any part of the said Lands belonging to Said Tuscaroras in Bertie County, which the Commissioners Shall direct.

****

THE STATE RECORDS OF NORTH CAROLINA
VOLUME XXIV
LAWS, 1777-1788
EDITED BY: WALTER CLARK

LAWS OF NORTH CAROLINA - 1778
CHAPTER XVI

An Act for quieting and securing the Tuscarora Indians, and others claiming under the Tuscaroras, in the Possession of their Lands.

I. Be it Enacted, by the General Assembly, and it is hereby Enacted by the Authority of the same, That Withmell Tuffdick, Chief or Headman of the Tuscarora Nation, and the Tuscarora Indians, now living in the County of Bertie, shall have, hold, occupy, possess and enjoy, all the Lands lying in the County of Bertie aforesaid, whereof they are now seized and

Chapter One
Tuscarora Records

possessed (being Part of the Lands heretofore allotted to the Indians aforesaid by solemn Treaty, and confirmed to them and their Successors by Act of Assembly, in the Year One Thousand Seven Hundred and Forty Eight) without Let, Molestation, or Hindrance, clear of all Quitrents, or any Public Demand by Way of Tax whatever, to them the said Tuscarora Indians, and their Heirs and Successors; and that they the said Tuscaroras, and their Heirs and Successors, shall for ever be clear and exempt from every Kind of Poll Tax.

II.   And whereas the said Tuscarora Indians, by Nature ignorant, and strongly addicted to drinking, may be easily imposed on by designing Persons, and unwarily deprived of their said Lands; Be it Enacted by the Authority aforesaid, That no Person, for any Consideration whatever, shall hereafter purchase, buy or lease, any Tract or Parcel of Land now claimed by, or in Possession of the said Tuscarora Indians, or any of them; nor shall any Person settle on or cultivate the said Lands, or any Part thereof, in his own Right, or under Pretence as acting as Overseer for the Indians, all such Purchases, Sales, Leases and Agreements, shall be, and they are hereby declared null and void; and the Person so purchasing, buying or leasing, settling on, or cultivating the said Lands, or any Part thereof, shall forfeit and pay the Sum of Three Hundred Pounds current Money for every Hundred Acres by him so purchased, bought or leased, settled on or cultivated as aforesaid, one Half to the Use of the said Tuscarora Indians, the other to the Use of him or her who shall sue for the same; to be recovered by Action of Debt, Bill, Plaint, or Information, in any Court having Cognizance thereof. Provided, That the said Tuscarora Indians may sell or dispose of their Lands, or any Part thereof, with Consent of the General Assembly first had and obtained.

III.   And whereas the Chieftains and Headmen of the Tuscarora Nation living in the County, did on the Twelfth Day of July, in the Year One Thousand Seven Hundred and Sixty Six, for the Consideration of Fifteen Hundred Pounds to them paid by Robert Jones, Jun., William Williams, and Thomas Pugh, by Indenture under their Hands and Seals, demise, grant, and to Farm let, unto the said Robert Jones, William Williams, and Thomas Pugh, a certain Tract of Land lying in the County aforesaid, containing about Eight Thousand Acres, more or less, bounded as follows, to-wit, Beginning at the Mouth of Deep Creek, otherwise called Falling Run; thence running up the said Creek, to the Indian Head Line; thence by the said Line South, Seventeen Degrees East, Twelve Hundred and Eighty Poles; thence a Course parallel with the general Current of the said Creek, to Roanoke River; and then up the River to the Beginning; together with

Chapter One
Tuscarora Records

the Appurtenances thereto belonging, to be held and enjoyed by the said Robert Jones, William Williams, and Thomas Pugh, their Executors, Administrators, and Assigns, in Severalty, for and during the Term of One Hundred and Fifty Years, as may more fully appear by the said Indenture, registered in the County Court of Bertie aforesaid, and ratified by Act of Assembly, passed at New Bern in the Year One Thousand Seven Hundred and Sixty-Six; Be it Enacted by the Authority aforesaid, That each and every of the Persons intitled to claim under the Demise afore mentioned, or by Grants from the Persons claiming under the same, or either of them, and their Heirs and Assigns, shall and may have, hold, occupy, possess and enjoy, the several Shares, Dividends, or Parcels of the said Land to them belonging, in as full, free, and absolute Manner, and with the same legal privileges and Advantages, in every Respect, and subject to the same Taxes, as if the said Land had been originally granted to the said Robert Jones, William Williams, and Thomas Pugh, by Lord Granville, or by this State.

IV. And whereas the said Tuscarora Indians, for good and sufficient Reasons, and for valuable Considerations, have since the Twelfth Day of July, One Thousand Seven Hundred and Sixty Six, and previous to the First Day of December last, demised, granted, and to Farm let, sundry Tracts or Parcels of Land lying in said County of Bertie, to sundry Persons, as by Indentures duly executed may more fully appear; Be it Enacted by the Authority aforesaid, That all the Lands contained in the last mentioned Demises, if the said Demises were fairly, bona fide, and without `Fraud, made by, and obtained from the said Tuscarora Indians, since the Year One Thousand Seven Hundred and Sixty Six, and previous to the First Day of December last past, shall not be deemed vacant Lands, or be liable to be entered as such in the Land Office, unless the General Assembly shall hereafter so direct, but nevertheless shall be subjected to the same Taxes as other Lands in this State are liable to.

V. And whereas it is suggested by the said Tuscarora Indians that unfair Dealing has been used in obtaining one or more of the Demises afore mentioned, and they the said Indians have at present no Mode for obtaining Redress in such Cases: Be it therefore Enacted by the Authority aforesaid, That the Commissioners herein after mentioned, or a Majority of them, shall and may, upon Complaint of the said Tuscarora Indians, in Court or Meeting assembled, that any Person or Persons has or have unfairly or fraudulently obtained any Grant or Demise for Lands to them belonging since the Year One Thousand Seven Hundred Sixty Six, and previous to the First Day of December last, summon the Person or Persons so

Chapter One
Tuscarora Records

complained against, or cause him or them to be summoned, to appear before them on a certain Day on the Land in Dispute (giving at least Ten Days Notice previous to the Day in such Summons appointed) then and there to answer the Complaints of the Indians for having fraudulently or unfairly obtained a Grant or Demise of the Land in Question; and shall also summon, or cause to be summoned, a Jury of Twelve Men, being Freeholders in the said County of Bertie, and not resident on, or Owners of any Lands purchased of the said Tuscarora Indians: And the said Commissioners, or a Majority of them, shall attend at the time and Place appointed, with the Jury aforesaid, and having first sworn the Jury to try and determine fairly between the said Indians and the Person or Persons complained against, shall and may cause Witnesses to be examined on both Sides, and receive the Verdict of the Jury, and return the same, with the Pannel, to the next County Court of the said County of Bertie, to be entered upon Record, and such Verdict shall be as good and effectual as if obtained in any Court of Record; and if the same be general, the said Commissioners, or a Majority of them, shall and may appoint one or more Person or Persons to carry the same into Execution; but if special, then the Court shall decide thereon, and cause the Sheriff of the County to carry such Decision into Execution.

VI. And whereas the said Indians are often injured by Horses, Cattle and Hogs, driven on their Lands by the white People, the said Horses, Cattle and Hogs, breaking into their Inclosures, and destroying their Corn and other Effects, and are also frequently deprived of their Property, and abused by ill disposed Persons: For Remedy whereof, and also for Recovery of Rents or Demands now due, or which may hereafter become due and owing to the said Tuscarora Indians; Be it Enacted by the Authority aforesaid, That William Williams, Thomas Pugh, Willie Jones, Simon Turner, and Zedekiah Stone, be and they are hereby appointed Commissioners for the said Indians; and they, or any Three of them, shall and may inquire into Complaints made by the said Indians, summon the persons complained against before them, and award such Restitution and Redress as to them shall seem just an necessary; and may appoint an Officer or Officers to serve Subpoenas, and to execute such Awards and Determinations as they shall or may make in Regard of the Premises: And the Court of the said County of Bertie is hereby authorized and required to fill up, from Time to Time, by new Appointments, any Vacancies which may happen among the Commissioners, by Death or Resignation; and upon Complaint of the Chief or Headman of the Nation, and the Rest of the Indians, in Court of Meeting properly assembled, against any one of the

Chapter One
Tuscarora Records

Commissioners for Misbehaviour, may inquire into the Conduct of the Persons or Persons complained against, remove him or them, if necessary, and appoint another or others in his or their Stead.

VII. And be it further Enacted by the Authority aforesaid, That the Lands leased by the said Tuscarora Indians to Robert Jones, Jun., William Williams, and Thomas Pugh, and to other Persons, shall revert to, and become the Property of the State, at the Expiration of the Terms the several Leases mentioned, if the said Nation be then extinct: And the Lands now belonging to, and possessed by the said Tuscaroras, shall revert to, and become the Property of the State, whenever the said Nation shall become extinct, or shall entirely abandon or remove themselves of the said Lands, and every Part thereof. Provided, That no Person shall have any Preference of Entry to any of the said Lands by Virtue of any Lease or Occupancy whatsoever since December, One Thousand Seven Hundred and Seventy-Six, whenever the General Assembly shall declare the said Lands to be vacant.

****

North Carolina State Archives
General Assembly Sessions Records
GASR, Box #1, Apr.-May, 1780

No. Carolina In Senate 2d May 1780
Mr. Speaker & Gent. of the House Commons
The Resolve of your House requesting His Excellency the Governor to issue a proclamation requiring all persons settled on the Indian Lands to move off in a certain Time you will herewith receive Concurred with.
By Order   Alex Martin SS
Jno Sitgreaves CS

In the Honourable Senate and House of Commons now met at Newbern
The Petition of Whitmell Tufdick Hed man and the rest of the Indians of the Tuskarorah Nation living in Bertie County in the State of North Carolina Humbly Sheweth

That Whereas at a former Assembly held at Newbern in the Year of our Lord one Thousand seven hundred and seventy eight you were Pleased to Pass an Act for the Tuskarorah Indians, and other under the Tuskarorah's,

Chapter One
Tuscarora Records

in the Possession of their Lands and thereby Appointed certain Commissioners who were to Determine all disputes which might happen between the white people and the said Tuskarorahs or any of them and also where the dispute was Concerning Lands to have a jury Summoned by the said Commissioners to try the Same, Notwithstanding all which your good intentions towards us, We your unfortunate Petitioners still Labour under many of the Inconveniences and hardships which you in your great goodness intended to remedy by the said Act by means of the Juries not Attending or not a Sufficient Number of them to compose a jury According to the directives of the said Act of Assembly. As your Petitioners conceive by reason of the artfull persuation or some other means made use of by the Parties who contend with your Petitioners.

Our Petitioners therefore most Humbly Pray that you would take their Case under your most Serious Consideration and lay such Penalty on such Jurors who do not attend when Lawfully Summoned & will compell them to attend or by a Law for that purpose give such an Allowance to be paid by the parties who fail in the disputes as will be an Incouragement to them to Attend when so Summoned or otherwise believe

[The rest of this petition is faded and cannot be accurately read or transcribed]

His Lewis XX Tufdick Mark	His John X Roggers Mark	His John X Pugh Mark
His John X Randolph Mark	Whitmell Tufdick	His West X Tufdick Mark
His William X Blount Mark		His Thomas X Thomas Mark
His James + Mitchell Mark	His Benj. X Smith Mark	His William X Roberts Mark
His Walter X Gibson Mark	His Billey X Pugh Mark	

Chapter One
Tuscarora Records

****

THE STATE RECORDS OF NORTH CAROLINA
VOLUME XXIV
LAWS 1777-1788
EDITED BY: WALTER CLARK
NASH BROTHERS BOOK AND JOB PRINTERS
GOLDSBORO, N.C., 1906

CHAPTER XXIII. 1ST SESSION.
1780. An Act to amend an Act, intituled "An Act for quieting and securing the Tuscarora Indians, and others claiming under the Tuscaroras, in the possession of their lands. (Page 335)

I. Whereas by the said Act there is no penalty imposed on jurors or witnesses, duly summoned, and failing to attend;

II. Be it enacted by the General Assembly of the State of North Carolina, and it is hereby enacted by the authority of the same, that the commissioners by the said Act appointed, or any three of them, assembled for the purpose of holding a court, shall and may inflict fines on jurors or witnesses so failing to attend, not exceeding one hundred pounds, at their discretion; and unless sufficient excuse be to them afterwards shewn, cause the same to be levied and applied towards defraying the county charges of Bertie: And the witnesses and jurors who shall attend on the trial of any disputes between the Tuscaroras and others, shall have and receive ten dollars per day for their attendance, to be paid by the party cast, with all other costs; and such trial may hereafter be had on any part of the lands belonging to said Tuscaroras in Bertie County, which the commissioners shall direct.

****

NORTH CAROLINA HISTORICAL AND GENEALOGICAL REGISTER
VOLUME III, PAGE 453, J.R.B. HATHAWAY, ED.
(EDENTON, 1900-1903)

At a Court of Indian Commission, held at the house of Wm. Blunt on the Indian Lands, Feby. 24, 1781, to try a matter of dispute between said Indians and Exrs. of Wm. King, decd., concerning a lease said to be

Chapter One
Tuscarora Records

obtained by said King during his life time. Present: Thomas Pugh, Simon Turner and Zedekiah Stone, Commrs. appointed by the Assembly, the Indians and Executors of Wm. King also present. The Sheriff returned the following Jury: Wm. Freeman, Jno. Walston, Peter Clifton, Hugh Hyman, Sam'l Milburn, James House, Henry Averit, Elisha Rhodes, Andrew Oliver, James Bentley, William Watson and Henry Smith, Freeholders, who being sworn say that Wm. King in his life time had no right to the premises in dispute nor his Executors since his death, said lease by which he held it and under which he claimed being fraudulent and fraudulently obtained. Whereupon the Court gave judgment according to verdict, and John Bryan was appointed to execute the judgment by putting the Indians in possession.

                                                    Thos. Pugh,
                                                    Sn. Turner,
                                                    Zed. Stone,
                                                    Commrs.

****

North Carolina State Archives
General Assembly Session Records
(Nov..-Dec. 1798)
House Bills (Dec. 13)

A Bill granting the Tuskarora Nation of Indians two other Commissioners, in addition to those now acting for them.

     Whereas the Chiefs of the Tuskarora nation of Indians have made it appear to this General Assembly by petition that it is indispensably necessary there should be two other Commissioners appointed for them in addition to those now acting & have recommended as their choice William Williams of Martin, & Samuel Johnston Junr. of Bertie County for that purpose.
     Be it therefore enacted by the General Assembly of the State of North Carolina, & it is hereby enacted by the authority of the same that the said William Williams of Martin & Samuel Johnston Junr. of Bertie County are hereby vested with the same power & authority with the Commissioners before appointed for the Tuskarora Nation of Indians --- & from & after the passing of this act shall be considered as Commissioners

Chapter One
Tuscarora Records

to act for them in addition to those now acting --- any law or custom to the contrary notwithstanding.

****

THE PUBLIC ACTS OF THE GENERAL ASSEMBLY OF NORTH CAROLINA
VOLUME II
CONTAINING THE ACTS FROM 1790 TO 1803
REVISED AND PUBLISHED UNDER THE AUTHORITY OF THE LEGISLATURE
BY FRANCOIS XAVIER MARTIN
NEWBERN; MARTIN & OGDEN, 1804

1798 LAWS
CHAP. 17

An Act granting the Tuscarora Nation of Indians two other Commissioners in addition to those now acting for them, (Page 122).

Whereas the Chief of the Tuscarora Nation of Indians have made it appear to this General Assembly by petition, that it is indispensably necessary there should be two other Commissioners appointed for them in addition to those now acting, and have recommended as their choice William Williams, of Martin, and Samuel Johnston, jun. of Bertie County, for that purpose;

II. Be it enacted by the General Assembly of the State of North Carolina, and it is hereby enacted by the authority of the same, That the said William Williams, of Martin, and Samuel Johnston, jun. of Bertie County, are hereby vested with the same powers and authorities with the Commissioners before appointed for the Tuscarora Nation of Indians; and from and after the passing of this act shall be considered as Commissioners to act for them in addition to those now acting; any law or custom to the contrary notwithstanding.

****

North Carolina State Archives
Governor's Papers
Governor Benjamin William Letter Book
Page 95/460 - 96/461

Chapter One
Tuscarora Records

War Department
3rd November 1801

Sir

    A deputation from the Tuscarora Nation of Indians, accompanied by an Interpreter, left the Seat of Government this morning, on their way to North Carolina, for the Purpose of opening a negotiation with that State, for the Cession or sale of their right to a tract of Land of ten miles square on the River Roanoke, from which the major part of the said Nation migrated about thirty five years since.
    The deputation represent that on this migration the aforesaid tract was reserved for the benefit of the Nation, & that their object now is to procure from the State of North Carolina, for the sale or Cession of the right which they suppose still to possess, a sum of money, with which they may purchase other Lands in the Vicinity of those on which they now reside.
    On their application, the President has been pleased to appoint the Honble. William R. Davie Commissioner to attend the Negotiation, and give the necessary consent & sanction of the United States to the compleation of the bargain, on such terms as the Agents or Representatives of the State of North Carolina & the Indian deputation may agree to consistently with the Laws and Constitution.
    It is presumed that Genl. Davie's compensation (eight dollars p Day) & reasonable expences in attending to the business, shall be paid by the State of North Carolina.

                               I have the honor to be,
                               with respectful consideration

His Excellency   Your Obt. humbl. Servt.
     Sir   H. Dearbourn
Govr. Williams

****

North Carolina State Archives
Governor's Papers
Governor Benjamin Williams Letter Book
Page 18/490   November 1801

Chapter One
Tuscarora Records

To the Honorable, the General Assembly
of the State of North Carolina

Gentlemen,

I have held a talk with the Deputation from the Tuscarora Indians: the result of which perhaps may be unnecessary to be detailed to your honorable body, I would however submit to the Legislature the propriety of appointing a Committee or Commissioner to treat with them respecting the objects explained in the Letter of the Secretary of War which a few days past I had the honor of laying before the General Assembly, and am

Gentlemen,
With due respect
Your Obt. Servt.
B. Williams

****

North Carolina State Archives
Private Manuscript Collection
David Stone Papers, 1795-1865
Call Number: P.C.82.1

Bertie 4th. Decr. 1801

Dear Sir

I wished to have had an opportunity of conversing with you before you set out to Raleigh upon a subject which I find a very unexpected event has brought to the notice of the Assembly I mean the Indian lands in this County.

That portion of County denominated Indian land in this County was by an Act of Assembly in the year 1744 (I believe) confirmed to the Indians so long as they should continue to occupy it - In the Year 1764, 5 or 6 a Tuscarora chief from the Mohawk Nation either came of his own accord or was brought by the procurement of the persons interested who prevailed upon one half of the Tribe living here to go with him to Canada. Those who removed wished to sell their Interest in the Land and the persons who after became.

Chapter One
Tuscarora Records

****

Duke University
Perkins Library, Manuscript Reading Room
Special Collections Department
Henry Alexander Scammell Dearborn Papers
1802-1848
Boston, Suffolk Co., Mass.

War Department
July 30, 1802

Sir,

      The bearer Capt. Lunt has been sent by direction of the President of the United States to be present with you, with the Tuscarora Indians, when and where a formal and explicit Power shall be executed by the voice of the Nation and executed by their principal Chiefs authorising such of their Chiefs as they may designate, to convey all the rights and title which that part of the Nation claims to lands in the State of North Carolina - Capt. Lunt must be a witness to the execution of the power and must appear in person, with the Chiefs who may be authorised to make the Conveyance at the seat of Government in North Carolina - You will please Sir to accompany Capt. Lunt to the residence of the Tuscaroras or follow him at such time as you may reasonably expect they may be prepared to execute the power, you will be pleased to attend to the form of the instrument and a formal execution of the same, and will certify on the back of the power that you were present at the execution and that it was done by the full consent and approbation of the Nation

                      I am respectfully your
                            Humbl. Servt.
                            H. Dearborn

Capt. Callender Irvine

****

North Carolina State Archives
Governor Benjamin William's Letter Book

Chapter One
Tuscarora Records

1799-1802, Part II, Page 195
G.L.B. 14

War Department

Sir, October 18th - 1802

    A Chief of the Tuscarora Nation of Indians, accompanied by an interpreter has left the Seat of Government for North Carolina for the purpose of making a Sale or cession of the tract of Land claimed by Said Nation on the River Roanoke, which was the object of the Visit of the deputation the last Season but being unsuccessful at that time he wishes now to renew the Negotiation.
    It is conceived that the authority that he now brings from his nation will be deemed sufficient for authorising the Sale.
    The Hon. Wm. R. Davie is Commissioned with full powers to attend the negotiation and give the necessary sanction and consent of the United States to Such terms as the Legislature of the State or their Agents and the Chief may agree on consistently with the laws and the Constitution.
    It is presumed that General Davie's compensation and expences in attending to the business will be paid by the State of North Carolina.

His Excellency
Benjamin Williams

I have the honor to be
respectfully, Your Hble. Servt
H: Dearborn

****

North Carolina State Archives
Governor's Papers
Governor Benjamin William's Letter Book
Page 195/671

War Department

October 18th 1802

Sir,

Chapter One
Tuscarora Records

A Chief of the Tuscarora Nation of Indians, accompanied by an interpreter has left the seat of Government for North Carolina for the purpose of making a Sale or Cession of the tract of Land claimed by the said Nation on the River Roanoke, which was the object of the Visit of the deputation the last Season but being unsuccessfull at that time he wishes now to renew the Negotiation. It is conceived that the authority that he now brings from his Nation will be deemed sufficient for authorising the Sale.

The Hon. Wm. R. Davie is Commissioned with full powers to attend the Negotiation and give the necessary sanction and consent of the United States to such terms as the Legislature of the State or their Agents and the Chief may agree on consistently with the laws and the Constitution.

It is presumed that General Davie's compensation and expences in attending to the business will be paid by the State of North Carolina

I have the honor to be
respectfully Your Obt. Servt.

His Excellency
Benjamin Williams   H. Dearborn

****

North Carolina State Archives
General Assembly Sessions Records
November-December, 1802, Box #1

North Carolina
    In Senate 30 Nov. 1802
Mr. Speaker
    We agree to your proposition for referring to a joint Committee the representation made by the Chiefs of the Tuscarora Tribe of Indians. We have for this purpose appointed on our part Mr. Outlaw, Mr. Gaither & Mr. Turner.

By order   Jo Riddick S.S.
M Stokes Clk

Chapter One
Tuscarora Records

House of Commons 3 December 1802
    Resolved that Mr Cameron and Mr Edward Harris be appointed Commissioners on the part of this State, to see the agreement to which this report refers
executed   S. Cabarrus Sp
By order   J Hunt CHC

In Senate Decemr 3rd AD 1802
    Read & concurred with & Resolved that Mr. Carney & Mr. Binford be appointed Commissioners on the part of this House to execute in behalf of this State the agreement or contract refered to in this report
By order   Jo Riddick SS
M Stokes Clk

****

North Carolina State Archives
General Assembly Sessions Records
November-December, 1802, Box #1

                      Report of the Committee
                 on the address of the Chiefs of
                       the Tuscarora Nation

The Committee to whom was referred the address of the Chiefs of the Tuscarora Nation, beg leave to report

       That on a conference with the said Chiefs agreeably to the instruction of the Committee, they agreed to relinquish on the part of their Nation, their claim to the said lands after the expiration of the lease made to Robert Jones and others in the year 1766 on the condition that the General Assembly would pass a law enabling them to lease the undemised part of their lands, and lengthen the short lease in the manner proposed in their address, and facilitate the payment and receipt of the rents on the present leases; your Committee are of opinion that it would be good policy to meet them on this ground, as the interest of all parties will be promoted by it, the Indians will be satisfied; such persons as may have grants located on that land before the year 1748 will now see a prospect of reducing their

Chapter One
Tuscarora Records

claims into possession and the State effects the extinguishment of the Indian claim without expence. The Indian Chiefs agree to carry this arrangement into effect in any manner that may be thought expedient. The Commissioners of the United States remains here to give such agreement the necessary sanction & form, and desires that two or three persons may be appointed as agents or as a Committee to see the agreement executed and to satisfy the Legislature that it is made in due Conformity with the propositions agreed on in Conference with your Committee.

Your Committee beg leave to report a Bill to carry this agreement into effect on the part of the State.

All which is Submitted
[Name?]

****

North Carolina State Archives
Governor's Papers
State Series, Volume XXV.
Benjamin Williams, Volumes 3 - 1802, Jan. 10 - Dec.4

4 DECEMBER 1802

Articles of a Treaty between the United States of America
and the Tuscarora Indians

Whereas a large part of the Nation now reside at so remote a distance from the State of North Carolina, that they are unable to derive any benefit from the lands, the use of which had been granted to the Nation by the Legislature of that State so long as they should occupy and live upon the same.

And Whereas the Legislature of the State of North Carolina in directing the use of said lands had heretofore permitted certain leases to be made of part thereof, and difficulties have arisen in the payment and receipt of the rents becoming due thereon.

And Whereas for the purpose of preventing any disputes that might arise respecting the future occupancy of said lands, or the direction of the use thereof, and to remove the difficulties aforesaid, the President of the United States by and with the advice and consent of the Senate thereof hath appointed William Richardson Davie of North Carolina

Chapter One
Tuscarora Records

Commissioner on the part of the United States for the purposes aforesaid, and the said William Richardson Davie on the part of the United States, and the undersigned Chiefs in their own names and in behalf of the whole Tuscarora Nation have agreed to the following Articles, namely.

Article 1st.

In consideration of the agreement on the part of the Legislature of the State of North Carolina that they will by certain Acts of the General Assembly of said State facilitate the collection of the rents due or to become due on the leases of said lands heretofore made: And on the condition that an Act or Acts of the General Assembly of the said State shall be passed authorising the said Tuscarora Nation or the Chiefs thereof in behalf of said Nation to lease on such terms as they may deem proper the undemised part of the lands alotted to them in the County of Bertie in the said State as well as other parts thereof now under a lease or leases for years, so that the term or terms of the leases made of the whole or any part thereof may extend to the twelfth day of July which shall be in the year of our Lord one thousand nine hundred and sixteen: And upon condition also that the Legislature of the said State shall by an Act or Acts for that purpose remove as far as the same can be done by Legislative interposition any difficulties or disputes that might arise respecting the future occupancy of said lands either by the Indians of the said Tribe or Nation of Tuscaroras or their lessees and assigns until the said twelfth day of July which shall be in the year of our Lord one thousand nine hundred and sixteen, and also declare and enact that the occupancy and possession of the Tenants under the said leases heretofore confirmed by Act or Acts of the General Assembly and such leases as may be made under the Act or Acts made in pursuance of this Treaty, shall be held and deemed in all cases whatsoever the occupancy and possession of the said Tuscarora Nation to all intents and purposes as if they the said Nation or the Indians thereof or any of them actually resided on said lands; the under signed Chiefs in their own names and in behalf of the whole of the Tuscarora Nation hereby stipulate and agree that from and after the said twelfth day of July which shall be in the year of our Lord one thousand nine hundred and sixteen all the right interest and claim of the said Nation or any of the Indians thereof by an Act of the General Assembly of the State of North Carolina of the State of North Carolina or otherwise to the use possession or occupancy of a certain Tract of Land alotted to them by the Legislature of the said State situated in the County of Bertie in the State aforesaid bounded as described as

Chapter One
Tuscarora Records

follows, Viz. Beginning at the mouth of Quitsnoy Swamp running up the said Swamp four hundred and thirty pole to a Scrubby Oak near the head of the said Swamp by a great Spring, then north ten degrees East eight hundred and fifty pole to a persimmon tree on Raquis Swamp then along the Swamp and pocoson main course North fifty seven degrees West two thousand six hundred and forty pole to a Hickory on the East side of the falling run on deep Creek, and down the various courses of the said run to Morattock or Roanoke river, then down the river to the first Station, shall cease and determine and shall be held and deemed extinguished forever.

Article 2nd.

This Treaty shall be considered as a final and permanent adjustment and settlement of all the differences, disputes and claims between the State of North Carolina, and the said Tuscarora Nation of Indians, as soon as the conditions stipulated in the forgoing article shall be fullfilled on the part of the State of North Carolina, and the Treaty shall be ratified by the President of the United States, by and with the advice and consent of the Senate of the United States.

In witness of all and every thing herein contained the said William Richardson Davie and the undersigned Chiefs in behalf of themselves and the Tuscarora Nation have hereunto set their hands and seals.

Done at the City of Raleigh in the State of North Carolina on the fourth day of December in the year One thousand eight hundred and two.

William R. Davie (Seal)

Witnesses
S. Cabarrus speaker of the
House of Commons

Jno. M. Binford } Agents for the State &
E. Harris   } Members of the Genl. Assembly

Dun. Cameron - Agent for the State & Member
    Of Gl. Assembly

S.W. Cearney Agent for the State & member
    of the General Assembly

Chapter One
Tuscarora Records

Wm. Hill   Secry.

Ezra Lunt[?]

H.L. Banner   Member of the Senate

Nat. C. Whitaker   Member of the House of Commons

B.H. Stith   Member of the House of Commons

                  his
      Saccorusa   +   (Seal)
                  mark

                  his
      Long Board   +   (Seal)
                  mark

                  his
      Samuel Smith   +   (Seal)
                  mark

****

North Carolina State Archives
General Assembly Sessions Records
November-December, 1802, Box #1

The Committee who were appointed to examine the Treaty proposed to be made between the United States and the Tuscarora Nation of Indians - Report
      That they have examined the same, and were present at the Signing and Execution of the said Treaty, and that the said Treaty has been made in exact Conformity to the Agreement made between the Chiefs and the Committee appointed to confer with them on that Subject, and the Report and Bill reported to the House
Submitted
                      D. Cameron

Chapter One
Tuscarora Records

Chairman

Reported in the House of Commons
6th December 1802
By order J Hunt CHC

North Carolina
    In Senate 9 Decr. 1802
The House taking into Consideration Resolved that they do concur therewith
By order   M Stokes Clk

North Carolina
In Senate Decemr. 13th 1802
Mr Speaker
    On the third & last reading of the bill entitled "a bill for the relief of the Tuscarora nation of Indians" we propose shall be amended by inserting the words forty shillings 40S instead of "twenty five shillings" in the fourteenth line of the third enacting clause.
    Should you agree two of your Members will attend & see the same done accordingly
                Jo Riddick S.S.
By order M Stokes Clk

In House of Commons Decr 1802
Mr Speaker
    We do not agree to amend the Bill for the relief of the Tuscarora Indians as proposed by the Senate
By Order   S. Cabarrus
J Hunt

****

North Carolina State Archives
General Assembly Sessions Records
November-December, 1802, Box #1

Chapter One
Tuscarora Records

Origl   1802
A Bill for the relief of the Tuscarora Nation of Indians

In House of Commons 2d December 1802 read the first time and passed
By Order   J Hunt

In Senate Decr 3rd 1802
Read the first time & passed
By Order   M Stokes Clk

Mr. Arrington & Mr. Hookes

In the H. Commons 6 Decemr 1802
Read the Second time amended & passed
By order   J Hunt CHC

In Senate Decemr 9th 1802
Read the second time, amended & passed
By order   M Stokes   Clk

House of Commons 11 Dec. 1802
read the third time, amended & passed
By order   J Hunt   CHC

In Senate Decemr 13th 1802
Read the third time & passed
Ordered to be Engrossed
By order
M Stokes   Clk

****

North Carolina State Archives
General Assembly Sessions Records
(Nov-Dec. 1802)

Chapter One
Tuscarora Records

House Bill (Dec. 2)

A Bill for the relief of the Tuscarora Nation of Indians

Whereas the Indians composing the Tuscarora Nation have by their chief Sacorusa and others regularly deputed and authorised requested the concurrence of the General Assembly of this State to enable them to lease or demise for a number of years the residue of their lands situate in the County of Bertie in such manner that the whole of the leases on said land shall terminate at the same period.

1. Be it enacted by the General assembly of the State of North Carolina and it is hereby enacted by the authority of the same, That the said chiefs Saccorusa, Longboard, and Samuel Smith, or majority of them be and they are hereby authorised to lease and to farm let the undemised residue of the lands allotted to the Tuscarora nation in Bertie County for a term of years that shall expire and end when the lease made by the Tuscarora nation to Robert Jones and others in the year one thousand seven hundred and sixty six shall end and expire; and also to extend the terms of the leases already made or granted for a shorter term to a term or terms which shall expire at thesame time with the said lease made in the year one thousand seven hundred and sixty six in such parcels and on such rents and conditions as may be approved by the Commissioners appointed in pursuance of this act, and which may best promote the interest and convenience of the said Indian nation

And whereas some difficulties have arisen respecting the receipt and payment of there rents on some of the present leases

2. Be it further enacted that the said chiefs or a majority of them be and they are hereby authorised to make such alterations by covenant or agreement respecting the payments and receipt of any of the rents due, or that may become due on any of the existing leases as the Commissioners appointed in pursuance of this act, or a majority of them shall approve

Whereas the said Indian Chiefs are ignorant of the usual forms of business, and may want advice and assistance in transacting the business respecting their lands for remedy whereof and to prevent their being injured

3. Be it further enacted That the Governor shall appoint three Commissioners for the purpose of carrying the provisions of this act into

Chapter One
Tuscarora Records

effect and no lease, grant, demise covenant or agreement made by said Indian Chief as aforesaid respecting said lands or the rents thereof, shall be good or sealed in law, unless the same shall be approved by said Commissioners or a majority of them, and such approbation shall be expressed in writing, and annexed or endorsed on Such lease covenant or agreement and registered in the Registers office of the County of Bertie together with said lease or agreement and the said Commissioners shall receive the sum of twenty five shillings per day for their compensation and expenses to be paid out of the monies received by the said chiefs on leasing said lands.

And be it further enacted that the occupancy and possession of the tenants under the said leases heretofore confirmed by act or acts of the General Assembly and such leases as may be made under this act, shall be held and deemed in all cases whatsoever the occupancy and possession of the said Tuscarora nation, to all intents and purposes as if the said nation or the Indians thereof or any of them actually resided on said land

Whereas the said chiefs Saccorusa, Longboard and Samuel Smith, being duly and fully authorised and empowered by the said Tuscarora nation, have consented that the Indian claim to the use possession and occupancy of said land shall cease and be extinguished, when the said lease made in the year one thousand seven hundred and sixty six to Robert Jones and others shall expire.

Be it enacted That from and after the twelfth day of July which shall be in the year one Thousand nine hundred and sixteen, the whole of the lands allotted to the said Tuscarora Indians by an act of the General Assembly passed Newbern on the fifteenth day of October in the year of our Lord one thousand seven hundred and forty eight shall revert to and become the property of the State, and the Indian claim thereto shall from that time be held and deemed forever extinguished

And be it further enacted, that after the said lands shall revert to the State, if the same or any part thereof shall be vacant, the same shall not be [?] to the entry or entries of any person or persons without an express act of the Legislature to that Effect, provided always that it shall not be lawful for any person or persons to make any entry or entries on the Said Lands after the passing of this act

Provided always that nothing in this Act Contained shall be construed so as to effect the Title of any Individual

Provided nevertheless, that no plat or parcel of land, laid off under the direction of the Commissioners shall exceed two hundred acres.

Chapter One
Tuscarora Records

And provided further that no lease shall be made but by public auction, of which due notice shall be such in the Halifax & Edenton news papers

A Bill for the relief of the Tuscarora nation of Indians

In the House of Commons 2d December 1802 read the first time and passed
By order   J Hunt

In Senate Decr 3rd 1802 Read the first time & passed
By order   M Stokes Clk

Mr Arrington, Mr Hooker
In the H. Commons the second time amended & passed
By order   J Hunt CHC

In Senate Decr 9th 1802 Read the second time, Amended & passed
By order   M Stokes Clk

In Senate 9 Decr. 1802 The House taking the forgoing report into consideration Resolved that they do concur therewith
By order   M Stokes Clk

House of Commons 11 Dec. 1802 read the third time, amended & passed
By order   J Hunt CHC
In Senate Decemr 13th 1802 Read the third time & passed
Ordered to be Engrossed
By order   M Stokes Clk

The Committee who were appointed to examine the Treaty proposed to be made between the United States and the Tuscarora Nation of Indians -- Report
    That they have examined the same, and were present at the Signing and Execution of the said Treaty, and that the said Treaty has been made in exact Conformity to the Agreement made between the Chiefs and the Committee appointed to confer with them on that Subject, and the Report and Bill reported to the House --
    Submitted

Chapter One
Tuscarora Records

D Cameron
Chairman

Reported in the House of Commons 6th December 1802
By order
J Hunt CHC

****

LAWS OF THE STATE OF NORTH CAROLINA
REVISED, UNDER THE AUTHORITY OF THE GENERAL ASSEMBLY
VOLUME II
HENRY POTTER
RALEIGH: PRINTED AND SOLD BY J. GALES, 1821

CHAP. 607.
1802. An act for the relief of the Tuscarora nation of Indians. (Pages 965-967).
    Whereas the Indians composing the Tuscarora nation, have by their Chief Sacarusa, and others, regularly deputed and authorised, requested the concurrence of the General Assembly of this state to enable them to lease or demise, for a number of years, the residue of their lands situate in the county of Bertie, in such a manner that the whole of the leases on said land shall terminate at the same period;
    1. Be it enacted, &c. That the said Chief Sacarusa, Longboard and Samuel Smith, or a majority of them, be, and they are hereby authorised to lease and to farm let, the undemised residue of the lands allotted to the Tuscarora nation in Bertie county, for a term of years that shall expire and end when the lease made by the Tuscarora nation to Robert Jones and others, in the year one thousand seven hundred and sixty six, shall end and expire, and also extend the term or terms of the leases already made or granted for a shorter term, to a term or terms which shall expire at the same time with the said lease made in the year one thousand seven hundred and sixty six, in such parcels and on such rents and conditions as may be approved by the commissioners appointed in pursuance of this act, and which may best promote the interest and convenience of the said Indian nation.
    And whereas some difficulties have arisen respecting the receipt and payment of the rents on some of the present leases,

Chapter One
Tuscarora Records

  2. Be it further enacted, That the said Chiefs, or a majority of them, be, and they are hereby authorised to make such alterations, by covenant or agreement, respecting the payment and receipt of any of the rents due, or that may become due on any of the existing leases, as the commissioners appointed in pursuance of this act, or a majority of them, shall approve.

  Whereas the said Indian Chiefs are ignorant of the usual forms of business, and may want advice and assistance in transacting the business respecting their lands, for remedy whereof, and to prevent their being injured,

  3. Be it further enacted, That the governor shall appoint three commissioners for the purposes of carrying the provisions of this act into effect; and no lease, grant, demise, covenant or agreement made by said Indian Chiefs as aforesaid respecting their lands, or the rents thereof, shall be good or valid in law, unless the same shall be approved by said commissioners, or a majority of them, and such approbation shall be expressed in writing, and annexed or endorsed on such lease, covenant or agreement, and registered in the register's office of the county of Bertie, together with said lease or agreement; and the said commissioners shall receive the sum of twenty five shillings per day for their compensation, and expenses, to be paid out of the monies received by the said Chiefs on leasing said lands.

  4. And be it further enacted, That the occupancy and possession of the tenants under the said leases, heretofore confirmed by act or acts of the General Assembly, and such leases as may be made under this act, shall be held and deemed, in all cases whatsoever, the occupancy and possession of the said Tuscarora nation, to all intents and purposes as if the said nation, or the Indians thereof, or any of them, actually resided on said lands.

  Whereas the said Chiefs Sacarusa, Longboard and Samuel Smith, being duly and fully authorised and empowered by the said Tuscarora nation, have consented that the Indian claim to the use, possession and occupancy of said lands, shall cease and be extinguished, when the said lease made in the year one thousand seven hundred and sixty six, to Robert Jones and others, shall expire.

  5. Be it enacted, That from and after the twelfth day of July, which shall be in the year one thousand nine hundred and sixteen, the whole of the lands allotted to the said Tuscarora Indians, by an act of the General Assembly passed at Newbern, on the fifteenth dat of October, in the year of our Lord one thousand seven hundred and forty eight, **(C. 43.)**

Chapter One
Tuscarora Records

shall revert to, and become the property of the state, and the Indian claim thereto, shall, from that time, be held and deemed forever extinguished.

6. And be it further enacted, That after the said lands shall revert to the state, if the same, or any part thereof, shall be vacant, the same shall not be liable to the entry or entries of any person or persons, without an express act of the legislature to that effect: Provided always, That it shall not be lawful for any person or persons to make any entry or entries on the said land, after the passing of this act: Provided always, That nothing in this act contained shall be construed so as to effect the title of any individual: Provided nevertheless, That no lot or parcel of lands laid off under the direction of said commissioners, shall exceed two hundred acres: And provided further, That no lease shall be made but by public auction, of which due notice shall be given in the Halifax and Edenton newspapers.

****

AMERICAN STATE PAPERS

DOCUMENTS

LEGISLATIVE AND EXECUTIVE

OF THE

CONGRESS OF THE UNITED STATES,

FROM THE FIRST SESSION OF THE FIRST TO THE THIRD SESSION OF THE
THIRTEENTH CONGRESS, INCLUSIVE:

COMMENCING MARCH 3, 1789, AND ENDING MARCH 3, 1815.

Chapter One
Tuscarora Records

SELECTED AND EDITED, UNDER THE AUTHORITY OF CONGRESS,

BY WALTER LOWRIE, *Secretary of the Senate*,

AND

MATTHEW ST. CLAIR CLARK, *Clerk of the House of Representatives*.

VOLUME IV.

WASHINGTON:

PUBLISHED BY GALES AND SEATON

1832.

Chapter One
Tuscarora Records

1803.
THE TUSCARORAS
685

7th Congress.   No. 103.
         2d Session

THE TUSCARORAS.

COMMUNICATED TO THE SENATE, FEBRUARY, 1803

Gentlemen of the Senate:
   The Tuscarora Indians, having an interest in some lands within the State of North Carolina, asked the superintendence of the Government of the United States over a treaty to be held between them and the State of North Carolina, respecting these lands. William Richardson Davie was appointed a commissioner for this purpose, and a treaty was concluded under his superintendence. This, with his letter on the subject, is now laid before the Senate for their advice and consent, whether it shall be ratified.

   February 21, 1803.
   TH: JEFFERSON.

Articles of a Treaty between the United States of America and the Tuscarora Nation of Indians.

   Whereas a large part of the Tuscarora nation of Indians reside at so remote a distance from the state of North Carolina that they are unable to derive any benefit from the lands, the use of which had been granted to the nation by the Legislature of that State, so long as they should occupy and live upon the same:
   And whereas the Legislature of the State of North Carolina, in directing the use of the said lands, had heretofore permitted certain leases to be made of part thereof, and difficulties have arisen in the payment and receipt of the rents becoming due thereon:
   And whereas, for the purpose of preventing any disputes that might arise respecting the future occupancy of said lands, or the direction of the use thereof, and to remove the difficulties aforesaid, the President of the United States, by and with the consent of the Senate thereof, hath

Chapter One
Tuscarora Records

appointed William Richardson Davie, of North Carolina, commissioner on the part of the United States, for the purposes aforesaid; and the said William Richardson Davie, on the part of the United States, and the undersigned chiefs, in their own names, and in behalf of the whole Tuscarora nation, have agreed to the following articles, namely:

Article 1. In consideration of the agreement, on the part of the Legislature of the State of North Carolina, that they will, by certain acts of the General Assembly of said State, facilitate the collection of the rents due, or to become due, on the leases of said lands heretofore made: And on the condition that an act or acts of the General Assembly of the said State shall be passed, authorizing the said Tuscarora nation, or the chiefs thereof, in behalf of said nation, to lease, on such terms as they may deem proper, the undemised part of the lands allotted to them in the county of Bertie, in the said State, as well as other parts thereof, now under a lease, or leases, for years, so that the term or terms of the leases made of the whole, or any part thereof, may extend to the 12th day of July, which shall be in the year of our Lord one thousand nine hundred and sixteen:

And upon condition, also, that the Legislature of the said State shall, by an act or acts, for that purpose, remove, as far as the same can be done by legislative interposition, any difficulties or disputes that might arise respecting the future occupancy of said lands, either by the Indians of the said tribe or nation of Tuscaroras, or their lessees and assigns, until the 12th day of July, which shall be in the year of our Lord one thousand nine hundred and sixteen; and also declare and enact, that the occupancy and possession of the tenants, under the said leases, heretofore confirmed by act or acts of the General Assembly, and such leases as may be made under the act or acts made in pursuance of this treaty, shall be held and deemed, in all cases whatsoever, the occupancy and possession of the said Tuscarora nation, to all intents and purposes, as if they, the said nation, or the Indians thereof, or any of them, actually resided on said lands:

The undersigned chiefs, in their own names, and in behalf of the whole of the Tuscarora nation, hereby stipulate and agree, that, from and after the said twelfth day of July, which shall be in the year of our Lord one thousand nine hundred and sixteen, all the right, interest, and claim, of the said nation, or any of the Indians thereof, by act of the General Assembly of the State of North Carolina, or otherwise, to the use, possession, or occupancy, of a certain tract of land, allotted to them by the Legislature of the said State, situated in the county of Bertie, in the State aforesaid, bounded and described as follows, viz: Beginning at the mouth

Chapter One
Tuscarora Records

of Quitsnoy swamp, running up the said swamp four hundred and thirty poles, to a scrubby oak, near the head of said swamp, by a great spring; then north ten degrees, east eight hundred and fifty poles, to a persimmon tree, in Roquis swamp, and along the swamp and pocoson, main course north fifty seven degrees west, two thousand six hundred and forty poles, to a hickory on the east side of the Falling run or Deep creek, and down the various courses of the said run, to Morattock, or Roanoke river; then down the river to the first station; shall cease and determine, and shall be held and deemed extinguished for ever.

Article 2. This treaty shall be considered as a final and permanent adjustment and settlement of all differences, disputes, and claims, between the State of North Carolina and the said Tuscarora nation of Indians, as soon as the conditions stipulated in the foregoing article shall be fulfilled on the part of the State of North Carolina, and the treaty shall be ratified by the President of the United States, by and with the advice and consent of the Senate of the United States.

In witness of all and everything herein contained, the said William Richardson Davie, and the under signed chiefs, in behalf of themselves and the Tuscarora nation, have hereunto set their hands and seals.

Done in the city of Raleigh, in the State of North Carolina, on the fourth day of December, in the year one thousand eight hundred and two.

W.R. DAVIE, [L.S.]
And a number of Indians.

686 **INDIAN AFFAIRS**
1803.

Halifax, *February* 3, 1803.

Sir:
The severity of the season, and the badness of the roads, prevented my return from South Carolina to this place, before the 21st of January; and I have delayed forwarding the treaty made with the chiefs of the Tuscarora nation of Indians, until I should receive the act passed by the Legislature of North Carolina, to carry the treaty into effect. They are both

Chapter One
Tuscarora Records

herewith enclosed, and commissioners have been appointed by the Governor, agreeably to the provisions of the said act of Assembly.

The agents of the State chose the form of the first article, as you will find it in the treaty, stipulating for the final extinguishment of the Indian claim, in preference to a cession of the lands, on the ground that the Indians had only a kind of usufructuary possession granted to them, so long as they should live upon the same; and that the legal title was, and always had been in the State; they were substantially the same in effect, and it seems a matter of no moment to the Government of the United States, which mode was preferred.

By your letter of the 28th of December, 1801, I was informed that the President approved of the arrangement I had made in the business of the Tuscarora lands. I am happy that the benevolent views of the Government, with respect to this nation of Indians, are now completely effected; they will dispose of their lands at their real value, and a little time will also operate an extinguishment of their claim, without any expense to the State or the United States.

I have the honor to be, &c.

W.R. Davie.

An act for the relief of the Tuscarora nation of Indians.

Whereas the Indians composing the Tuscarora nation, by their chief, Sacarusa, and others, regularly deputed and authorized, requested the concurrence of the General Assembly of the State, to enable them to lease or demise, for a number of years, the residue of their lands, situate in the county of Bertie, in such a manner that the whole of the leases on said land shall terminate at the same period:

Be it enacted by the General Assembly of the State of North Carolina, and it is hereby enacted by the authority of the same, That the said chief, Sacarusa, Longboard, and Samuel Smith, or a majority of them, be, and they are hereby, authorized to lease and to farm let the undemised residue of the lands allotted to the Tuscarora nation, in Bertie county, for a term of years, that shall expire and end when the lease made by the Tuscarora nation to Robert Jones and others, in the year one thousand seven hundred and sixty six, shall end and expire; and, also, to extend the term or terms of the leases already made or granted for a shorter term, to a

Chapter One
Tuscarora Records

term or terms which shall expire at the same time with the said lease, made in the year one thousand seven hundred and sixty six, in such parcels, and on such rents and conditions, as may be approved by the commissioners appointed in pursuance of this act, and which may best promote the interest and convenience of the said Indian nation.

And whereas some difficulties have arisen, respecting the receipt and payment of the rents, on some of the present leases,

Be it further enacted, That the said chiefs, or a majority of them, be, and they are hereby, authorized to make such alterations, by covenant and agreement, respecting the payment and receipt of any rents due, or that may become due, on any of the existing leases, as the commissioners appointed in pursuance of this act, or a majority of them, shall approve.

Whereas the said Indian chiefs are ignorant of the usual forms of business, and may want advice and assistance, in transacting the business respecting their lands: For remedy whereof, and to prevent their being injured,

Be it further enacted, That the Governor shall appoint three commissioners, for the purpose of carrying the provisions of this act into effect; and no lease, grant, demise, covenant, or agreement, made by the said Indian chiefs, as aforesaid, respecting said lands, or the rents thereof, shall be good or valid in law, unless the same shall be approved by said commissioners, or a majority of them; and such approbation shall be expressed in writing, and annexed or endorsed on such lease, covenant, or agreement, and registered in the Register's office of the county of Bertie, together with said lease or agreement; and the said commissioner shall receive the sum of twenty five shillings per day, for their compensation and expenses, to be paid out of the monies received by the said chiefs, on leasing said lands.

And be it further enacted, That the occupancy and possession of the tenants, under the said leases, heretofore confirmed by the act or acts of the General Assembly, and such leases as shall be made under this act, shall be held and deemed, in all cases whatsoever, the occupancy and possession of the said Tuscarora nation, to all intents and purposes, as if the said nation, or the Indians thereof, or any of them, actually resided on said lands.

Whereas the said chiefs, Sacarusa, Longboard, and Samuel Smith, being duly and fully authorized and empowered by the said Tuscarora nation, have consented that the Indian claim, to the use, possession, and occupancy of said land, shall cease and be extinguished, when the said

Chapter One
Tuscarora Records

lease, made in the year one thousand seven hundred and sixty six, to Robert Jones and others, shall expire.

Be it enacted, That, from and after the twelfth day of July, which shall be in the year one thousand nine hundred and sixteen, the whole of the lands allotted to the said Tuscarora Indians, by an act of the General Assembly, passed at Newbern, on the fifteenth day of October, in the year of our Lord one thousand seven hundred and forty eight, shall revert to, and become the property of , the State, and the Indian claim thereto shall, from that time, be held and deemed forever extinguished.

And be it further enacted, That, after the said lands shall revert to the State, if the same, or any part thereof, shall be vacant, the same shall not be liable to the entry or entries of any person or persons, without an express act of the Legislature to that effect: *Provided, Always*, That it shall not be lawful for any person or persons to make any entry or entries on the said lands, after the passing of this act: *Provided, always*, That nothing in this act contained shall be construed so as to affect the title of any individual: *Provided, nevertheless*, That no lot or parcel of lands, laid off under the direction of said commissioners, shall exceed two hundred acres. *And provided further*, That no lease shall be made, but by public auction, of which due notice shall be given in the Halifax and Edenton newspapers.

Read three times, and ratified in General Assembly, the sixteenth day of December, anno Domini 1802.

JO. RIDDICK, *S.S.*
S. CABARRUS, *S.H.C.*

State of North Carolina:

Secretary's Office, 6th *January*, 1803.

This certifies that the foregoing act of the General Assembly, entitled "An act for the relief of the Tuscarora nation of Indians," is a true copy, taken from the original, deposited in this office.

Given under my hand, at Raleigh, the date aforesaid.

WILL. WHITE, *Secretary.*

Journal of the Executive Proceedings of the Senate, in The Congressional Journals of the United States
Part I of the National State Papers of the United States Series, 1789-1817

Chapter One
Tuscarora Records

The Journal of the Senate, Including The Journal of the Executive Proceedings of the Senate, Thomas Jefferson Administration, 1801-1809, Volume 2, Seventh Congress, Second Session, December, 1802-March, 1803 (Wilmington, Delaware: Michael Glazier, Inc., no date)

Monday, February 21, 1803

The following written message was received from the President of the United States, by Mr. Lewis, his Secretary:

Gentlemen of the Senate:

The Tuscarora Indians having an interest in some lands within the State of North Carolina, asked the superintendence of the government of the United States, over a treaty to be held between them and the State of North Carolina, respecting these lands. William Richardson Davie was appointed a Commissioner for this purpose, and a treaty was concluded under his superintendence. This, with his letter on the subject, is now laid before the Senate, for their advice and consent, whether it shall be ratified.

TH: JEFFERSON.

****

February 21st, 1803

The message, and papers referred to, except the treaty, were read.

Ordered, That they lie for consideration, and that the treaty be printed for the use of the Senate.

****

Tuesday, February 22, 1803

The treaty, made under the authority of the United States, with the Tuscarora nation of Indians, on the 14th day of December, 1802, was read the first time

****

Saturday, February 26, 1803.

The treaty between the United States of America and the Tuscarora nation of Indians, was read the second time

****

Chapter One
Tuscarora Records

Tuesday, March 1, 1803.
The treaty between the United States and the Tuscarora nation of Indians, of 4th December, 1802, was resumed; and, by unanimous consent, the rule was dispensed with; and, on the question, will the Senate consent and advise to the ratification of this treaty?

It passed unanimously in the affirmative: Yeas, 21.

Those who voted in the affirmative, are--Messrs. Anderson, Bradley, Breckenridge, Clinton, Cocke, Ellery, T. Foster, Howard, Jackson, Logan, S.T. Mason, Morris, Nicholas, Olcott, Ross, Stone, Sumpter, Tracy, Wells, White, and Wright.

So it was
"*Resolved*, (two-thirds of the Senators present concurring therein,) That the Senate do advise and consent to the ratification of the treaty, made under the authority of the United States, between the United States and the Tuscarora nation of Indians, at Raleigh, in the State of North Carolina, on the fourth day of December, in the year one thousand eight hundred and two."

Ordered, That the Secretary lay this resolution before the President of the United States.

****

North Carolina State Archives
General Assembly Sessions Records
November-December, 1802, Box #1

The Memorial of the Chiefs of the Tuscarora Nation of Indians

A resolution in favor of the Chiefs
deld. Jere. Slade
by J Hunt

To the Honorbl. the Genl Assembly of North Carolina

Brothers, we the undersignd. Cheifs of the Tuscarora Nation of Indians; Beg Leave to address your Honorble. Body in behalf of our Selves & Nation.

Chapter One
Tuscarora Records

Brothers, we feel Sensibly the obligation your Honorable. Body Layd us under the past year in Discharging our Ball. of Expence while in this town, as well as for the Sum of Money Granted us by your Honorble. Body, to help us on our way home & in Pertinkler for the Pains & Troble your Honorble. Body has ben att the present Year on passing a Law to Enable us to Dispose of our Lands in this State to the Best Advantage.

Brothers we beg you to accept of Senecar thanks for the above favours & be asured that you Shall have our prayer to the Great Spirit for your wellfair & Happyness.

Brothers we are Short of money, we have therefore to Request your Honorble. Body to Consider us & Grant us a small Sum to help Defray our Expence, Since we have been at this place.

Your Honorble. Bodys Complience with the above Request will Lay us your Brothers under a new obligation.

his
Saquaresa X
mark

his
Longboard X
mark

his
Saml. X Smith
mark

Raleigh Decemb. 14th: 1802

****

North Carolina State Archives
Governor's Papers
State Series, Volume XXVI.
James Turner, 1802-1803, Dec. 8 - Dec. 31

Halifax   15th Jany. 1803

Chapter One
Tuscarora Records

I hasten to acknowledge your favor of the 10th. Inst. accompanying a Commission for me, under the "Act for the relief of the Tuscarora Nation of Indians. I am so circumstanced at the present that I cannot possibly act under the commission you have been pleased to honor me with

With great respect
I am your mst. Obt.
Hble. Servant

L. Burges

****

North Carolina State Archives
Governor's Papers
State Series, Volume, XXVI.
James Turner, 1802 - 1803, Dec. 8 - Dec. 31

Governor Turner   No. Hampton 23rd. Jany. 1803

Sir

your favour of the tenth Inst. come to hand yesterday; I hasten to inform you, agreeable to request, That in honour to the appointment, I accept the commission for carrying into effect the law for the relief of the Tuscarora Indians. I return you my thanks, for the great Confidence, you have reposed in me.

I am with due respect
Your Most Obt.
John M. Binford

****

North Carolina State Archives
Governor's Papers
State Series, Volume XXVI.

Chapter One
Tuscarora Records

James Turner, 1802 - 1803, Dec. 8 - Dec.31

Sir,
    I was this day honour'd by the receipt of your polite Letter of the 10th. Ulto. mentioning that you had appointed me one of the Commissioners contemplated by the Act passed last Session of the General Assembly, "entitled an act for the relief of the Tuscarora Nation of Indians"; and a Commission to that effect.
    There is no doubt that by accepting the appointment with which you have been pleased to honour me, I shall draw on myself some trouble and inconvenience -- But feeling as I do an Interest for the Indians, and a regard for your choice, I have Ventured to accept said Appoint. flattering myself that the business tho' troublesome, will require no great share of abilities, and that I shoud be in this deceived, the abilities of the worthy Gentlemen with whom you have been pleased to associate me, will be fully equal.

                      I have the honour to be
                      with much respect & esteem
                      Your Mt. Obt. Sert.

                      J. Slade

His Excellency
    James Turner Esqr.

****

North Carolina State Archives
Private Manuscript Collection
David Stone Papers, 1795-1865
Call Number: P.C.82.1

                    Indian Woods 23rd May 1803
    We have fixed on Thursday the 26th Inst. for the purpose of extending and thereby confirming those leases which were obtained from the Tuscarora Indians subsequent to the 12th of July 1766 and prior to the first day of December 1777; and also of commuting the rents arising from said leases and settling the arrearajes of rents. We shall with the authorised Chiefs, meet in Ceasar's Islands at the residence of the late Samuel Smith.
    At your leave a desire to negotiate respecting your lease dated the 10th of Feby 1777, you may attend at the time and place above mentioned.
                    We are with consideration

Chapter One
Tuscarora Records

Mr. Stone

Yours
Jno. M. Binford
J Slade
William Hawking

Letter of the Commissioners relative to the extension of the lease of the Tuscarora Indian Lands on Roanoke
                       23rd May 1803. A.D.
                       David Stone Esqr.
                       Bertie County

Jno. M. Binford
Mr. Hawkins &
J Slade

                       Commissioners Concerning extending
                       the lease on leased lands

                       23 May 1803

****

Duke University
Perkins Library, Manuscript Room
William Slade Papers, 1751-1929

Received of John M. Binford Jeremiah Slade and William Hawkins Commissioners for the Tuscarora Nation of Indians seven hundred and seventy dollars and 50 cents for the purpose of defraying the expenses of the Indians to the City of Washington, it being a part of the monies arising from the leasing their lands
17th of June 1803

Test
Wm Wilson

         Sacarusa   X}
                                  }Chiefs
         Longboard   X}

         Ezra Lunt Acct.

****

Chapter One
Tuscarora Records

Duke University
Perkins Library, Manuscript Room
William Slade Papers
1751-1929

      Jeremiah Slade In Acct. with the Tuskerora Indians

Dr.
19th June 1803

To Amt. of Bond left with me	$17224.65
To amt. of Col. Thos. Pughs Bonds for the extention of the black gut Lease	650.00
To amt. of Saml. W. Johnstons Bonds for the extention of his lease	506.66
To Amt. of Judgmt. recovered agt. Pugh & others for the trespass on the lands of the Indians	95.00
To amt. of John McCaskeys Bond for the extention of his lease	236.00
To amt. of Pugh & Williams Bonds for the extention of their part of Lease to Messrs. Jones Pugh & Williams	<u>3175.62</u>
	21887.93
To amt. of Allen Jones & Willie Jones Bond for the Extention of their Lease	1588.88
	23476.81
To amt. of Int. Rec'd on the several debts due on Instalments of 1805.6	<u>355.19</u>
	23832.00
The [?] agt. McCaskey if made use of will make the balance	$2116.28.

Chapter One
Tuscarora Records

Cr.

By Cash paid colector at Petersburg	$4670.68
By Cash paid John McClary	4964.32
By Cash paid into the Bank at Richmond	5900.00
By Commissrs. 5 pct. on $23476.81	1173.84
By Cash paid Atty	48.00
By Cash in conveying money to Richmond	75.00
By Cash pd. David Clark on Bond given by Sam Smith the Indian to sd. Clark	50.00
By Cash paid Indian Girl for support	10.00
	16941.84
By balance of the debts due the Indians still uncollected	5009.88
	21951.72
Balance due the Indians	1880.28
	23832.00

5900.00
  56.65
  60.00
  30.14
  75.00
6121.79
     5
30608.95

****

North Carolina State Archives

Chapter One
Tuscarora Records

North Carolina Map Collection
Search Room

Editor's Note: The following is a copy of printed text from a map of the Tuscarora lands after they were surveyed on 17 June 1803. The surveyor appointed by the State of North Carolina was W.H. Bruce. The Indian Commissioners appointed by the State to supervise the survey were Jeremiah Slade and William Hawkins.

State of North Carolina } The above is a Correct
                         } Plan of the Lands allotted
Bertie County   } to the Tuscarora Nation
of Indians, the bounds of which are expressed in an Act of the General Assembly of the State aforesaid Passed in the year of 1748, and which was as follows, Viz, Beginning on Roanoke River at the Mouth of Quitsney Swamp, thence up the various Courses of the said Swamp to an oak near the Head, at the great spring, thence N 10 E 904 poles to a Persimman on Rockquis Swamp, thence N 57 W 2888 Poles to a Hickory at the head of Falling Run on Deep Creek, thence down the various Courses of said Creek to Roanoke River, thence down the River to the first Station, Containing Forty one Thousand, one-hundred thirteen Acres the Subdivisions Represent the Several Leases which appears to have been obtained from the said Indians Subsequent to the 12 day of July 1755 & Prior to the first day of December 1777 as well as the undivided Residue, Which was, in Pursuance of an Act of the General Assembly of the State aforesaid, Leased on the 9th day of Instan, Certified under my Hand this 17th of June 1803.

The above plan and surveys were made under our inspection
and are correct 17th June 1803

W.H. Bruce Surveyor
J. Slade Commissioner for the the Tuscaroras
William Hawkins   [?] Indians

Editor's Note: The following excerpts from the map list the number of acres leased to individuals versus what they actually claimed.

1. James Pughes, Williams 150 Years Lease - 21,752 1/2 Acres by Actual survey - Note. The Lease calls for only 8000 acres.

Chapter One
Tuscarora Records

2. James Pughs & Williams 99 years Lease 12,533 1/2 Acres by actual survey - Note. The Lease calls for only 2000 acres.

3. Churtons Lease 478 Acres - 200 Acres Called for.

4. Edwards Lease 117 Acres - 10 Acres called for.

5. Col. Pughes Lease 547 Acres - 100 Acres called for.

6. Stones Lease 670 Acres - 100 acres called for.

7. McCaskeys Lease 1934 Acres - No Quantity called for.

8. Undemised claimed by David Stone - 151 Acres.

[Editor's Note: According to Jeremiah Slade (Indian Commissioner), David Stones claim to this land was illegal and unfounded.]

****

NorthCarolina State Archives
Governor James Turner's Letter Book
1802-1805, Part I, Pages 80-82
G.L.B. 15

Indian Woods

Sir,　　　　　　Bertie County 20th June 1803.

　　We arrived at this place on the 6th of April and entered on the duties of our appointment. Since that period we have caused the lands alotted to the Tuscarora nation of Indians and all the Leases which have been obtained from the said Indians subsequent to the year 1766 and prior to the 1st of December 1777 to be surveyed.
　　As we had good reasons to believe that all those Leases contained many more acres in their bounds than called for, and as all of them except that confirmed to Robert Jones, William Williams and Thomas Pugh for 150 years, were, if the authorised Chiefs deemed it advisable, to be extended, our object for adopting this plan was not only to ascertain with

Chapter One
Tuscarora Records

pricision the quantity of undemised Lands, but also the exact number of acres in each Lease, in order that the Indians if they did extend might receive compensation for every acre which would be their property at the expiration of 99 Years from the dates of the Several leases.

The number of acres in the whole tract, in each Lease with the names of all the Leases and the quantity called for in their respective Leases, are marked in the plan which accompanies this.

The undemised residue amounts to 3411 acres, of which we have leased 2916 1/2 for $20966_6. of which we have received $3741.51 - for the balance we have taken Bonds with good and sufficient Securities, of which $15724_65 are to be paid by three annual instalments, the residue Vizt $1500 on the 15th day of June 1807. The balance of the undemised Lands is held as being within the bounds of David Stone's, Johnston's and McCaskey's Leases.

We have extended but one Lease, containing 117 acres, for which we received &180.17 prompt payment. We have not commuted the rents arising from any of the Leases or Settled the arrearages of rents nor could we have acceded to any of the propositions of the Leasees without doing injustice to the Indians.

After defraying all the expences of surveying the lands, refunding money which Cheifs Sacarusa and Longboard had borrowed, paying some accounts, furnishing money to purchase horses, carts &c and for the expenditures of the Cheifs and their Charge on the road, we have sent to be deposited in the Bank of Norfolk $2000 for which they are to receive a check on the Bank of Columbia which is to be delivered to the Secretary at War.

We deem it unnecessary to make remarks on the unfairness of any of the Leases, or on the unjust claim set up by David Stone Esquire, to a part of the undemised Lands, as we expect that the validity of them will be ascertained by a judicial determination.

We are with consideration Your
His Excellency   Excellency's most Obt. & Humbl
Servts
James Turner Esquire   J. Slade   William Hawkins

****

Journal of the Executive proceedings of the Senate, in The Congressional Journals of the United States
Part I of the National State Papers of the United States Series

Chapter One
Tuscarora Records

1789-1817

The Journal of the Senate, Including The Journal of the Executive Proceedings of the Senate, Thomas Jefferson Administration, 1801-1809, Volume 2, Seventh Congress, Second Session, december, 1802-March, 1803 (Wilmington, Delaware: Michael Glazier, Inc., no date)

Monday, February 21, 1803

The following written message was received from the President of the United States, by Mr. Lewis, his Secretary:
Gentlemen of the Senate:
The Tuscarora Indians having an interest in some lands within the State of North Carolina, asked the superintendence of the government of the United States, over a treaty to be held between them and the State of North Carolina, respecting these lands. William Richardson Davie was appointed a Commissioner for this purpose, and a treaty was concluded under his superintendence. This, with his letter on the subject, is now laid before the Senate, for their advice and consent, whether it shall be ratified.

TH: JEFFERSON.

****

February 21st, 1803
The message, and papers referred to, except the treaty, were read.
Ordered, That they lie for consideration, and that the treaty be printed for the use of the Senate.

****

Tuesday, February 22, 1803
The treaty, made under the authority of the United States, with the Tuscarora nation of Indians, on the 14th day of December, 1802, was read the first time.

****

Saturday, February 26, 1803

Chapter One
Tuscarora Records

The treaty between the United State of America and the Tuscarora nation of Indians, was read the second time.

****

Tuesday, March 1, 1803

The treaty between the United States and the Tuscarora nation of Indians, of 4th December, 1802, was resumed; and, by unanimous consent, the rule was dispensed with; and, on the question, will the Senate consent and advise to the ratification of this treaty?

It passed unanimously in tha affirmative: Yeas, 21.

Those who voted in the affirmative, are--Messrs. Anderson, Bradley, Breckenridge, Clinton, Cocke, Ellery, T. Foster, Howard, Jackson, Logan, S.T. Mason, Morris, Nicholas, Olcott, Ross, Stone, Sumpter, tracy, wells, White, and Wright.

So it was
"Resolved, (two-thirds of the Senators present concurring therein,) That the Senate do advise and consent to the ratification of the treaty, made under the authority of the United States and the Tuscarora nation of Indians, at Raleigh, in the State of North Carolina, on the fourth day of December, in the year one thousand eight hundred and two."

Ordered, That the Secretary lay this resolution before the President of the United States.

****

Duke University
Perkins Library, Manuscript Room
William Slade Papers
1751-1929

Rec'd of Jeremiah Slade one of the Commissrs. for the Tuskerora Indians two Thousand Dollars in Bank Notes. No. & amt. as follows Viz

thirty two $50 Notes No. 4195. 4209. 6260. 4180. 4721. 4221. 4737. 4265. 4779. 4137. 4293. 6208. 4606. 4679. 6242. 6279. 4689. 4647. 4768. 4755. 4743. 6247. 4105. 4614. 4736. 4144. 4296. 4608. 4228. 4666. 4795. (73.) Four $100 Bank Notes No. 5895. 5821. 3642. (20) It being Notes rec'd for the $2000 sent to be deposited in the Norfolk

Chapter One
Tuscarora Records

Bank for a Check on the Bank of Columbia, for the use of the Tuskerora Nation of Indians. N.B. Those included in satchels are on the Bank of Columbia and the others on the United States Bank at Washington   June 27th 1803

Test Ezra Lunt

                         X   Sacarusa

                         X   Longboard

****

University of North Carolina
Southern Historical Collection
Manuscript Department, Collection # 716
Lewis Thompsom Papers

Folder # 2

To Jeremiah Slade   War Department
                                      July 20th 1803

Sir

       By certain documents placed in my hands by Sacarusa and Longboard, it appears that they have constituted you, Agent and Attorney for the Tuscarora Nation of Indians, for collecting monies due them on bonds and for extending leases heretofore given of their undemised lands in the State of North Carolina. From the extreme jealousy which the Indians entertain towards their civilized neighbors in all pecuniary transactions, it has ever been found necessary to conduct towards them with the utmost circumspection, and from their ignorance as to the modes of transacting business, it is frequently difficult to convince them of its fairness, however obvious it may appear to other better informed -- These considerations induce me to suggest a wish, that you would not extend the leases of their lands without first having notified the President of the United States or myself, that you have it in contemplation. In doing this you will be pleased to state the quantity of lands, the price for which it stands leased, and the price at which the lease is proposed to be extended.

Chapter One
Tuscarora Records

Possessed of this information, it may be in the power of the Executive at all times to remove any wrong impressions, or ill founded jealousies which the Indians receive or cherish.

I am &c

I certify that the foregoing is a true copy from the records of the War Office - Given under my hand and the Seal of the said Office this 6th March 1809-

Jno Smith C.C.
Acting Secy. of War

****

North Carolina State Archives
Governor James Turner's Letter Book
1802-1805, Part I, Pages 171-174
G.L.B. 15

Washington 4th Decembr. 1803

Dr. Sir,

Understanding from the Report of Mr. Slade & Mr. Hawkins two of the Commissioners for superintending the sale of Indian Lands that they have much misrepresented a circumstance relating to me the respect I have for the State and for yourself induces me to correct the impression.

If those Gentleman mean by this expression in their report (Vizt "the balance of the undemised Lands is held as being within the bounds of David Stone's Lease to which they afterwards allude when they say "we deem it unnecessary to make remarks on the unfairness of any of these Leases, or on the unjust claim set up by David Stone Esquire to a part of the undemised Lands" they will I presume be able to explain what they mean by an unjust claim set up by a Tenant to Lands within the bounds of his Lease.

For me I hope it will not be considered improper to declare that I do not hold or claim one foot of land under a Lease made by the Indians to me.

That my father did in the Year 1777 Lease from the Indians a tract of Land then supposed to be 500 Acres for the Term of 99 Years at the rent of œ12 - a year - that afterwards and as well as I now recollect, in the year 1793 I purchased this Lease from my Father, that from the time when the

Chapter One
Tuscarora Records

Lease was made in 1777 until the Land came to my possession my father held to the bounds to which I now claim and paid the rent reserved.

That uniformly since the land has been in my possession, I have held to the same bounds and paid the rent. The boundaries being natural ones have been as well known in the Neighborhood and as much respected as the boundaries of any tract of Land in the County.

As Mr. Slade & Mr. Hawkins seem desirous some matters should be examined, they will I hope the more readily excuse the liberty I take in making some remarks upon certain parts of their reports, which do not immediately relate to the Lands of David Stone.

1st. I have been told by a Gentleman of respectability who kept a list of the sales and who I have no doubt told me the truth that the Land Sold for more than $20966.6 the sum reported - Why the sum reported does not exactly correspond with that of the actual sales, Mr. Slade & Mr. Hawkins can certainly explain - & I hope they will.

2nd. The Terms of Sale or Leasing advertised, and announced by the Person who cried the Land were - "one fourth of the purchase money to be paid before the execution of the Leases, the balance at three annual instalments the purchaser giving bond with approved security - and the only lot of the Land Sold for $1500 was one to Ebenezer Slade a Brother to Mr. Commissioner Slade - now the Reporters can doubtless inform whether it be for those $1500 that a further credit was after given till June 1807 - and whether that after extension of credit was gratuitous and if not, the inducements for it.

3rd. Mr. Commissioner Slade bid off at the sale between five and six thousand dollars worth of the said Land himself and can I am satisfied also inform whether that was the reason why a full fourth part of the purchase money was not paid as the terms of the Sale required.

I will only add further that the permission granted to the Indians and more especially to those of them so long since removed from that Land to make either a Sale or Leases for a long term of Years has always appeared to me an extraordinary act of liberality.

For without taking into the account the obvious effect of the seeming countenance given to a postponement of the patent Rights secured by the Act of 1748, it appeared to me that any act recognising the right of the Indians to dispose of lands for such a length of time was at least hasardous in precedent for a State, so many of whose Citisens are interested in the Lands of Tennessee now occupied by the Indians.

I have the honour to be, with
the highest respect & consideration

Chapter One
Tuscarora Records

Your humble Servant,
David Stone

His Excellency
James Turner Esquire

****

North Carolina State Archives
Governor James Turner's Letter Book
1802-1805, Part I, Page 175
G.L.B.15

To the Honourable, the General Assembly
of the State of North Carolina,

Gentlemen,

    I have the honour of laying before you a general return of the Militia of North Carolina for the present Year.
    I also at the particular of David Stone Esquire, lay before you a letter relative to the report of the Commissioners appointed under the Act for the relief of the Tuscarora nation of Indians.

I am respectfully,
Your obt. hble. Servant
J. Turner

Raleigh 12th Decemr. 1803

****

North Carolina State Archives
Governor James Turner's Letter Book
1802-1805, Part I, Pages 176-179
G.L.B. 15

Raleigh 14th Decemr. 1803

Dr. Sir,

Chapter One
Tuscarora Records

Mr. Hawkins & myself are called on by the Honble David Stone in his letter of the 4th Instant directed to your Excellency to explain the remarks of that Gentleman on certain parts of the Report of the Commissioners.

First. Why the sum reported does not exactly correspond with that of the actual Sales? I beg leave to inform that Gentleman that it does, and that if he had taken one half the trouble to examine the Report that he did to write to you Sir, he would have discovered that the undemised Lands Sold for the sum of $20966.6. and the extension of Titus Edwards lease $180.17. making the aggregate amount of receipts $21,146:23. But if he means by these words "that the undemised lands Sold for more than $20966.6." that the undemised lands sold for me, or that the aggregate amount exceeded $21,146.23. I can only say that, that Honble. Gentleman's Informant is mistaken as will appear by the account of Sales attested by John King & William Wilson, and which can be supported by the Several Purchasers, as also by Genl. W.R. Davie, under whose inspection the sales were conducted -- I can but admire the address, tho' I am shock'd at the design of the Honourable Gentleman in giving the above information as coming from a third person, when if he had have appropriated ten minutes of his time to a calculation on this subject he could have stated of his own knowledge whether it was founded in truth or not, as he was present at the Sales and did not know the price given for each lot of Land.

Secondly, Why there was an extension of credit on the $1500. mentioned in the Report of the commissioners contrary to the terms of leasing advertised: Previous to my explaining the reasons which induced the Commissioners to give the credit alluded to, I hope you will indulge me with one or two remarks on the base insinuation of that Honble Gentleman, where he states "that the only lot of Land that sold for $1500 was one to Ebenezer Slade" I can believe that this assertion of the Hnble Gentleman is a willful pervertion of the truth, for he must know, unless his powers of recollection have greatly failed him, that Ebenezer Slade bid off but one lot of land & the fishery, and that the purchase money of both did not exceed $950; my reasons for believing this is that he was the principal bidder against the said Eb. Slade while the said lot of Land was crying.

Chapter One
Tuscarora Records

Having premised thus much I will proceed to give the reasons which induced the Commissioners to give credit on the $1500, -- until Januy 1807. The only persons who were able & willing to purchase to any extent were David Stone Esquire, Col. Thomas Pugh and General William Williams, that by the experience of the first day's sales it was manifest that they would not bid against each another; it was equally obvious that unless this plan was counteracted the Lands of the Indians would not sell for near their value, to obviate this difficulty I was made choice of by the Indians to bid for their use on each lot of Land as far as it was reasonably worth which was agreed to by the other Commissioners & General Davie, who had acted as Agent on the part of the United States: and I accordingly bid on each Lot as much as was considered by the Commissioners it's reasonable value; in the course of the sale there was struck off to me eight hundred acres of Land for the sum of $5,600, which Lands were afterwards sold by the Commissioners to General Wm. Williams for $6000. on the Commissioners agreeing to give him a further credit of one Year on one fourth part of the $6000 -- which is the $1500 alluded to by that Honble Gentleman.

Now Sir, I leave it with you to determine whether the inducement of the Commissioners were such as to justify their conduct.
I might here in the same eccentric manner, that the honourable Gentleman attacked the Characters of the Commissioners submit with propriety a number of remarks, on the title to, & made of acquiring the lands of Dav'd Stone Esqr, which I should be glad he could explain without exposing the dark side of his own & his Father's character, but neither your patience nor my time will admit of them at present, I shall therefore drop the subject for the present: -- And beg leave to consider myself,
Your Most obt. hble servant

J. Slade

His Excellency
James Turner

****

North Carolina State Archives
Private Manuscript Collection
David Stone Papers, 1795-1865
Call Number: P.C.82.1

Chapter One
Tuscarora Records

David Stone Esq.
J. Slade about extending Lease

Should Mr. Stone feel inclined to extend and settle the business of his Lease for the [?] Land. I attend for that purpose.
I am Yrs
J. Slade

Jeremiah Slade does not recollect any offer by Mr. David Stone to extend his Lease previous to this day, but be that as it may he does not put himself authorised to acced to the offer now made, but will forward Mr. David Stone's proposition to the secretary at War, and should he think that the offer is such as ought to be closed with Jere. T. Slade readely acqui[?]
14th Augt. 1804

Byrd & Clark

Byrd & Clark Witnesses for pltff

Durham Davis Surveyor   those persons proves the
John M hoon[?]   bounds of shivy patten
Thomas Sutton

Silas Ballard---- proves Byrds possessions of Claime
         up to the deep gut

William Byrket----Do Isaack Wimberlys to be the oldest
         son of Joseph

Saml. Johnson proves---- Maurice Moore to be Judge

Wimberly, Deed older than the deed to pierce
pierces deed does not Correspond with Clark's Deed
pierce faild to notice by when he made the line to Clark

****

North Carolina State Archives
Private Manuscript Collection

Chapter One
Tuscarora Records

David Stone Papers, 1795-1865
Call Number: P.C.82.1

J. S. W. Johnson
to
John Allen
Copy of Courses
of Deed

Courses of a Deed from John Johnston and Samuel W. Johnston to John Allen - 11th May 1795

    A Tract or Parcel of Land containing 400 Acres be the same more or less, beginning at three White oaks standing in Col. Pugh's line being the dividing Corner between S. Williams and John Johnston then running south 59 East to the old Indian line a pine then along said Line N. 10 E. to a Persimmon standing on Roquist then N. 57 W. to Pugh's Corner then along Pugh's line S. 20 W. to the beginning.

Rec'd upon obligations	1406.81
of J. Maer	400
of Doctor Cooper	160
of E. Outlaw	300
	2266.81
of F. James	90
	2356.81
Paid away	
To Lawyers Fee	600
To Bakers for Land	300
To M. Oliver for Land	100
	1000
Paid at Windsor	200
Paid for Cotton gin	50
Paid for goods sent N. York 100	
Paid for goods sent to Philadelphia	54
Paid Mr. Hancock	50
Paid Moses Gillam	120
	1574

Chapter One
Tuscarora Records

Still have	425
Jo Cartey	150
for Coffee to Hubbell	33
To James Walles	40
	2202

****

Duke University
Perkins Library, Manuscript Room
William Slade Papers
1751-1929

    Collectors Office Petersburg 22d August 1804

Received from Mr. J. Slade the sum of Four thousand six hundred and seventy dollars and sixty eight cents, being money in his hands belonging to the Tuscarora Indians, for which I have this day signed duplicate receipts for.

       Henry Dearborn Sec. at War
       Chas. Turnbull D Coll.

  4670.68
  4964.32
  5900.00
 15535.00
 13752.80
  1782.20

****

Duke University
Perkins Library, Manuscript Room
William Slade Papers, 1751-1929

   Dr. Jeremiah Slade In acct with the Tuskerora Indians

Chapter One
Tuscarora Records

1805
June 15th

To the amt of the debts due the Indians for the sale of the undemised Lands & payable the 15th June 1805 $5235.30

To the amt. of Col. Thos. Pugh's Bond for the Extention of his Lease, payable 15th June 1805. -$ 650.00

To the amt of Gnl. Wm Williams & Col. Thos. Pughs Bonds for the Extention of their part of the Lease to Messrs. Jones Pugh & Williams and payable 15th June 1805. -----------$2381.72

To the amt. of Samuel W. Johnstons Bonds for the extention of his Lease, due 15th June 1805. $ 253.33

To the amt. of John H. Pughs Bond payable 15th June 1804 with Interest. ---
$ 335.49

Total	$8855.84
Balance due J Slade	$ 38.11
	$8893.95

Cr.
By the amt of Int. of John McClarys rect. $4964.32   **
4964.32

By the Amt of Saml. Johnstons Bonds due   553.33   **
not pd.
15th June 1805 not collected

By the Amt. of Gnl. Wm Williams & Col.
Pughs Bonds for the extention of their
part of the Lease to Messrs. Jones Pugh
& Williams payable 15th June 1805
not collected $2381.72   **
pd.

By the Amt. of Jno. H. Pughs Bond payable

Chapter One
Tuscarora Records

15 June 1805 not collected $250 pd.	316.50	**
By the balance due on Thos. Speller & others Bond payable 15th June 1805 not collected pd.	286.16	**
By the amt. of William Johnstons Bond payable 15th June 1805 not collected pd.	30.65	**
By the amt. of Hardy Boyce's Note payable 15th June 1805 not collected 3588.47	22.11	**
By cash paid Joseph B. Littlejohn Assistant for the Indians	24.00	
By cash paid Esther Gibson the Indian	10.00	
By cash expended in carrying the money for the Indians to Petersburg in the year 1804	50.00	
By Cash notes on $5123.29 at 5 pb 340.16	256.16	**
	8893.95	

****

Duke University
Perkins Library, Manuscript Room
William Slade Papers, 1751-1929

Williamston N.C.   Augt. 24th 1805

Then rec'd of Jeremiah Slade the Sum of four Thousand nine Hundred & Sixty four Dollrs. & thirty two cents, it being the Money due the Tuskr. Indians & remaining in his hands.

Chapter One
Tuscarora Records

Jno. McClary

****

North Carolina State Archives
Private Manuscript Collection
David Stone Papers, 1795-1865
Call Number: P.C.82.1

State of North Carolina   Superior Court of Law
Edenton District   October Term 1806

      John Den complaint of Richard Fen in custody For that whereas Penelope Lowther on the second day of september in the year of our Lord one thousand eight hundred and five at Bertie county State & District aforesaid had demised granted and to farm let to the said John Den one undivided moiety of a certain tract or parcel of Land situate lying or being in Bertie county State and District aforesaid butted and bounded as follows to wit. Beginning at a White oak standing on the upper side of the mouth of Quitsney Swamp thence up the various courses of the said Swamp to a marked tree standing in the swamp in the swamp in the Indian line from thence No. and by Et. along the Indian line 200 poles to an oak thence No. 320 poles to an Hickory thence West 340 poles to a Cypress standing on Morratock River Bank, thence the various courses down the River to the first station containing six hundred and forty acres more or less with the appurtenances, As Also one other undivided moiety of one other tract or parcel of Land Situate lying or being in Bertie County aforesaid State and District aforesaid butted and bounded as follows to wit Beginning at a Cypress an upper corner of the tract of Land first above mentioned thence East 340 poles to an Hickory an another corner of the tract of Land first above mentioned thence North to the southern Branch of Rotsutskey 300 poles thence the various courses of the said Branch and Rotsutskey Swamp to a white Oak standing in the mouth of the said Swamp thence the various courses down the River to the Cypress the first station, containing six hund'd and forty acres more or less with the appurtenances to have and to hold the said undivided Moiety of each of the aforesaid two tracts of Land with the appurtenances to the said John Den and his assigns from the said second day of September unto the full end and term of seven years thence

Chapter One
Tuscarora Records

next ensuing fully to be completed & ended - And Also that whereas William McKenzie and Margaret his wife on the second day of September in the year of our Lord one thousand eight hundred and five at Bertie County aforesaid State and District aforesd had demised granted and to farm let to the said John Den one undivided fourth part of each of the aforesaid two tracts of Land with the appurtenances, to have and to hold the said undivided moiety of each of the aforesd two tracts of Land with the appurtenances to the said John Den and his assigns from the said second day of September unto the full end and term of seven years thence next ensuing fully to be completed and ended And also that whereas Penelope Swann on the said second day of September in the year of our Lord one thousand eight hundred and five at Bertie county District & State aforesaid had demanded granted and to farm let to the said John Den one undivided sixteenth part of each of the aforesaid two tracts of Land with the appurtenances to have and to hold the said undivided sixteenth part of each of the aforesaid two tracts of Land with the appurtenances to the said John Den and his assigns from the second day of September unto the full end and term of seven years fully to be completed and ended. And also that whereas James C. Johnston on the second day of September in the year of our Lord one thousand eight hundred and five at Bertie county state and District aforesaid had demised granted and to farm let to the said John Den one other undivided sixteenth part of such of the aforesaid two tracts of Land with the appurtenances, to have and to hold the said undivided sixteenth part of each of the aforesaid two tracts of Land with the appurtenances to the said John Den and his assigns from the said second day of Septr unto the full end and term of seven years thence next ensuing and fully to be completed and ended. And also that whereas Francis A. Johnston an Infant under the age of 21 years by her next friend James C. Johnston on the second day of September in the year of our Lord one thousand eight hundred and five at Bertie county State & District aforesaid had demised granted and to farm let to the said John Den one other undivided sixteenth part of each of the aforesaid two tracts of Land with the appurtenances to have and to hold the said undivided sixteenth part of each of the two tracts of Land with the appurtenances to the said John Den and his assigns from the said second day of September the full end and term of seven years thence next ensuing fully to be completed and ended.And Also that whereas Helen S. Johnston an Infant under the age of 21 years by her next friend James C. Johnston on the said second of September 1805 at Bertie county State & District had demised granted and to farm let to the said John Den one other undivided sixteenth part of each

Chapter One
Tuscarora Records

of the aforesaid two tracts of Land with the appurtenances to have and to hold the said undivided sixteenth part of each of the aforesaid two tracts of Land with the appurtenances to the said John Den and his assigns from the said second day of September unto the full end and term of seven years thence next ensuing fully to be completed and ended By virtue of which several demises the said John entered into the said two tracts of Land with the appurtenances and was possessed thereof until the said Richard Fen afterward to wit on the same day and year last mentioned by force and arms entered into the said two tracts of Land with the appurtenances which the said Penelope Lowther, Wm McKenzie and Margaret his wife, Penelope Swann & James C. Johnston Francis A. Johnston an Infant under the age of 21 years by her next friend Jas. C. Johnston demised to the said John Den Granted to farm aforesd. which are not yet expired and Ejected the said John out of his farm and other wrongs to him did to great damage of said John Den and against the peace of the said State, whereby the said John saith that he is injured and hath sustained damage to the amount of one hundred pounds, therefore he bringeth suit.

John Doe
    Pledges
Richard Roe   P. Browne atto
                                  J. Haywood Pltff

To David Stone Esquire

Sir
    I am informed that you are in possession or claim title to the premises mentioned on the within declaration of Ejectment or some part therof and I being sued in this action as a casual ejector and having no claim to the same, do advise you to appear at Edenton at the court house therein being the Court house of Edenton District on the sixth day of April next by some attorney of that court then and there to cause yourself to be made defendant in my stead otherwise I shall suffer judgment to be entered against me and you will be [?] out of Possession

                    Your loving Friend
                    Richard Fen
1st March 1806

Chapter One
Tuscarora Records

****

Duke University
Perkins Library, Manuscript Room
William Slade Papers, 1751-1929

Jeremiah Slade has this day deposited in the Bank of Virginia Five thousand nine hundred Dollars, subject to the order of the Honorable Henry Dearborn Secretary of the War Department.

       Richmond 16th January 1807

       John Breckenbrough Cashier
       of the Bank of Virginia

****

University of North Carolina
Southern Historical Collection
Lewis Thompson Papers
Collection No. 716

I do hereby Certify that I have rec'd on Acct. of the Tuskr. Indians of Genl. William Williams the sum of Ten Thousand Seven Hundred & Twenty Two Dollars & Twenty nine Cents, and of Colo. Thomas Pugh, & his Exrs. the Sum of Eleven Thousand one Hundred & Eighty one Dolrs. & forty five Cents, making in the whole the sum of Twenty one Thousand Nine hundred and three Dollrs. & Seventy four Cents

April 23d 1807   J. Slade Commssr.

$21903..74

Thomas Pugh Dr.
To the purchase of land	$8918..64
To the Extension of large Lease	1587..81
To Extension of Black Gut Lease	650..--
To Amt of Compromise of the Suit While & the Indians agt. him	<u>25.</u>

Chapter One
Tuscarora Records

$11781..45

Gnl. William Williams
To the Indians   Dr.

To the purchase of Land	$9134..48
To the Extension of Lease }	
Jones Pugh & Williams }	1587..81
	$10722..29

E.E.   J. Slade Commssr.

****

Duke University
Perkins Library, Manuscript Room
William Slade Papers
1751-1929

(Copy)   Canandaigua August 24th 1807 **[?1817]**

Sir,
    I received your letter of the 9th instant, with the enclosed check for Eleven hundred and twenty dollars and fifty Cents, on the Office of Discount and Deposited at New York, which Sum I will pay over to the Chiefs of the Tuscarora Indians as soon as possible.

I have the honor
(Signed) Jasper Parrish

I hereby Certify that the within is a true Copy from the Original letter on file in the Department of War.

****

Duke University
Perkins Library, Manuscript Room
William Slade Papers, 1751-1929

Chapter One
Tuscarora Records

Jeremiah Slade in Acct. with the Chiefs of the Tuskerora Indians
Dr.

To amt. of the sales of the undemised Lands	2[Torn]
To amt. of the extention of the Leases	4[Torn]
To amt of the Judgts. recovered agt. White Pugh et al for trespass on the Indian Lands	[Torn]
To amt. of Interest rec'd of bonds that became due in the years 1805, 1806	$355.[Torn]
	$2592.[Torn]

3177.76	3809.5
506.66	708.65
650.00	4617.70
4334.42	

Cr.

1803 By cash paid Indians	3921.58
1804 By cash pd. to collector at Petersburg	4670.68
1805 By cash pd. To John McClary	4964.52
1807 By cash deposited in Bank at Richmond	5900.00
By Bonds Still due & uncollected	3809.50
1805 By cash pd. J.C. Guion & Joseph Littlejohn Atty	44.00
1807 By amt of the charges for carrying the money of the Indians to Petersburg & Richmond	125.00
1807 By cash paid Esther Gibson at different time	40.14
1807 By cash pd. Kenneth Clark & Co. for Indians as will appear by Bond taken up	56.65
1807 By cash pd. Samuel Williams Executr. for money borrow'd by the Indians	40.00
By Commissioners on amt. of Debts	1296.43
By amt. of acct. for board Cloathing &	

Chapter One
Tuscarora Records

Schooling of John Cain from July 180[?] untill June 1808	312.00
	25219.85
Baln. due the Indians	708.65
	25928.70
Sup C.	
By cash pd. Chiefs	250.00
	655.[?]

A List of Debts due the Indians

For the year 1805	
Gl. William Williams	$793.91 - $21.38
John Williams	396.95 - 396.95
Col. Thos. Pugh	1207.95 - 703.56
John H. Pugh	316.5
John McCaskey	118.5 1/2
Slade Speller & Griffin	427.75 - 285.16
Saml. W. Johnston	300.00
" " "	253.33
William W. Johnston	30.65 - 30.65
Hardy Boyce	22.11
Judgt. for Trespass for Pugh	
Johnston White & others	95.00 95.00
	3962.20 - 1532.70
For the year 1806	
Gl. William Williams	1968.62 1/2
" " "	264.64
Col. Thos. Pugh	2229.66 1/2
" " "	379.86
Gl. Allen Jones	794.44
Slade Speller & Griffin	427.75
John H. Pugh	316.50
Saml. W. Johnston	300.00
[Faded]	253.33
Due in the year 1805	3962.20
due in the year 1806	7377.93 1/2

111

Chapter One
Tuscarora Records

For the year 1807} Gl. William Williams $1500.00
            } Gl. Allen Jones   794.44
                                                  $2294.44
                                                  $13494.57 1/2

Gl. William Williams Dr.
To amt of Bond payable 19th June 1805   793.91
To Int. on the above 1 year   46.35
To amt of Note payable 15 June 1806   264.64
To amt of Bond Do   Do Do Do   1968.62 1/2
                                                3073.52 1/2
Sup By cash   21.38
Balance due Indians $3052.14 1/2

John Williams Dr.
To Note payable 15th June 1805   396.95
To Do Do   15th Do 1806   132.31
                                              529.26
[?]   396.95

Jeremiah Slade in Acct. with Sacarusa & Longboard, Chiefs of the Tuskerora Indians.

Dr.
To Amt. of the sales of the undemised Lands   20966.60
To Amt. of the Execution of the Leases   4512.45
                                                          2.14
                                                          4514.59
To Amt. of Judgts. Recovered of White & [?]
for trespassing on the Indian Lands   95.00
To Amt. of Interest Rec'd on Lands that
became due in the Years 1805 - 1806   255.19
                                                        25928.70

Rec'd of Jeremiah Slade

Cr.

Chapter One
Tuscarora Records

June 1, 1803		
By Cash paid Indians As p Rec't	3928.50	
Aug. 22d 1804		
By Cash paid to Collector at Petersburg	4670.60	
Aug. 24th 1805		
By Cash paid to John Clarey as p Rec't	4964.52	
Janry 16, 1807		
By Cash deposited in the Bank at Richmd.	5900.00	
By Bonds still due and unsettled	3809.50	
1804-5		
By Cash paid to J.C. Guion & Joseph Littlejohn	44.00	
1804-7		
By Acct. of Charges for Carrying the Money of the Indians to Petersburg & Richmond	[Torn]	
1805-8		
By Cash paid Esther Gibson at different times	[Torn]	
June 11th 1807		
By Cash paid Kenneth Clark & Co. for Indians as will appear by Bond taken up	[Torn]	
June 11th 1807		
By Cash paid Samuel Williams Exectr. form money borrowed by the Indians	[?]	
By Commission on Amt. of Debts	1296.43	
By Amt for Board Cloathing and Schooling of John Cain from July 1803 till June 1808	312.00	
Novr. 29th 1808		
By Cash paid Sacarusa & William Printup	250.00	
	25469.85	
By balance due Tusk Nation remaining in my hands & unaccounted for	458.85	
	25928.70	

****

University of North Carolina
Southern Historical Collection
Lewis Thompson Papers
Collection No.: 716
Copy of the Tuscarora Treaty of 1717

Chapter One
Tuscarora Records

No. Carolina Ss.

Whereas the Tuscarora Indyans by their Articles of Peace with this Government were bounded and limited for their future settlement to a certain tract of land lying between Onion Quits=tah Creek on Pamplico River and Neuse River to which Settlement they were to repair so soon as the Warr should be over, But for as much as the Indyan Warr is since broken out in South Carolina, the aforesaid Tuscarora Indyans have signified to this Government that they are in danger of being attacked and destroyed by those Indyans and therefore has prayed to be allowed a settlement on Marrattuck River for their further security. Now be it known that it is hereby mutually agreed on between the Honble. Charles Eden, Governor. Capt. Genl., and Admr. of this province, by and with the advice and consent of the Council for and on behalf of himself and the Inhabitants of this Governmt. and King Blount - for and on behalf of himself and ye rest of the Tuscarora Indyans, that forasmuch as the said Blount his Indyans, have been very serviceable to this Government and still Continues so to be and as a particular mark of favours from this Government they do hereby Give unto him the said Blount for his further and better support of himself and his Indians all the Land Lying between Mr. Jones's lower line on the North side of Marrattock River to Quitsnah Swamp and the said King Blount doth hereby agree to remove all his Indyans from off the other lands down to Rosoosskee by Christmas next and that they shall not molest nor disturb the Inhabitants nor their Stocks in hunting in any of the adjacent grounds, but that they shall take all the due care therein they can and that they shall not nor will not claim any right or property to any other lands hereafter on either side of the Said Marrattock river

In Witness whereof the said Parties have interchangably set their hands and seals this fifth day of June 1717

State of North Carolina
Secretary's office 13th Oct. 1808

This certifies that the afore going treaty or Grant to the Tuscarora Indians is a true Copy taken from the journal of the Governor and Council noe in this office

Given under my hand
at Raleigh the date Aforesaid
Will White Sec

a copy from Mr. White's copy by W.W. Jones

/Copy/

Chapter One
Tuscarora Records

Governor Eden & King Blount, of the Tuscarora Indians
Treaty
A. Dom. 1717

****

Duke University
Perkins Library, Manuscript Room
William Slade Papers
1751-1929

November 29th 1808

    Then rec'd of Jeremiah Slade two hundred & fifty Dollars on acct. of monies which he hath collected for the Tuskerora Indians which Sum is past to his Credit in the acct. by him render'd this day.

Tukin[?] Cuin

                    Sacarusa
                    William Printup
                    Nicholas Cusick

****

Duke University
Perkins Library, Manuscript Room
William Slade Papers, 1751-1929

12 July 1816

The Chiefs of the Tuscarora Nation Indians [?]
been with me by whom I rec'd your favours [?]
I have taken all the means in my power to [?]
understand the Situation of their business in this State
which I am Sorry to say is an embarrassing situation.
The Legislature in the year 1748 passed a law conferring
the Tuscaroras the lands within the bounds therein [?]
to the Chiefs of the Tuscarora Nation of Indians & their
Successors forever with a proviso That it shall not be
lawful for any person or persons that have formerly obtained

Chapter One
Tuscarora Records

any Grant or Grants under the late Lords Proprietors for
any tract or parcels of land within the aforesaid bounds
upon the sd Indians deserting or leaving the sd lands
to enter Occupy & enjoy the same according to the bounds [?]
their sd several Grants between the years 1723 [?] Grants
were obtained from the Lords Proprietors for [?] the
whole of the sd. lands allotted to the sd Nation of Indians
the whole or a part of the sd Nation continued to
live on the sd. Land until the year 1802 the Legislature
of this State passed a law authorising the sd. Nation by
their Chief & three Commissioners to lease & farm let
the undemised residue of the Lands allotted to the Tuscarora
Nation in Bertie County for a Term of years that will expire
[Faded] when the Lease **[Faded]** by the Tuskerora **[Torn]** Robert Jones
and others in the year 1766 shall **[Faded]** and also extend the term or
Terms of the Leases already made or granted for a shorter Term, to a term
of leases which shall expire at the same time of the Lease made in the year
1766, And further to make such attestation by covenant or agreement
respecting the payment & receipt of any of the [**Fade**] that may be
coincident[?] on any of the existing Leases the Chiefs & commissioners
shall approve **[Faded]** The Chiefs of the Tuskerora Nation of Indians did
agree that from and after **[Faded]** July in the year 1916 the whole of the [
Faded] Tuskerora Nation as by an Act passed in the year 1748 shall
revert to and become the property [**Faded**] thereto shall from [
Faded] be held & [?] forever extinguished [**Faded**] should not
opperate against or affect the title of any individual By virtue of an Act of
the Legislature the Chiefs with the Commissioners have sold all the
undemised lands (save a tract in the possession of David Stone Esq.) for
the sum of $20966.50 and have extended the short leases & commuted the
rents thereon to Jones Pugh & Williams to Pugh (alone for Black Gut
Lease)[?] and Johnston up to the 12 day of July 1916 for the sum of
$4512.45. I as the Agent of the Indian

[Editors Note: This document is badly torn, faded and incomplete. It may be a rough draft of a letter dated 3 December 1808.]

Sir
                      Williamston
                    December 3d 1808

Chapter One
Tuscarora Records

I rec'd your Letter of 13th Ultimo from the Tuskerora Chief; I have taken every measure in my power to make them acquainted with the situation of their business in North Carolina, which is Some what imbarrassing.

The Legislature of No. Carolina in the year 1748 passed a Law confirming the title to the Lands allotted the Tuscarora Indians in Bertie County to James Blount Chief of the sd. Nation and the people under his charge their Heirs & Successors forever; "Provided that it shall & may be lawful for any person or persons that have formerly obtained any Grant or Grants, under the late Lords Proprietors for any tracts or parcells of Land within the aforesaid boundaries, upon the sd. Indians deserting or Leaving the said Land to enter occupy and enjoy the same, according to the tenor of their said Several Grants." The Tuskerora Nation continued to occupy the said Lands untill the year 1766 when the Chiefs of the sd. Nation made a Lease for 150 yrs to Robert Jones William Williams and Thomas Pugh for about one half of the Lands alloted them and a part of the Nation removed off. Some time in the year 1775 the Chiefs of the Nation who remained on the Land, Leased to Jones Pugh and Williams about 12533 acres more of their Land for 99 years To Thomas Pugh for 547 acres To William King 540 acres To Hunter & McCaskey 1934 acres To Titus Edwards 117 acres To John Johnston 478 acres and to Zekiah Stone 625 acres of Land all for 99 years Leaving but 3000 acres of Land undemised for the Nation to live on, where they resided untill July in the year 1803 The Legislature in the year 1802 having authorised the Chiefs of the Tuskerora Nation with the advice of the Commissioners to Lease & to Farm let the undemised residue of the Lands alloted to the Tuskerora Nation in Bertie County for a term of years that shall expire & end when the Lease made by the Tuskerora Nations to Robert Jones & others in the year 1766 shall end & expire. And also extend the term or terms of the Leases already made or Granted for a shorter Term, to a Term or Terms which shall expire at the same time of the Lease made in the year 1766. And further to make such alterations by Covenant or agreement respecting the payments & receipts of any of the rents due or that may become due on any of the existing Leases as the Chiefs of sd. Nation & Commissioners shall approve. And also that the occupancy & possession of the Tenants under the said Leases heretofore confirmed by Act or Acts of the General Assembly, and such Leases as may be made under this Act, shall be held & deemed in all cases whatsoever, the occupancy & possession of the said Tuskerora Nation to all intents and purposes as if the said Nation, or the Indians thereof or any of them, actuall resided on the said Land. In consideration whereof the sd. Chiefs of the Tuskerora Nation did agree that from & after the 12th day of

Chapter One
Tuscarora Records

July in the year 1916 the whole of the Lands alloted to the Tuskerora Nation of Indians by an Act passed in the year 1748 shall revert to & become the property of the State, & the Indian claim thereto shall from that time be held & deemed extinguished Provided that nothing therein should effect the title of any individual" - By virtue of the last mentioned act of the Legislature the Chiefs by & with the advice of three Commissioners did Lease to Farm let all the undemised Land (except a tract in the possession of David Stone Esq.) for the sum of $20966.60 and have extended the short Leases for a Term which will expire on the 12th day of July in the year 1916 to Jones Pugh & Williams, to Thomas Pugh Samuel Johnston heir of John Johnston & Titus Edwards for the sum of $4512.45; I as the agent of the Tuskerora Nation recovered agt. White Pugh & others for trespassing on the Lands of the sd. Nation the sum of $95 and I also rec'd by way of Interest on the [?] that were not punctually paid the further sum of $355.19 forming an aggregate of $25928.70, of which sum I have collected and accounted for, as will appear by my acct. with the Chiefs of the Tuskerora Nation of Indians the sum of $21410.80. The balance of $3809.50 Still remains due & uncollected. Soon after the Bonds became due I brought suit on all that were not paid, and have recovered Judgts. in the Court of Common Law for the most of the money, and shall (I expect) at the next setting of the Fedl. Court for the District of No. Carolina obtain Judgts. for the balance. And should have been soon able to have finally adjusted & settled the business of the Tuskerora Nation of Indians in North Carolina, but the sd. Nation having after the sale of their undemised Lands all (except John Cain) removed to Niagara, those persons who held Grants from the Lords Proprietors bearing date anterior to the year 1748 brought suits agt. Jones Pugh & Williams for the Lands purchased of the sd. Nation of Indians Alledging that the Indians were untitled to the Lands alloted them in Bertie County only during their occupancy & therefore could not sell; Whereupon those who had not paid filed Bills in Equity against me as agent of the sd. Nation to stay the proceedings untill the decision of the suits for the Land should be Known, and praying a perpetual Injunction in case the Lands should be recovered from them.

   I have a lively hope that the Injunction will be dismissed on the Spring Circuit next, and that I shall be able to collect the money still due soon after. But the balance of the short Leases cannot be extended unless the decision of the suit for the Lands should be favourably determined for the Tuskerora Nation. From the foregoing Statements It will be readily

Chapter One
Tuscarora Records

discovered that the business of the Indians in No. Carolina cannot be finall adjusted at this time however desirable it may be.

It will appear from my acct. Stated that there is a balance of $458.85 in my hands unaccounted for; which sum I have retained to defray the costs & charges of the several suits, should the decrees be against me.

I have been induced to trouble you with long & circumstantiall acct. that the Chiefs of the Indian Nation might be correctly informed of the situation of their business.

> With the highest respect I am Sir
> Yr. Mt. Obt. Hble. Sert.
> J Slade

****

Duke University
Perkins Library, Manuscript Room
William Slade Papers
1751-1929

> Williamston N. Carolina
>
> October 4th 1809

Sir,

I this day rec'd your letter of the 29th Augt. last and avail myself of the earliest opportunity offered, to answer your enquiries. The Injunctions filed against myself & the Indians were dismissed according to my expectations and I obtained Judgts. on all the Bonds, save two, [Torn] but during the last session [Torn] an act was passed [Torn] to stay the Execution [Torn]

You mention in your letter, that the Indians "feel greatly disappointed in the result of their business & think they have been wronged". The uncertainty who is in the above communication, of who the Indians consider as the agent of their wrong precludes me from making any statement that might lend [Torn] shew that the Indians have had every Justice [Torn] done them so far as respects the State [Torn] the Agents of the [Torn]

Chapter One
Tuscarora Records

[Editors Note: Most of this letter is missing and has not yet been found.]

****

North Carolina State Archives
Manuscript Collection
P.C. 928
Jeremiah Slade Papers

To all our Right Worshipful and Well Beloved
BRETHREN
GREETING:

KNOW YE, that by the Powers and Authorities vested in me as Grand Master of Masons of North Carolina and Tennessee, and others under the Jurisdiction of the Grand Lodge, I do hereby and nominate and appoint Colonel Jeremiah Slade Deputy Grand Master of Masons under our Jurisdiction, for the Year 5812. AD 1812.

This is therefore to empower the said Jeremiah Slade to act as such in all Cases whatsoever, carefully attending to the Discharge of his Duty, agreeable to the ancient Land Marks of our Order.

It is hereby required of all Free and Accepted Masons and Lodges duly constituted to obey every Order and Summons of the said Deputy Grand Master, and to discharge Duties as may be by him required of the Craft according to the ancient Principles of our Institution. We do require of you, our Right Worshipful and Well Beloved Brother Jeremiah Slade strictly strictly to attend to the several Duties of your Office of Deputy Grand Master; that you will visit the respective Lodges under our Jurisdiction, and govern the Craft wheresoever you go; that you will teach and impress the several Duties of Morality and Religion, and strongly inculcate the Principles of Charity and Brotherly Love in the Mind of everyone; that you will cause Lectures on Symbolic Masonry to be frequently practised in the several Lodges; that the Pillars of our Order be carefully supported by the Exercise of every Christian and Moral Duty.

Given at Raleigh, under the Hand and Seal of the Grand Master, the 13th Day of December A.L. 5812   A.D. 1811.

Chapter One
Tuscarora Records

WITNESS   Robt Williams   GRAND MASTER

Test.   A. Lucas   Grand Secretary

****

Duke University
Perkins Library, Manuscript Room
William Slade Papers, 1751-1929

Williamston 1 July 1816

Jeremiah Slade (for Jno Cain)

Bot[?] of Saml. H. [?]

4 yards drab cord	/6	$5.--
2 1/2 " casimere (blk)	25/	6.25
1 rist patron		1.50
1 " "		1.25
3 1/2 yds homespun	4/6	1.57 1/2
2 Doz. mose[?]	1/	20
1 " "		15
5 skeins silk	1/	50
2 s. Twist	1/5	25
Thread		10
Do		50
14 yds Shirting	5/	7.--

Chapter One
Tuscarora Records

1 1/2 Doz Shirt Buttons	2/	30
	Dolls. 24.47 1/2	
Augt. 1 pair Shoes	2.50	
	26.97 1/2	

****

Duke University
Perkins Library, Manuscript Room
William Slade Papers
1751-1929

The Tuskerora Indians

To Jere Slade   Dr

To the Amt of Saml.[Torn]	$ 50.55
To George Pollards Amt [Torn]	15.--
To cash paid John Cain	108.75
To John Cains amt with Hyman &c	5.60
	179.90
To cash for making fou[Torn]	2.40
	182.30
To cash at Washington	4.60
To trunk to put his cloaths in	4.00
	$ 190.90

Augt. 11th 1816

I acknowledge the [Torn] acct to be correct & [Torn] Cain

****

Chapter One
Tuscarora Records

Duke University
Perkins Library, Manuscript Room
William Slade Papers
1751-1929

Williamston

The Chief of the
Tuskerora Indians   August 11th 1816.

Brothers

    Having heard nothing from **[Torn]**
20th Decr. 1809; And John Cain the boy left with me **[Torn]**
Chiefs Sacarusa & Longboard, being uneasy and anxious **[Torn]**
to trust his friends, I have furnished him with clo**[Torn]**
and money for that purpose. I heartily join **[Torn]**
in prayer to the great Spirit that he may **[Torn]**
his friends all alive & well, but the great leng**[Torn]**
of time and the many alarming difficulties tha**[Torn]**
have happened since we have heard from you are calculated in us many fears.
    In the month of April 1812 I wrote **[Torn]**
that I had completed the collection of all the **[Torn]**
due you in this State except the rents on the unextended lease to Wm **[Torn]** John McCaskey & David Stone who all refused to pay - six or seven years since I brought suit against the Kings and those holding under them, and at July **[Torn]** 1815 of the Supreme Court of No Carolina **[Torn]** a decision in your favour against them but before I could obtain an Execution for **[Torn]** collect the money one of the defendants died and I am obligded to revive the suit again **[Torn]** McCaskey has agreed to pay without a suit if I recover against King Mr. Stone wholly refuses and there being no rent reserved in his leases I cant compell him. The attempt to collect the rents has been verry troublesome to me and will continue to be so; And should John Cain be unwilling to live with the Nation, I am of opinion that you will do well to give it to him, and let him **[Torn]** to the collection. The Rent is due from **[Torn]**8. You can see the amt. in the said Leases copies of which are in your possession. I feel anxious to close the business so far as I am concerned as soon as possible: You are informed by my Acct. rendered the Chiefs on 29th November 1808 and my letter of the

Chapter One
Tuscarora Records

[Torn] date to Gl. Henry Dearborn the amt of the balance due you which you can draw from or come & receive, which you may prefer; The only request I have to make is that you would be so good as to let me know four to six months before you come or send; as it is a large sum of money and I may not be prepared without that notice.

****

Duke University
Perkins Library, Manuscript Room
William Slade Papers
1751-1929

Williamston

Tuskerora Indians   August 11th 1816

Brothers

    Having heard nothing from you since the letter of Erastus Granger Esqr. of the 20th of Decr. 1809 and John Cain the Indian boy left with me by the Chiefs Sacarusa & Longboard being anxiuos and desirous to visit his friends I have furnished him with cloaths & money for that purpose, who is the bearer of this letter. He goes with anxious hopes and earnest prayers with me that it may please the great Spirit to enable him to find his friends all alive and well, the great length of time that has intervened since we heard from you is calculated to excite in us many fears.

    In the month of April 1812 I wrote you that I had completed the collection of all the debts due you in this State except for the rents due upon the leases to David Stone William King and John McCaskey all of them have refused to pay and a suit has been depending in Court against William King & his tenents for six or seven years. In July 1815 in the Supreme Court of No. Carolina obtained a decision in favour of your further rents but before I could get an execution one of the tenants died and I am oblidged to revive the suit again before I can get the money. The persons claiming under McCaskey have agreed to pay **[Editor's Note: The second page of this document was not found, but it is referring to the fact that David Stone refused to pay the Tuskeroras.]**and there is no rent reserved in the lease to him and I can't make him pay.

Chapter One
Tuscarora Records

There is due on Kings Lease forty Dollars a year from June 1803 untill this time say thirteen years will amt to $520. On McCaskeys for the same length of time Twenty four Dollrs. a year will amt in all $312. It has been extremely troublesome to Settle and will continue to be so. I am therefore of opinion should John Cain be unwilling to live with the Nation that you would do well to give it to him and let him attend to the collection.

I feel anxious to close the business so far as relates to me; you are informed by my Amount rendered to the Chiefs 29th Novr. 1808 and my Letter of the same date to genl. Dearborn of the amt of the balance due you which sum you can draw for; or come on and receive it, which ever you prefer. I have only this request to make that you will give me four or six months notice before you come or draw on me for the money as it a considerable sum and I may not be in funds unless you give me Notice time enough for me to prepare.

****

Duke University
Perkins Library, Manuscript Room
William Slade Papers
1751-1929

Buffalo Nov. 10th 1816

J Slade Esqr.

Brother

Your letter by John Cain, dated Augt. 11th last past has been rec'd. He arrived at our Village in Good health and is now about returning for North Carolina.

We hope he will have a good Journey home.

We have given him a power to Collect the back rents due from Wm. King, Jno. McCaskey, and David or Zekiah Stone **[Torn]** to his time, at his own expense.

You mention of having Wrote us in April 1812 which we never received. We understand our agent has Wrote you, but no answer to his last letters. We believe letters have Misarrived.

Chapter One
Tuscarora Records

We have in our hands your letters to the Secrty of War and your Statements of our Business in your State.

We have also your letter to our agent. We feel thankful for your attention to our business. The Tuscarora Nation has authorised us to Write you, and request you to send the Money in Your hands to the Sectry of War at Washington, from whence we **[Torn]** get it with out expe**[Torn]** to us. The Tuscaroras intend to prosecute their further Claims.

      your friends & Brothers

Sacarusa   his + Mark
Nicholas Cusick

In presence of
Erastus Granger   Indn. Agt.

      Duplicate

P.S. the Tuscarora Indns. do not intend to relinguish their Claim. They intend once More to apply to the Legislature of your State to have Justice done them **[Torn]** they with Jno. Cain **[Torn]** and say he **[Torn]**   enjoy with others of their Nation the property in Common.

The Chiefs appointed to attend to their Business think of visiting N.C. once More.
      E Granger

****

Duke University
Perkins Library, Manuscript Room
William Slade Papers
1751-1929

      Sacarusa & Cusick
      Cheifs of the T Ind
      Bu

      Williamston
Williamston   December 2d. 1816

Brothers

Chapter One
Tuscarora Records

I this day recd. your esteemed favour of the 10th Novr. last and I am of a loss for language to express my feelings at the pleasing intelligence that the Great Spirit had prolonged the lives of persons for whom I entertain so sincere a regard; when John Cain left me to go to the Village of his friends & Nation I awfully fear'd that those of them with whom I was acquainted had gone to the World of Spirits for from no other ground could I account for your long Silence; for not one word have I heard from you since the letter of Mr. Granger of the 20th day of Dec 1809; it is however with some fear and anxiety that I read the Signature of my much respected & venerable friends Sacarusa and Nicholas Cusick only, to the letter, it was with anxiety I looked for the names of Longboard & Printhrop But being vain, they are not there. I however hope they have not left us to visit their friends in the other World, if they have peace to their Manes [Names] they have rested from their labours & their works will follow them. I received no small consolation from the information that John Cain had arived to your Village in health and I join with you in the hopes & prayer that he may safely return. I could wish and have often pressed him to settle with his friends & the Nation, but I fear that his attachments to the place of his Nativity is so strong that he never will quit it, I shall however continue to urge him to settle with you.

With regard to the monies which I have in my hands I shall make the earliest possible arrangement to remit it to the Secretary of War agreeable to your instruction and will let you know when I have done it that you may know when to apply.

It is with no small pleasure that I anticipate the time when you will visit North Carolina again and I hope you will do me the favour to make my house your Home during your stay in this part of the Country: It will give me particular pleasure to ack you in your wishes in every respect.

With feelings of Love & esteem I am
Yr. Mt. Obt. Hble. Sert.
    J Slade
The Cheifs of the Tuskerora Indians

****

North Carolina State Archives
North Carolina Reports
Volume 4, Pages 336-340

Chapter One
Tuscarora Records

Sacarusa & Long Board VS. William King's Heirs. &C. Page 451.

The grant made by the Governor in 1717 to the Tuscarora tribe of Indians is absolute and unconditional, and does not require the residence of the Indians upon the land.
The proviso in the act of 1748 ch. 3, sec. 3, being in derogation of rights actually vested in the plaintiffs, cannot be regarded. But if the act of 1748 could rightfully superadd the condition contained in the proviso, subsequent legislatures had an equal right to modify or abrogate it. And the acts of 1778 ch. 16 and 1802 make a different appropriation of the land, on the happening of either of the events mentioned in the act of 1778, from that made by the act of 1748.
He, who accepts a lease from another, and those claiming under him, are estopped during the continuance of the lease, to deny the title of the lessor.

On the 5th of June, 1717, Governor Eden, by and with the advice of the Lords Proprietors' deputies, made a grant of a tract of land, lying on the south side of Morrahock (now Roanoke) River, To King Blount, for himself and the Tuscarora tribe of Indians.
On the 13th of Dec. 1775, Whitmill TuffDick, King of the said tribe of Indians, for himself and his nation, made a lease in writing under seal, of a part of the aforesaid tract, to Wm. King, for 99 years-the lease contains a covenant on the part of said Wm. King, his heirs, &c. to pay to the lessors, their heirs and successors, the yearly sum of **[Blank]** during the continuance of the lease.
King took possession of the land described in the lease, immediately after its execution-and he, and those who claim under him, have had the undisturbed possession of said land, from that time continually up to the bringing of this suit.
In April, 1726, **[Blank]** obtained a grant from the Lords Proprietors' deputies for the same land mentioned in the lease from the Tuscaroras to Wm. King-and on the 21st of October, 1777, the said Wm. King obtained a conveyance in fee-simple for the same land, derived from the grant of 1726.
Some of the Indians of the aforesaid tribe remained in actual possession of part of the land comprehended in the grant of 5th June, 1717, until June, 1803, when they finally removed from the said land to the state of New York, leaving one of their tribe in the county of Martin (not on the lands granted to them) to attend to their concerns, receive their rents, &c.

Chapter One
Tuscarora Records

After their removal from the lands so granted on the 5th of June, 1717, in June, 1803 the defendants refused to pay the rent reserved by the lease. This action was brought on the covenant contained in the lease, to recover the rents in arrear. The defendants opposed the plaintiff's claim for the rents, on the following grounds: 1. That by the act of 1748, c. 3, S. 3, it is enacted, "that it shall and may be lawful for any person or persons, that have formerly obtained any grant or grants, under the Lords Proprietors, for any tracts or parcels of land within the aforesaid boundaries (meaning the boundaries of the land described in the grant to the Indians of the 5th June, 1717) upon the said Indians deserting or leaving said lands, to enter, occupy and enjoy the same, according to the tenor of their several grants, any thing herein to the contrary notwithstanding." 2. That the Indians having removed themselves from the said land, the defendants claim the possession of that which they occupy, under the title derived from the grant of April, 1726, and not under the lease made to their ancestor by the Indians in Dec. 1775.

The jury, under the charge of the court, found for the plaintiffs, the amount due for the arrears of rent. A motion for a new trial was made for misdirection of the court which being overruled, the defendants appealed to this court.

Cameron, J. delivered the judgment of the court:

If the title of the Tuscarora tribe of Indians to the lands leased by them to the defendant's ancestor, depended solely on the confirmation it received by the 2 S. of c. 3, acts 1748, to which the 3 S. (relied on by the defendants) is added, by way of proviso, the grant and the condition annexed to it, would now be regarded as forming one entire contract between the sovereignty of this State and the tribe of Indians. Their title, however, rests on higher grounds. The Governor and the deputies of the Lords Proprietors, having full and competent powers for that purpose, did, by the grant of the 5th June, 1717, vest the lands thereby granted, in the Tuscarora tribe, absolutely and unconditionally. The grant recites, that it is made "in consideration of great services rendered by the said tribe of Indians to the Government, and of their agreeing to relinquish all claims to other lands, which had been before allotted to them." It contains no condition by which the Indians are bound to reside actually and perpetually on it. It is a conveyance (in substance) in fee simple, by those having power to convey, to persons capable of taking and holding lands in fee.

The acts of the General Assembly confirming their title, providing for their comfortable enjoyment of it, by prohibiting white persons from hunting and tresspassing on their lands, were such as policy and justice

Chapter One
Tuscarora Records

dictated, and are entitled to approbation and support; but the proviso in S. 3 c. 3, 1748, under which the defendants claim, being in derogation of rights actually vested in the plaintiffs by the highest authorities, cannot be regarded, or allowed to have any weight in deciding this case.

If, however, the Assembly of 1748, had the power to annex the condition contained in the proviso referred to, they had equally a right afterwards, to modify, alter, or abrogate that condition. It cannot be contended, that the aforesaid 3 S. 3 c. 1748, is irrepealable, and that all which has been done by subsequent assemblies for the modification of it, is void, because repugnant to that proviso.

Pursuing the acts of Assembly on this subject, we find that by c. 16 of acts 1778, certain leases made by the Indians were rendered valid- that the lands leased to Jones, and to other persons, shall revert to, and become the property of the State, at the expiration of the leases, if the nation be extinct; and the lands now belonging to, and possessed by the Tuscaroras, shall revert to, and become the property of the State, whenever the said nation shall become extinct, or shall entirely abandon, or remove themselves off the said lands, and every part thereof."

The lease made by the Indians to Wm. King, is within the operation of this act; and if any effect is to be allowed to legislative will on this subject, a very different appropriation is made of the land granted to the Indians, on the happening of either of the events mentioned in the act of 1778, from that made by the act of 1748; under which the defendants claim.

We further find, that by the act of 1802, c. **[Blank]**, the Indians were authorized to lease out their unleased lands, to extend other leases. Commissioners were appointed under its authority to superintend and direct the management of their concerns; and they finally agreed by treaty with this State (with the approbation and consent of the General Government) at the expiration of the leases, to abandon all claims to the lands, to the State. It is expressly declared and provided by said act, "that the possession of the lessees shall be considered the possession of the Indians."

At the time the act of 1802 passed and took effect, the plaintiff's, either by themselves or their lessees, were in possession of all the land comprehended in the grant of the 5th of June, 1717. The General Assembly were apprized that the Indians intended to remove from it; they had agreed to renounce all claim to the land on the expiration of the leases made, and to be made under the said act, for the purpose of securing to them the full benefit of the leases; to allay their apprehensions that their removal from

Chapter One
Tuscarora Records

the land might destroy their claims to the rents secured by their leases; in short, to obviate the very objection made by the defendants against the plaintiff's demand, under color of the proviso in the 3d sect. 3d c. 1748, the General Assembly, with a proper regard to liberality and justice, enacted and declared that the possession of the lessees should be considered the possession of the plaintiffs; - In effect saying that the removal of the Indians from the land should not prejudice their claim to the rents due on leases made and to be made by them.

Viewing this case with reference merely to the acts of Assembly passed on this subject, and admitting that the plaintiff's claim must be governed by those; it is very clear to us that they are entitled to recover.

There is however, another ground, on which the plaintiffs are entitled to prevail. Admitting (for the sake of argument) that the fee-simple of the land comprehended in the lease, vested by the grant of 1726, the mesne conveyances under it, coupled with the actual removal of the Indians, in Wm. King, the ancestor of the defendants (on which point we give no opinion): yet, as he accepted the lease on which this action is brought, and took possession of the land under it, he could not, and those claiming under him cannot, during the continuance of the lease, say that the plaintiff's have no right to recover the rents reserved and secured by it. Lord Coke says, "if a man take a lease of his own land, by deed indented, reserving rent, the lessee is concluded." Co. Lit. S. 58. 47 B. - The court is unanimously of opinion, that the motion for a new trial be overruled, and that there be judgment for plaintiff.

****

Duke University
Perkins Library, Manuscript Room
William Slade Papers
1751-1929

Williamston May the 23rd 1817

Erastus Granger Esqr.   Williamston

Sir your favours of the 15th March last was duly recd. and in answer I beg you will inform the Chiefs of the Tuskerora Indians, that at the time I recd. your letter I was from Home and did not return untill the last of April, that on the 29th of Apl. I purchased a Bill on John Maybin

Chapter One
Tuscarora Records

Esqr. of Philadelphia payable in 60 days after the 24th Apl. 1817 for $1500 of which I directed my agent to deposit in the Bank of the United States at Philadelphia which sum the Chiefs will be at liberty to draw for thro' the medium of the Secretary of War as soon as the bill is paid of which you will be informed by Mr. John Maybin of Philadelphia. This is the only bill that I have been able to procure that would place the money more convenient to the Indns. than in No. Carolina. I have no doubt but that the Bill will be duly Honored & paid by the 24th June. I am prepared to deposit in the State Bank of North Carolina at the Branch Bank of Edenton two thousand Dollars, which you can draw for thro' the medium of the Secretary of War, so soon as the Indns. will authorise me to do so. The balln. still due the Indians in my hands say five Hundred Dollars I am not prepared to deposit nor do I know that I shall be able untill next winter or fall. When the Chiefs were in this State last I gave them a Statement shewing the amt of money due them in No. Carolina (to viz) $3809.5 and $458.85 retained in my hands to meet the expences of the several Lawsuits about their business, forming an agregate sum of $4267.90 this sum has been reduced by the expences attending their business but how much I am not now prepared to say but not more than $267.90 and probably not so much. I am extremely sorry for the situation of the Indians and more so as it is not in my power to send their Money to them which would afford them relief.

With consideration of respect &c
J Slade

****

Duke University
Perkins Library, Manuscript Room
William Slade Papers
1751-1929

11 July 1817

Know all men by these presents that we Saccarusa and Nicholas Cusick chiefs of the Tuscarora Nation of Indians, residing in the County of Niagara and State of New York by our Letter of Attorney bearing date some time in the year 1816 did make constitute and appoint John Cain one of the said Nation of Indians resident in the State of North Carolina our

Chapter One
Tuscarora Records

attorney for recovery of all rents of land due to the said Nation from divers persons in the said State of North Carolina as by the said letter of attorney may appear: Now Know ye that we the said Saccarusa and Nicholas Cusick for that the said John Cain hath abused the authority by us in him reposed have revoked, countermanded, annulled and made void and by these presents do revoke, countermand and make void the said letter of attorney, and all power and authority thereby given or **[Faded]** to the said John Cain. In witness whereof we have hereunto let our hands and Seals this eleventh day of July in the year of our Lord one thousand eight hundred and seventeen.

	his
Signed Sealed	Saccarusa x
in presence of	mark
B[?] Cooke	Nicholas Cusick

State of New York
Court of Niagara   Personally appeared before me Gideon Frisbee one of the Justices of the Peace in and for the County of Niagara State aforesaid Sacarusa and Nicholas to me known to be the persons who are described in and who executed the above instrument and acknowledged the same to be their voluntary act and deed for the uses and purposes therein mentioned - Witness my hand the day and year above written.

G. Frisbee

State of New York
Niagara County
Clerks Office
   I Frederick B. Merrell
Clerk of the County aforesaid hereby Certify that Gideon Frisbee Esquire before whom the Acknowledgement Appears to have been made is a Justice of the Peace in and for said County Acting under the Authority of the State and that the same so signed is his signature.

In Testimony whereof I have hereunto Set my hand and affixed the County Seal at Buffalo this 17th day of July 1817

F.B. Merrell Clerk

****

Chapter One
Tuscarora Records

Duke University
Perkins Library, Manuscript Room
William Slade Papers
1751-1929

                        Jeremiah Slade Esqire

                           Williamston
Lewiston   Martin Co. North Carolina
22 July

                    Lewiston 11 July 1817

Brother, Your letter of 18 June last we have received and the contents have been made known to the Nation, it is accepted. Sir, as an additional evidence of the interest you have taken in our behalf - receive our most hearty thanks and through us the thanks of the Nation - although we are in extreme want of the money and anxiously await its arrival yet we are sensible you have done all you could to expedite it. We hope the Secretary of War will comply with your request - if he should not our situation would be deplorable - all you propose to the settlement of accounts we are satisfied with and hope to have the pleasure of seeing you the next fall or beginning of winter - With respect to John Cain we wish him to return to us and request you to furnish him with the necessary means, if he refuses to return we wish to deprive him of the chance of receiving and expending the money belonging of right to the nation and in order that you may do so we enclose you a revocation of the power of attorney we gave him - we are sorry he has abused the trust reposed in him - may the great spirit preserve your valuable life and afford you the means of doing good is the anxious prayer of your much oblidged friend

                                       his
                                 Sacarusa x
                                 mark

                           Nicholas Cusick

J. Slade Esq.

****

Duke University

Chapter One
Tuscarora Records

Perkins Library, Manuscript Room
William Slade Papers
1751-1929

Buffalo 5th Sept. 1817

We the Sachems and Chiefs of the Tuscarora Nation of Indians , do acknowledge to have received J. Slade of North Carolina our agent through the War Department by the hands of Jasper Parish, the sum of Eleven hundred and Twenty Dollars & fifty Cents on account of moneys Collected by him for us

$1120. 50/100

          Sacarusa   his mark x
          William Prantup   his mark x
          Solomon Longboard his mark x

Triplicates

H.B. Potter
   his
Young x King
   mark
   his
Colonel x Pollard
   mark

Horatio Jones

****

Duke University
Perkins Library, Manuscript Room
William Slade Papers, 1751-1929

22 October 1817

Know all men by these presents that we the Sachems Chiefs & Warriors of the Tuscarora Nation of Indians, for divers good causes and considerations, us hereunto moving, have made, ordained, authorised

Chapter One
Tuscarora Records

nominated & constituted & by these presents do make, authorize, nominate & constitute Nicholas Cusick & Solomon Longboard two of our principal Chiefs to be our lawful attorneys for us & in our names to ask demand sue for, recover & receive of & from every person or persons resident or living in the State of North Carolina all such sum or sums of money debts or demands whatsoever which are now due or owing to us the said Tuscarora Nation of Indians by and from any person or persons living or residing in said State of North Carolina and to have, use & take all lawful means and ways in our name or otherwise for the recovery thereof by attachment arrest distress or otherwise & to compound & afree for the same, & acquittances or other sufficient discharges for the same; for us & in our names to make seal & deliver, to appoint & employ other attornies & to do all other lawful acts & things whatsoever concerning the premises as fully & in every respect as we ourselves might & could do, were we personally present at the doing thereof; hereby ratifying & confirming all such attachments arrests distresses agreements acquittances & discharges which for us & in our names & done by our said attornies touching & concerning the said sum or sums of money, debts & demands which are noe due to the said Tuscarora Nation of Indians by any person or persons living or residing in said State of North Carolina as fully and effectively as if we ourselves were personally present & the actors & docrs thereof.

In witness hereof we have hereunto set our hands & seals at Tuscarora Village in the County of Niagara & State of New York this twenty second day of October in the year of our Lord, one thousand eight hundred & seventeen.

Signed, Sealed & delivered in presence of

The words arrests distresses agreements interlined after the fifteenth line noticed before signing
James Young
Teacher among the Tuscaroras   Sacarissa, Sachem   his mark "x"
Jas C. Crane
Missny to Tuscaroras
Robert Fleming   William Printup, Sachem   his mark "x"
Jasper Parrish   Thomas, Sachem   his mark "x"
Sub Agent to the
Six Nations of Indians

    Abraham Chief Warrior   his mark "x"
    Paulus: War Chief: his mark "x"

Chapter One
Tuscarora Records

Obediah do	his mark "x"
William do	his mark "x"
Jacob War Chief	his mark "x"
Big Fish Warrior	his mark "x"
William do	his mark "x"
David Cusick Warrior	his mark "x"
Jacob do	his mark "x"
George Lovedenny War Chief	his mark "x"
John Mountpleasant do	his mark "x"
Edward Johnson Warrior	his mark "x"
Isaac Green do	his mark "x"
Lewis do	his mark "x"
Adam Patterson do	his mark "x"
John Billy do	his mark "x"
Solomon Longboard do	his mark "x"
John Green do	his mark "x"

Niagara County Ss:

    On this twenty second day of October in the year of our Lord, One thousand eight hundred & seventeen personally appeared before me Robert Fleming one of the Assistant Judges of the court of common pleas & justice of the peace for the county of Niagara, the Sachems Chiefs and warriors of the Tuscarora nation of Indians above mentioned to me personally known to be the same persons described in, & who executed the preceding power of attorney who acknowledged that they executed the same as their act and deed for the uses & purposes therein mentioned

                Robert Fleming

State of New York   }
                            }   Frederick B. Merrill
Niagara County }

Clerk of the County aforesaid do hereby Certify that Robert Fleming before whom the within acknowledgments appear to have been made is one of the Assistant Justices of the Court of Common pleas   in and for said County and Justice of the peace acting under the Authority of this State and that the within is his Signature
                In Testimony Whereof

Chapter One
Tuscarora Records

I have hereunto Set my hand and Affixed the County Seal at Buffalo this Twenty fourth day of October in the year of our Lord One thousand Eight hundred and Seventeen

Frederick B. Merrill

****

Duke University
Perkins Library, Manuscript Room
William Slade Papers
1751-1929

RECEIPT

Rec'd of Jeremiah Slade agent of the Tuskerora Indians the sum of seven hundred Dollars. Feby. 2d 1818

Nicholas Cusick

Solomon + Longboard
his
mark

Test. A.M. Slade

****

Duke University
Perkins Library, Manuscript Room
William Slade Papers, 1751-1929

WILLIAMSTON NO. CAROLINA
February 4th 1818

Tuskerora Nation
Brothers,

Your Chiefs Nicholas Cusick and Solomon Longboard arived here on the 2d ult and laid their papers before me; from which I discovered

Chapter One
Tuscarora Records

the objects of their mission were, 1st, to apply to the Legislature of this State, for a modification of their law of 1802 so as to entitle the Nation to a fee simple in the lands which belonged to them in Bertie County after the expiration of the Leases (Viz in year 1916) or for some compensation in lieu thereof; and 2dly the collection of the monies due the Nation in No. Carolina.

With regard to the first, the Chiefs arived here too late to make an application to the Legislature it having adjourned about the 24th Decr. last; But I have taken great pains to procure and furnish them with all the documents which can in any degree ilustrate the extent and nature of your claims, and there is nothing deficient except the Treaty signed by your Chiefs in Raleigh in the year 1802, which the Chiefs will be able to procure at Washington as they return home.

It may be expected that I should state to you my opinion relative to the Success of an application to the Legislature. With that view I will take the liberty of Stating that, as the Legislature, or the State of No. Carolina had no interest in nor derived any benefit from the Treaty of 1802 but acted merely as Arbitrators between the Tuskerora Nation, and the citizens of this State claiming the lands under old Patents which they were assured by the Act of 1748 should take effect so soon as the Nation should remove off the sd. Lands, or become extinct; which event was obviously likely to happen in a short time by the death of the small portion of the Nation then remaining on the lands; it was with great difficulty the Legislature was prevailed on to agree to the compromise solicited in the memorial of the Chiefs to the Legislature and which form'd the basis of the Treaty of 1802 (to wit) the rendring certain their then precarious title untill 1916, to sell their undemised lands and extend their short leases for a term which should expire at that time; also to commute their rents which would become due yearly during the term of the Several Leases for a sum to be paid by short instalments; and this the Legislature would not have done unless the chiefs had agreed to relinquish all claim to the Lands after that time, it is at least problamatical whether they will again interfere. Your title at that time was very imperfectly understood by all parties for it was believed that the act of 1748 was the foundation of your title; but since that time the Treaty of 1717 has been found, which conveyed to the Nation an estate in fee simple, and I do not think the Legislature had the power to limit or qualify that estate to a base fee without your Consent. Notwithstanding the Act of 1748 I think you had an estate in fee simple in the lands untill you parted with it by the treaty of 1802; but since then you are only tenants for years.

Chapter One
Tuscarora Records

As connected with the foregoing Subject I will call your attention to the claim of David Stone Esqr. to a part of the undemised lands of the Nation. Mr. Stone has in his possession about one hundred & fifty acres which if sold would bring from $1500 to $2000; Your Chiefs being disposed to bring suit for it if they could ascertain that your title was good. I have collected all the papers necessary, made a plot of the land with such remarks as I deem'd material and have made a statement of the case, and given them to the Chiefs, that they may not only take the advice of their Nation but also such Counselors learned in the law as they may think proper.

With regard to the collection of the monies due you in this State, I have only to say that your Chiefs and myself have settled as will appear by my Acct. Signed and given to the Indians a Copy of which they have signed and given me leaving a ballance of $362.21 Cents still due you in my Acct. it will be seen that I have not charged myself with the Interest on the money which I held belonging to the Nation, because I was at all times ready to pay, and tho' I derived some advantage from the occasional use of the money yet it was not more

[Editors Note: The rest of this letter has not been found.]

****

Duke University
Perkins Library, Manuscript Room
William Slade Papers
1751-1929

Jeremiah Slade's Day Book

Rec'd of John Griffin for Indians	40.75
2nd Feby 1808	
Esther Gibson for the Indians	Dr.
To cash pd. to Mr. Stone	30.40
29th Novr. 1808	
The Chiefs of the Tuskerora Nation	Dr.
To Cash	250.00
To attention to their business over & above	

Chapter One
Tuscarora Records

commissions	458.85
To board for 3 persons 9 days at 30p	27.00
To three horses boy & chair	20.00
The Indians	Dr.
To cash pd John Cain to go to Raleigh	15.00
8th June 1818	
The Tuskerora Indians	Dr.
To Cash paid John Cain	5.00

Settled with John Cain for 7 months work

[Editor's Note: John Cain may have been a shoemaker.]

****

ACTS PASSED BY THE GENERAL ASSEMBLY
OF THE STATE OF NORTH CAROLINA AT ITS SESSION
COMMENCING ON THE 15TH OF NOVEMBER, 1824
RALEIGH: PRINTED BY J. GALES & SON - STATE PRINTERS.
1825

CHAPTER XIII.
1824. An Act concerning the Lands held under leases from the Tuscarora Tribe Indians. (Page 13).
Whereas it is represented to this General Assembly, in behalf of persons holding lands under leases for a long term of years from the Tuscarora tribe of Indians, that they are subject to great inconveniences from their estates being mere chattel interest: For remedy whereof,

Be it enacted by the General Assembly of The State Of North Carolina, and it is hereby enacted by the authority of the same, That the estates in land now held by certain individuals, under leases for a term of years from the Tuscarora tribe of Indians, made in pursuance of certain acts of the General Assembly of this State, shall be hereafter considered real estate; shall descend to, and be divided among the heirs of any intestate, subject to dower and tenancy by curtesy, and other incidents to real estate, and its liability to execution, and its conveyance and devise, shall be governed by the same rules as are now prescribed in the case of real estate held in fee simple: Provided, that nothing herein contained, shall be so

Chapter One
Tuscarora Records

construed as to give to the individuals holding the said terms for years, a right to enjoy the same for a longer period than is designated in the leases executed by the said Tuscarora Indians, in pursuance of acts of the General Assembly of this State, nor so as to give to said individuals any right which, by the constitution of this State, is exclusively confined to freeholders.

****

Journals of the Senate and House of Commons
of the General Assembly of the State of North Carolina
At its Session in 1824.
Raleigh: J. Gales & Son, 1824.

Page 40.
House Journal
Resolved, That a select committee be appointed to enquire into the expediency of making provision, by law, for the sale of the lands now held under lease in the County of Bertie, from the Tuscarora tribe of Indians; and that they report by bill or otherwise.
    Resolved, that Mr. Mhoon, Mr. Stanley, Mr. McFarland, Mr. Meredith and Mr. Iredell, form the Committee.

****

North Carolina State Archives
Governor's Letter Book, VOL. 27
James Iredell (1827-1828), Page 160-161

Washington Novr. 12th 1828

Sir
    This will be handed to your Excellency by Cusack & Long Board, two principal Tuscarora Chiefs who with a Grand son of the former, are on their way to North Carolina for the purpose of adjusting some claim, which that Nation supposes itself to have on lands within your State, from whence they formerly emigrated.
    The Tuscaroras now inhabit a village in the State of New York but a few miles distant from my late residence. I have long been acquainted with these two Chiefs & take pleasure in recommending them as worthy &

Chapter One
Tuscarora Records

Correct men; and without pretending to know any thing of the Merits of this claim. I feel confident they will receive from your Excellency & the other constituted Authorities of North Carolina, that consideration which is due to a people, who have no other means of enforcing their rights, than the moral obligation, which such rights, when established, impose.

      I have the honor to be
      Your Mo. Ob. Servt.
      P.B. Porter

His Excellency
Govr. Iredell

PAGE 161

      Ex. Dept. N.C.
      Raleigh 26th Novr. 1828

To the Hon:
  the General Assembly
    Gentlemen

  I transmit to you a memorial from the Chiefs of the Tuscarora nation, which is addressed to you & which has been placed in my hands by Carseck & Longboard two of the Chiefs now in this City, together with a letter of introduction, which they have brought from the Honorable P.B. Porter Secretary of War.

      I have the honor to be
      With the highest Consideration
      Your obed. Servt.

      Ja. Iredell

****

PRINTE
ACTS PASSED BY THE GENERAL ASSEMBLY
OF THE STATE OF NORTH CAROLINA AT THE SESSION OF **1828**
-1829

Chapter One
Tuscarora Records

RALEIGH: PRINTED BY LAWRENCE & LEMAY RS TO THE STATE. 1829

CHAPTER XIX.
1828-1829. An act concerning the lands formerly occupied by the Tuskarora tribe of Indians, lying in Bertie county, on the north side of Roanoke river. (Pages 11-13).

Whereas the Tuskarora Indians have for more than a century been the firm and undeviating friends of the white people of this country, insomuch that the State of North Carolina is disposed not only to render to them full and complete justice, but also to exercise towards them that spirit of generosity which their conduct has merited: Therefore,

Be it enacted by the General Assembly of the State of North Carolina, and it is hereby enacted by the authority of the same, That William R. Smith, of Halifax; Simmons J. Baker, of Martin; and William Brittain, of Bertie,be, and they are hereby appointed commissioners for the purpose of advertising and selling, in manner hereinafter directed, the above named tract of land, lying in Bertie county, butted and bounded as follows, to wit: Beginning at the mouth of Quoitsney Swamp; running up the swamp 480 poles to a scrubby oak, near the head of said swamp by a great spring; thence north 10 degrees east 850 poles, to a persimmon tree, on Raquis Swamp; thence along the swamp and pocosin, main course north 57 degrees west 2640 poles, to a hickory on the east side of Falling Run or Deep Creek, and down the various courses of said run to Roanoke River; then down the river to the first station.

II. And be it further enacted, That the title so to be sold by said commissioners shall be understood to extend only to the reversion of the State in said lands after the expiration of the leases from the Indians under which they are now held; and that immediately after the ratification of this act, and notice thereof to the commissioners, it shall be their duty to proceed forthwith to advertise in the newspaper most convenient to the premises, and also at five of the most public places in the counties of Bertie, Halifax and Martin, including the court houses in said court houses in said counties, that a sale of land, according to the provisions of this act, will take place on Tuesday of the ensuing March term of the Superior Court of Bertie county, that is, on the 17th day of March next; and it shall be the duty of the said commissioners to attend at the aforesaid time and place, and offer, in the court house yard, at public sale, to the highest bidder, the said lands according to advertisement, subject however to the leases as aforesaid; and the commissioners shall have power to continue or

Chapter One
Tuscarora Records

postpone the sale from day to day until the end of that week; and should they, by unavoidable accident or otherwise, be prevented from selling all or any part of said lands during the said week, it shall be their duty to advertise in like manner for two months next preceding the following September term of Bertie Court and to sell at said term as is heretofore directed, at March term; and said commissioners shall be empowered to put up said lands in such parcels as they may deem most advantageous for selling; and that they shall give the purchasers a credit of twelve months on one half of the purchase money, and a credit of twenty-four months on the other half: Provided always that the purchaser shall deliver to the commissioners bonds with good and sufficient security for the same, payable to the Governor of the State.

    III. And be it further enacted, That should the commissioners upon offering said lands as aforesaid, perceive that they were likely to be sacrificed, or to sell for an amount greatly below the real value, it shall be their duty forthwith to discontinue the sale; and that it shall be the duty of the commissioners, after making sale, or if no sale be made, immediately after September next, to make report to the Public Treasurer of the State of all such proceedings as they may have had under this act, and also to hand over to him all such bonds as they may have taken from purchasers; and it shall be the duty of the Secretary of State, upon certificate from the Treasurer of payment of the purchase money and a certificate from the commissioners of the boundaries of the land so purchased, to grant a title of release from the State of North Carolina to such persons as may be reported as purchasers by said commissioners under this act of Assembly.

    IV. And be it further enacted, That it shall be the duty of the Public Treasurer to collect the money on said bonds when they shall become due, and to hold the same subject to the order of the Tuskarora tribe of Indians; and whenever such order shall be presented properly and duly authenticated, by the said tribe or nation of Indians, it shall be his duty to pay the same over accordingly: Provided always, that upon paying over such monies, the Public Treasurer shall take from the Indians, or their properly authorised agent or agents, a full and complete release of all such claim or pretence of title, as they now make, or ever may have to the aforesaid tract of land.

    V. And be it further enacted, That the commissioners shall be allowed each the sum of three dollars for every day they shall necessarily be employed in examining said lands, or in attending to the sale of the same, to be paid out of the funds arising from the sales.

Chapter One
Tuscarora Records

VI. Be it further enacted, That if it should appear at any time hereafter that the said Indians have parted with their claims, or contracted for the same, so that in fact the benefit of the sale would go to some stranger, then the benefit of the sale shall, agreeable to the provisions of this act, enure to the State.

****

ACTS PASSED BY THE GENERAL ASSEMBLY OF THE STATE OF NORTH CAROLINA AT THE SESSION OF 1829-1830
RALEIGH: PRINTED BY LAWRENCE & LEMAY
PRINTERS TO THE STATE. 1830

CHAPTER XI.
1829-1830. An act directing the removal of certain papers from the office of the Treasurer to that of the Secretary of State. (Pages 16-17).
Be it enacted by the General Assembly of the State of North Carolina, and it is hereby enacted by the authority of the same, That the descriptive list accompanying the report made to the Public Treasurer by the commissioners under the act of one thousand eight hundred and twenty-eight, entitled an act concerning the lands formerly occupied by the Tuscarora tribe of Indians, lying in Bertie County, on the north side of Roanoke river, authorising them to sell the reversion of certain lands therein named, containing the boundaries of the several tracts of land by them sold, be, and the said descriptive list is hereby directed to be transferred by the Treasurer from his office to that of the Secretary of State; and that the Secretary of State, upon the payment of the purchase money, grant titles according to the boundaries therein contained, and agreeably to the provisions of the before recited act.

CHAPTER XV.
1829-1830. An act concerning the bonds in the office of the Public Treasurer for the purchase of the Cherokee and Tuscarora lands. (Pages 20-21).
Whereas, according to the provisions of the several acts of Assembly prescribing the mode of surveying and selling the lands lately acquired from the Cherokee Indians, the Comptroller is directed to raise an account against the several obligors for their respective purchases; and the bonds given by them were deposited with the Treasurer by the

Chapter One
Tuscarora Records

commissioners who took the same, without any statement or receipt therefor being filed with the Comptroller, so as to enable him to perform his duty: and whereas the check intended to be preserved upon the Treasurer in the discharge of his duty in this respect, as required by the several laws passed for that purpose, does not exist: Therefor,

Be it enacted by the General Assembly of the State of North Carolina, and it is hereby enacted by the authority of the same, That it shall be the duty of the Public Treasurer to prepare a full and particular statement of the bonds in his office given for the purchase of the lands lately acquired by treaty from the Cherokee Indians, as they were at the time he received the same from the committee of investigation of the Treasury Department in one thousand eight hundred and twenty-seven, which shall be certified by him to be and contain a true and correct statement thereof as aforesaid; and it shall be his duty to deliver the same to the Comptroller, to be by him filed in his office, who shall raise an account against the Public Treasurer for the same, and debit his bond account with the interest that has or may hereafter accrue on said bonds, as the same shall have been or may hereafter be paid, and credit his said account with such sums of principal or interest as may have been by the Public Treasurer heretofore paid according to receipts on file in the Comptroller's office, and for all sums that may hereafter be paid agreeably to law, for and on account of said bonds.

II. And be it further enacted, That it shall be the duty of the Comptroller to make out and complete the books in his office, on which the accounts of the obligors in the bonds for the purchase of the lands acquired as aforesaid are opened and kept up to the end of each fiscal year, in the same manner as the same are now kept in the office of the Public Treasurer, so as to exhibit the different amounts of principal and of interest to the time of the payments heretofore made, or which may hereafter be made, and the true and actual amount of each debt, and the balance due the State on account thereof.

III. And be it further enacted, That a statement and certificate of the bonds in the office of the Public Treasurer for the purchase of the Tuscarora lands, shall be made out by him and filed with the Comptroller; and that the same accounts shall be raised and general course pursued in regard to them as is required in the first and second section of this bill as to those therein referred to.

Chapter One
Tuscarora Records

Statement of cash received in the Treasury on bonds given for sales of Tuskarora Indian lands from the first of Nov. 1829 to the first of Nov. 1830.

William S. Mhoon
Mary Mhoon
James G. Mhoon
Jesse A. Powell
William M. Clark
William Williams
Thomas Ruffin
Alfred M. Slade
John Young
Francis K. Pugh
John S. Smallwood
Noah B. Hinton
Joseph J. Williams
Lewis A. Williams
Thomas I. Pugh
William Pugh
J.B. Outlaw
R.H. Cowan and
David Stone
Robert A. Jones
Robert F. Purrington

****

North Carolina State Archives
Private Manuscript Collection
David Stone Papers, 1795-1865
Call Number: P.C.82.1

                    Date of Lease
10 Feby 1777 for 99 years expires 10 Feby 1876
from 10 Feby 1830 has 46 years to [?]
A principal of 300 Dollars at compound Interest for 45 years would amount to - say that in doubles every 12 years which is will rather more than do-
300   250

Chapter One
Tuscarora Records

600	in 12 years	500	12 years
1200	in 24	1000	24
2400	in 36	2000	36
144		120	
2544	37	2120	37
152.64		127.20	
2696.64	38	2247.20	38
161.79.8		134.83.2	
2858.43.8	39	2382.03.2	39
171.50.5		142.92.1	
3029.94.3	40	2524.95.3	40
181.79.6		151.49.7	
3211.73.9	41	2676.45	41
192.70.3		160.58.7	
3404.44.2	42	2837.03.7	42
204.26.6		170.22.1	
3608.70.8	43	3007.25.8	43
216.52.2		180.42.5	
3825.23.0	44	3187.68.3	44
229.51.3		181.26.0	
4054.74.3	45	3368.94.3	45

The present value of an annuity for a limited period is a sum which if put at interest will at the and of that period give an amount equall to the sum of all the payments of the annuities and interest

****

North Carolina State Archives
Private Manuscript Collection
David Stone Papers, 1795-1865
Call Number: P.C.82.1

Rents due for balance of term on [?] Lands
paid A M Slade
9 Novr 1830
150 for Cowan
150 Outlaw pd. for use
300

1.80 - 1	13 - 23.40	25 - 45.00	37 - 66.60

Chapter One
Tuscarora Records

3.60 - 2	14 - 25.20	26 - 46.80	38 - 68.40
5.40 - 3	15 - 27.00	27 - 48.60	39 - 70.20
7.20 - 4	16 - 28.80	28 - 50.40	40 - 72.00
9.00 - 5	17 - 30.60	29 - 52.20	41 - 73.80
10.80- 6	18 - 32.40	30 - 54.00	42 - 75.60
12.60- 7	19 - 34.20	31 - 55.80	43 - 77.40
14.40- 8	20 - 36.00	32 - 57.60	44 - 79.20
16.20- 9	21 - 37.80	33 - 59.40	45 - 81.00
18.00- 10	22 - 39.60	34 - 61.20	664.20
19.80- 11	23 - 41.40	35 - 63.00	
21.60- 12	24 - 43.20	36 - 64.80	
140.40	399.60	658.80	

664.20
399.60
658.80
140.40
1863.00   Interest
1380.00   Principal
3243.00

Gave 300 for the Term balance if for 46 years Release from Alfred M. Slade Agent of Tuscarora Indians - Bertie Co Ct & fees for registration paid 60 Cts to E.A. Rhodes Clk - paid for Cowan by me 150 Dollars to be Credited on J. N. Outlaws note held by me - for money due me on Settlement

****

**ACTS PASSED BY THE GENERAL ASSEMBLY
OF THE STATE OF NORTH CAROLINA
AT THE SESSION OF 1831-1832
RALEIGH: PRINTED BY LAWRENCE & LEMAY
PRINTERS TO THE STATE. 1832**

Statement of cash received in the Treasury on bonds given for sales of Tuskarora Indian lands.
From whom received Bonds paid Principal Interest Total

Joseph J. Williams

Chapter One
Tuscarora Records

Lewis A. Williams
Robert A. Jones
Willie Bridger
John T. Johnston
W.M. Clark
John S. Smallwood
William Blanchard
Joseph B. Outlaw
Francis E. Ward
Noah B. Hinton
Robert F. Purrington
William Williams,
John B. Griffin
John Critchlow
Lewis Bond

I. WETMORE, Cl'k T. D.

****

**North Carolina State Archives
Search Room
NORTH CAROLINA REPORTS
*VOLUME 51, PAGES 210-216***

JOSEPH H. BURNETT VS. JOHN THOMPSON

A call from the mouth of the swamp, down a swash, to the mouth of another swamp, was held to mean a straight line from one point to the other through the swash.

Where A has an estate for life in possession, in a term for 99 years, B has an estate in remainder for the residue of the term after the death of A, and A has the reversion after the expiration of the term, in an action of tresspass, Q.C.F. against a stranger, for entering and cutting down trees and taking them off, it was held that, by means of the per quod, A might recover the entire value of the timber, and that B was not entitled to any part of such value, though he also could bring an action on the case and recover damages for the same act, as lessening the value of his expectancy.

The act of 1824, by which the long terms for years, created by the Tuscarora Indians, are, for certain purposes, made real estate, has no effect upon the reversions expectant on those terms.

Chapter One
Tuscarora Records

Action of trespass, Q.C.F., tried before Shepherd, J., at the last Fall Term of Washington Superior Court.

The action was brought cutting cypress trees and making them into shingles. The plaintiff claimed the premises south of the line between Town Swamp, and Coniot Swamp, marked in the diagram as "Swash," and the defendant owns the lands to the north of it marked "Caesar's Island."

The first question raised by the exceptions of the defendant was as to the boundary designated in his deed; the calls important to be noticed, are as follows: "thence to the run of Town Swamp, (G,) thence down the Town Swamp to the Swash, A, thence down the Swash to Coniot Swamp, to the first station." The question between the parties was, whether the line should be run straight from the mouth of Town Swamp, (A,) to the Coniot Swamp, or whether it should follow the course of some running water, called "Broad Water," through the Swash, which would lead to Coniot Creek, which creek the defendant insisted was reached by Coniot Swamp at C. The plaintiff insisted that the mouth of Coniot Swamp was at B. It was conceded that if the mouth of Coniot Swamp was at B, and a straight line was run from A to B, the defendant would be a trespasser.

The Court charged the jury, "that they must determine where Coniot Swamp was, at the date of the call; that having determined this, "the course of running from Town Swamp would be to start from the Swash and then proceed in a straight line through to Coniot Swamp." The defendant excepted to this instruction.

All the lands on both sides were claimed under leases from the Tuscarora Indians. The plaintiff had a life estate in a lease of the lands which he claimed (the locus in quo being a part) for 99 years, which would expire in the year 1916, and a reversion after the expiration of the term. The residue of this lease between the plaintiff's death, and the end of the term, belonged partly to the children of one Martin Ballard, and partly to one Barrington.

The Court assumed that the Act of Assembly of 1824, converting the estates or interests in the long leases made by the Tuscarora Indians into real estate, did not affect the reversion, and instructed the jury that if the plaintiff was entitled to recover at all, he was entitled to the full value of the timber cut and sawed up and made into shingles. Defendant's counsel again excepted. Verdict and judgment for the plaintiff. Appeal by the defendant.

Smith and Wm. A. Moore, for the plaintiff.
Winston, Jr., Hines and H.A. Gilliam, for the defendant.

Chapter One
Tuscarora Records

Pearson, C.J. The special instructions upon the question of boundary, and also in reference to the damages asked for by the defendant, are not set out, and, consequently, this Court is unable to say there was error in refusing to give them.

The general instruction "to run a straight line from Town Swamp, through the swash to Coniot Swamp," is, of course, to be understood to mean the shortest line through the Swash that would strike the Swamp; and although this leaves the question of boundary still open, (inasmuch as the fact, whether Coniot Swamp extended to Coniot Creek, or stopped some distance before reaching it, at the point indicated on the map, was not put to the jury in such a manner as to make it appear, from the verdict, how it was found,) still the statement of the case does not show any error of which the defendant has a right to complain.

Assuming that the plaintiff's title covered the locus in quo, his Honor held he was entitled to recover the full value of the trees cut and taken off by the defendant.

The act of 1824, by which the long terms for years created by the Tuscarora Indians, are, for certain purposes, made real estate, is confined, in its operation, to "the terms" and to the persons by whom they are held; and has no operation or effect upon the reversions which are expectant upon the term: so the matter may be simplified, and the question is this: A has an estate pur autre vie in possession, in a term for 99 years, B has an estate in remainder for the residue of the term, after the death of the cestui que vie: and A has an estate in reversion, after the expiration of the term, (the intermediate estate of B preventing a merger,) a stranger enters and cuts down cypress trees, makes them into shingles, and takes them off. Is A, in an action of trespass quare [?], entitled to recover the full value of the trees?

If there be tenant for years or for life, and a stranger cuts down a tree, the particular tenant may bring trespass, and recover damages for breaking his close, treading down his grass, and the like. but the remainderman, or reversioner in fee, is entitled to the tree, and if it be converted, may bring trover and recover its value. The reason is, the tree constituted a part of the land, and its severance was waste, which is an injury to the inheritance, consequently the party in whom is vested the first estate of inheritance, whether in fee simple or fee tail, (for it may last always,) is entitled to the tree, as well after it is severed, as before; his right of property not being lost by the wrongful acts of severance by which it is converted into a personal chattel.

Chapter One
Tuscarora Records

Such remainderman or reversioner has his election either to bring trover for the value of the tree after it is cut, or an action on the case in the nature of waste, in which, besides the value of the tree considered as timber, he may recover damages for any injury to the inheritance which is consequent upon the destruction of the tree. Williams v. Lanier, Busbee 30. In the instance of a cypress tree, the damages over and above the value of the timber of the tree cut in a swash, may be only nominal. But take an ornamental shade tree for the instance, and the difference between its value as timber, and the additional injury to the inheritance by its destruction is great; indeed, it is so much as to call into application the preventive jurisdiction of equity against irreparable damage. If there be an intermediate estate in remainder for life or years, the owner thereof may also bring an action on the case for the injury done to his estate, for, although it may never be enjoyed in possession, still its value may be affected by a destruction of something which constitutes a part of the land, and if disposed to sell, he would not be able to get as good a price for it. The remedy which is given to an intermediate tenant in remainder for life or years, by the introduction of the action on the case in the nature of waste, is one of its advantages over "the action of waste which it has superseded," 2 Sanders Uses, 252 at note 7. For the sake of illustration, suppose, in such a case, a stranger enters and pulls down a house on the land, and carries away the materials; the tenant for life or years in possession may bring trespass, and recover damages for breaking his close, and for the injury done by depriving him of the use of the house during the continuation of his estate; the intermediate remainderman may bring case and recover damages for the depreciation in the value of his estate, caused by the destruction of the house, whereby his estate would sell for less, and the use of the land, should it come into possession, would be of less value for the want of the house; and the remainderman in fee may bring case and recover the value of the materials of the house, and also additional damages for the injury to the inheritance caused by its destruction, or he might bring trover and recover the value of the materials.

Assuming these positions of law, Mr. Winston argued that the plaintiff, although he was the owner of the first estate, and also of the remainder in fee, was not entitled to recover the entire damage caused by the wrongful act of the defendant, inasmuch as the intermediate remainderman was entitled to recover some part of it, however small it might be. The fallacy of the argument, as applied to our case, lies in not distinguishing between the entire damage resulting from the act, and the full value of the trees, considered merely as timber. The latter is not at all

Chapter One
Tuscarora Records

affected by the fact of their being an intermediate estate; for if the remainderman in fee is content to take the value of the trees as timber, whether they be cypress or ornamental shade trees, or the mere value of the materials of the house, he is certainly entitled to the full value thereof, and could recover it in trover.

Another question is presented by the case, and we have considered of it, although it was not made on the argument. The plaintiff, as owner of the first estate, may maintain trespass for breaking his close, and as owner of the fee, he may maintain case or trover for the value of the timber. Is it necessary for him to bring two actions, or can he recover the value of the timber under a per quod in the action of trespass? The law seeks to avoid a multiplicity of suits, and we are of opinion that he may recover all the damage in the one action, by means of a per quod; because it all results from one wrongful act, and the commission of the tort in fact constituted the main part of the res gestoe. the per quod was invented to save the necessity of two actions. In Scott v. Shepherd, 2 Blackstone's Rep. 897, it is said, "every action of trespass, with a per quod, includes an action on the case." In trespass, damages for all ulterior injuries beyond the immediate injury, may be recovered under a per quod, Chitty's Plead. 442, and the most usual action for seduction is trespass, Q.C.F., with a per quod; so damages for the loss of hogs that escaped because a fence was let down, may be recovered in trespass, Q.C.F.; Welch v. Piercy, 7 Ire. Rep., 365, see Sedgwick on damages, 135, where the cases are collected. So damages for the loss of an eye, resulting from a cold contracted by exposure caused by tearing off the roof of a house, may be recovered in trespass, Q.C.F.; Hatchell v. Kimbrough, 4 Jones' Rep. 164.

In this discussion, we have put cypress trees on the same footing with shade and fruit trees, and buildings, in respect to the relative rights of particular tenants and remainderman. It may be, there is a difference where the trees grow in a swash, which is fit for nothing but its timber, for in such case, unless the tenant is allowed to "work up" a reasonable number of trees, he can have no benefit of his estate. A tenant, by the courtesy or dower, is allowed to work mines that have been opened.

We will not enter upon this subject, as its consideration is not necessary for our decision, and it was not alluded to in the argument, and the facts are not stated in reference to it. It is suggested merely to prevent misapprehension and exclude a conclusion.

Per Curiam,   Judgment affirmed.
December Term 1858

Chapter One
Tuscarora Records

****

North Carolina State Archives
Secretary of State Papers
Call Number: S.S.1033
File Name: A Letter Concerning the Lands Formerly Held by the Tuscarora Indians in Bertie County

State of North Carolina
Department of state
Raleigh, april 5, 1911

Mr. Luther W. Jack,
Secretary People's Rights Society,
Lewiston, N.Y., R.F.D. 18.

Dear Sir: Your communication to the Governor has been referred to me, with the request that I give you information concerning the claim of the Tuscarora Indians to a reversionary interest in certain lands in Bertie County.

After the Tuscarora Indian War, about 1712-1715, most of that Nation moved to join the Iroquois in New York. A part of the Tuscaroras in this State were friendly to the whites and aided them in the war. The chief of this branch of the tribe was known as "King" Tom Blount, and in recognition of his services to the whites he was on the 5th day of June, 1717 (see Colonial Records of N.C., vol. 2, page 283), granted by the province of North Carolina certain lands on Morratock (later Roanoke) River in North Carolina.

In 1748 the General Assembly passed an act, chapter 3 (see State Records of N.C., vol. 23, page 209), entitled "An act for ascertaining the bounds of a certain tract of land formerly laid out by treaty to the use of the Tuscarora Indians, so long as they or any of them shall live upon the same; and to prevent any person or persons taking up lands or settling within the said bounds by pretense of any purchase or purchases made, or that shall be made from the said Indians." These lands were described as follows:

"Beginning at the mouth of Quitsnoy Swamp, running up the said Swamp Four Hundred and Thirty Poles to a Scrubby Oak, near the Head of the said Swamp, by a Great Spring; then North Ten Degrees East, Eight Hundred and Fifty Poles to a Persimmon Tree on the Raquis Swamp; then

Chapter One
Tuscarora Records

along the Swamp and Pocosin main Course, North Fifty seven Degrees West, Two Thousand Six Hundred and Forty Poles to a Hickory on the East Side of the Falling Run, or Deep Creek, and down the various Courses of the said Run to Morratock River; then down the River to the first Station."

This was "confirmed and assured" unto James Blount, "Chief of the Tuscarora Nation and the people under his charge, etc." Section three of this act provided that parties who had taken up grants in that area could enter and occupy and enjoy the same upon the said Indians deserting or leaving the said lands.

In 1766, chapter 29 (see State Records of N.C., vol. 25, page 507), the General Assembly passed "An act confirming a lease made by the Tuscarora Indians to Robert Jones, Jr., William Williams, and Thomas Pugh, Esquires." The lease to Jones, Williams and Pugh was for a large part of the Indian lands on Deep Creek, the consideration being fifteen hundred pounds proclamation money. It was signed by about forty of the chieftains and head men of the Nation on behalf of themselves and the rest of the Tuscarora Indians. The term of the lease was for one hundred and fifty years, and was to secure money "in order to defray the expense of removing themselves and their effects from this province to the settlements on the River Susquehanna." This act was also for the protection of the Indians in the enjoyment of the use and rights to their lands. Section six of this act provided that nothing contained therein should be so "construed as to invalidate the title or titles to any to any person or persons who have obtained a grant or grants for any tract or parcel of land within the limits within the boundaries of the the land of the said Tuscarora Indians before the 15th day of October, one thousand seven hundred and forty-eight."

In 1778 the General Assembly of North Carolina passed an act (see State Records of N.C., vol. 24, Acts of 1778, chapter 16, page 171), entitled "An act for quieting and securing the Tuscarora Indians and others claiming under the Tuscaroras in the possession of their lands." This act confirmed a lease made by the Tuscaroras to Robert Jones, Jr. (Father of Allen and Willie Jones), William Williams, and Thomas Pugh, Esquires, for one hundred and fifty years. It provided that Whitmell Tuffdick, Chief or head man of the Tuscarora Nation, and the Tuscarora Indians now living in Bertie County, should hold and occupy, possess and enjoy all the lands lying in Bertie County, which had heretofore been assigned to them. It forbade the leasing or purchasing of lands from Indians except by consent of the General Assembly. It confirmed the lands leased, demised, granted, or "farm let" to sundry persons between July 12, 1766, and December

Chapter One
Tuscarora Records

1777, except such as were obtained by fraud. It appointed William Williams, Thomas Pugh, Willie Jones, and Simon Turner, and Zedekiah Stone commissioners for the Indians, and empowered the said commissioners to hold courts, for the redress of the grievances of the Indians. It further enacted that to other persons prior to '77' "shall revert to and become the property of the State at the expiration of the terms of the several leases mentioned, if the said Nation be then extinct. And the lands now belonging to and possessed by the said Tuscaroras shall revert to and become the property of the State whenever the said Nation shall become extinct, or shall entirely abandon or remove themselves off the said lands and every part thereof."

In 1780 an act was passed amending the act of 1778 as to penalizing jurors and witnesses failing to respond when summoned by the commissioners mentioned in the act of 1778.

In 1798, chapter 17 (Martin's Laws, page 122). two other commissioners--William Williams of Martin and Samuel Johnston, Jr., of Bertie--were added to the number of commissioners named in the act of '78'.

On November 3, 1801 (Letter Book, page 95). H. Dearborn, Secretary of War, in a letter to Governor Benjamin Williams, informs him that a deputation from the Tuscarora Indians, accompanied by an interpreter, was on the way to Raleigh to wait on him with the object "to procure from the State of North Carolina for the sale and cession of the right which they suppose still to possess, a sum of money with which to purchase the lands in the vicinity of those in which they now reside." He further notified Governor Williams that the President of the United States had appointed Hon. William R. Davie commissioner for the Indians, and that the United States gave its consent and sanction to such bargain and agreement as the State and the Indians might make.

In November, 1801, Governor Williams (Letter Book, page 18) recommended to the General Assembly the appointment of a commission to treat with the Tuscarora Indians.

This visit of 1801 seems to have been unsuccessful, for on October 18, 1802 (Letter Book, page 195), another letter from the Secretary of War, Mr. Dearborn, to Governor Benjamin Williams, recites the fact that the chief of the Tuscaroras, with an interpreter, is on his way to Raleigh to "renew the negotiation." and that "the authority that he now brings from his Nation will be deemed sufficient for authorizing the sale." He further states that the Hon. W. R. Davie "is commissioned with full powers to attend the negotiation and give the necessary sanction and

Chapter One
Tuscarora Records

consent of the United States to such terms as the Legislature of the State or their agents and the Chief may agree on."

The General Assembly of 1802 (Martin's Laws, chapter 4, page 194) passed "An act for the relief of the Tuscarora Nation of Indians." This act authorized the chiefs to lease the lands and extend leases already made, which leases were to be confirmed by an act of the General Assembly in such manner that the whole of the leases on said land should terminate at the same period. (After the Jones-Williams-Pugh lease for 150 years, subsequent leases had been made for 99 year.) The act authorized the Governor to appoint commissioners for carrying the act into effect. The act further recites that "Whereas the Chiefs, Sacarusa and Longboard, and Samuel Smith, being duly and severally authorized and empowered by said Tuscarora Nation, have consented that the Indian claim to the use, possession, and occupancy of said lands shall cease and be extinguished when the said lease made in the year 1766 to Robert Jones and others shall expire: Be it further enacted, That from and after the 12th day of July which shall fall in the year 1916 the whole of the lands allotted to the said Tuscarora Indians by an act of the General Assembly passed at New Bern on the 15th day of October in the year of our Lord one thousand seven hundred and forty-eight, shall revert to and become the property of the State, and the Indian claim thereto shall from that time be held and deemed forever extinguished." Section six of this act relates to entries and rights of individuals. Under this act the Governor appointed commissioners to lease and sell these lands.

On the part of these commissioners. Jeremiah Slade and William Hawkins made a report to Governor James Turner dated June 20, 1803. This report can be found in the Governor's letter book for that year at page 80, and is too long to copy here. The commissioners acted in cooperation with Chiefs Sacarusa and Longboard. They sold the lands, or the undemised portions of them, which amounted to less than 4,000 acres, for $21,146.23.

Settlement for these lands was made with the Secretary of War.

A map of the Indian land, dated June 17, 1803, was made by these commissioners, showing an area of 41,113 acres, and showing the various leases, with lengths of term, and filed in this office, which can be exhibited to interested parties. The metes and bounds of the map are as follows:

"Beginning on Roneoke River at the Mouth of Quitsney Swamp, thence up the various courses of the said swamp to an oak near the head at the great spring, thence No. 10 E 904 poles to a posseman on Rockquis swamp, thence N. 57 W. 2888 poles to a Hickory at the head of Falling

Chapter One
Tuscarora Records

Run or Deep Creek., thence down the various courses of said Creek to Roneoke River, thence down the River to the first station, containing forty-one thousand one hundred and thirteen acres."

The report, map, and papers accompanying them are unique and interesting documents.

All the acts in reference to the Tuscarora Indian lands provided that the reversions after the expiration of the leases in 1916 should be vested in the State.

In 1816 the Supreme Court of North Carolina held, in the case of Sacarusa and Longboard against William King's heirs, that the grant made by Governor Eden in 1717 to the Tuscarora Tribe of Indians was absolute and unconditional, and that the Indians had a fee-simple right to the lands, and not an "Indian title." (See Supreme Court Reports of North Carolina, vol. 4, p. 316.)

In 1825 the General Assembly passed an act, chapter 13, page 13, entitled "An act concerning the lands held in leases from the Tuscarora Tribe of Indians." The preamble of the act stated that persons holding these leases were subject to great inconvenience from their estates "being mere chattel interest," and for the remedy thereof the General Assembly enacted a law declaring that the land should be considered as real estate in fee simple for the term of their leases, but "Provided, that nothing in this act shall be so construed as to give to the individuals holding the said terms of years a right to enjoy the same for a longer period than is designated in the leases executed by the Tuscarora Indians."

On November 12, 1828, P.B. Porter, Secretary of War, notified Governor James Iredell that Sacarusa and Longboard, two principal Tuscarora Chiefs, with the grandson of the former, were on their way to North Carolina "for the purpose of adjusting some claim which that Nation supposes itself to have on lands within your State, from which they formerly emigrated." He further says: "I feel confident they will receive from your Excellency and the other constituted authorities of North Carolina that consideration which is due to a people who have no other means of enforcing their rights than the moral obligations which such rights when established impose." (See Governor's Letter Book, 1828, page 160.)

On November 26, 1828, Governor Iredell transmitted to the General Assembly a memorial from the Chiefs of the Tuscarora Nation. This memorial was referred to a special committee of the House and Senate, and the report of that committee, signed by George E. Spruill, chairman, is to be found in the Journal of the General Assembly of North

Chapter One
Tuscarora Records

Carolina, beginning at page 275. Acting upon that memorial and report the General Assembly (see Laws of N. C., session 1828-'29, chapter 19 page 11) passes "An act concerning the lands formerly occupied by the Tuscarora Tribe of Indians lying in Bertie on the south side of Roanoke River." This act recited that "Whereas the Tuskarora Indians have for more than a century been the firm and undeviating friends of the white people of this country, insomuch that the State of North Carolina is disposed not only to render to them full and complete justice, but also to exercise towards them that spirit of generosity which their conduct has merited, therefore, etc." In this act William R. Smith of Halifax, Simmons J. Baker of Martin, and William Brittain of Bertie were appointed commissioners for the purpose of advertising and selling these lands. "The title so sold by the said commissioners shall be understood to extend only to the reversion of the State in said lands after the expiration of the leases of the Indians from which they are now held." The Public Treasurer was to collect the money due on the lands and to pay the money over to the tribe or nation of Indians, or other properly authorized agent or agents; upon which the Indians surrendered and made "a full and complete release of all such claim or pretense or title as they now make or ever may have to aforesaid tract of land." Under this act these lands were sold, and the Treasurer in 1832 paid to Bates Cook, he being appointed agent of the Tuscarora Indians, the sum of $3,220.71. The record of this voucher, No. 258, is to be seen in the Treasurer's office, book of 1832, page 377.

The Treasurer's reports show two other small items paid to the Tuscarora Indians about this time, the reason for which payments I have not looked into.

On the 19th day of November, 1831, William Chew, Nicholas Casie, George Warchief, Jonathan Printup, Mathew Jack, William Johnson, and Isaac Miller, Chiefs of the Tuscarora Nation of Indians, of the first part, in consideration of $3,250 lawful money of the United States to them in hand paid, executed to the State of North Carolina a deed by which they granted, bargained, sold, demised, released, aliened, and confirmed unto the people of the State of North Carolina, "in their actual possession now being and to their assigns forever, all their lands, tenements, and hereditaments situate, lying, and being in the County of Bertie in the said State of North Carolina, together with all and singular the appurtenances thereunto belonging or in any wise appertaining, and the reversion and reversions, remainder and remainders thereof, and the estate, right, title, interest, claim and demand whatsoever of the said parties of the first, either in law or equity, of, in, and to the above bargained premises,

Chapter One
Tuscarora Records

with the hereditaments and appurtenances." This deed was properly witnessed by the Indians in person coming before Robert Fleming, First Judge of the Niagara County Court of Common Pleas of New York. The signature of Judge Fleming was authenticated by Enos. T. Throop, Governor of the State of New York.

These are all the leases and papers that I find that I think will be of use to you in determining the status of your claim for the reversionary interest in the Tuscarora lands in Bertie County.

If you desire an investigation of this matter by an attorney representing the Indians, it seems to me that it would be wise for you to select some man of standing in this State who can go into the details of the matter very carefully for you. I shall be glad to assist him in finding all records connected with this transaction. I understand from Chief Mount Pleasant that an attorney at Washington City has been employed, which probably means useless expense to you all in the prosecution of an untenable claim.

Respectfully,   J. BRYAN GRIMES,
Secretary of State

Chapter Two
General Assembly Sessions

Chapter Two

General Assembly Sessions

North Carolina State Archives
General Assembly Sessions Records
November-December, 1790, Box #3
House Joint Resolutions

1790
Geo Ogg, Letter
To The Genl. Assembly

The Speaker of the General Assembly of the State of North Carolina.

Gentlemen,
    I beg leave to lay before you the papers on which the demand of the State of North Carolina is founded against Mr. Bryan Ward of the State of Georgia on account of my transactions with him on the part of the State,
    That Mr. Ward is yet a debtor to the State of North Carolina to a Considerable amount will Appear by the Bond, and Accounts herewith delivered you and it is owing to the heavy loss Sustained by the depreciation of paper money and the Sudden and unexpected fall in the

Chapter Two
General Assembly Sessions

price of Skins[?] that he is [Faded] His ability to pay is notwithstanding at this time Sufficient, for to my Knowledge he is possessed of a Valuable landed property [Faded] When he Contracted this debt his Credit was equal in goodness to any Other Man in the State in the same line and under all his Misfortunes he still Supports the Character of an honest Man, you will [Faded] Permit me to inform you that he is an aged Man.
I am with due Respect, Gentlemen, Your Hbl. Servant.
Geo. Ogg
Fayetteville [Faded] 1790

1790
Deposition of Geo. Ogg, Respecting Goods sold by Wm. Blount As Agent for No. Ca. &c.

Fayetteville 29th Novbr. 1790

George Ogg of full age first being Sworn on the holy Evangelist of Almighty God Deposeth that he was present at Tugalo River in the County of Franklin in the State of Georgia on the 16th day of Jany. 1786 with William Blount Esqr. then Agent for the State of North Carolina and a Certain Bryan Ward an Indian Trader and at the same time & place the Sd. William Blount Sold & Delivered Goods Wares & Merchandise to the Sd. Ward to the amount of Nine hundred & Seventy Nine pounds five Shillings & Seven pence Sterling Money for which the Sd. Ward then and there Entered into one Bond payable to Sd. Blount as Agent for the State for three hundred & twenty nine pounds fifteen Shillings & two pence Sterling payable on the first day of April 1786 & Which bond bears date on the 16th Jany 1786 and one Other bond of the same date for the Sum of Six hundred & Seventy None pounds fifteen Shillings & five pence like Sterling Money and payable on the first day of April 1787 as Expressed in the face of the bond but which as this Deponant Conceives to be a Mistake in the Writing of the Bond, as he this Deponant was present at the time that the Contract was made between the Sd. Blount & Ward & when the goods were Delivered & the Bonds before Mentioned were taken & I well remember that the agreement between the Sd. parties was that, that the first towit that for £329..15..2 was to have been paid on the first day of April then next ensuing & the Other one for £679..10..5 was to have been paid on the first of April 1787, to both of which before mentioned Bond he this Deponant was a Witness & did then believe the time of payment Mentioned in Sd.

Chapter Two
General Assembly Sessions

bonds was according to the agreement of Sd. Parties and never discovered the contrary till the last Evening when it was presented him by the Committee when to his great Astonishment he Discovered that the Large bond Mentioned to be paid on 1st April 1787 when the bonds bears date Jany. 1786, but this Deponant Deposeth that those two bonds above Mentioned & which were presented him by the Committee are the two Identical bonds taken by the Sd. Blount of the said Ward at the time and place above Mentioned and for and on Account of the Goods Wares &c so Sold by the Sd. Blount & Purchaded by the Sd. Ward and at no other time & for No Other use or purpose than what is above Mentioned, so far as this Deponant knows & Verily believes and further this Deponant Saith Not.
Geo. Ogg
Sworn to before me at Fayetteville this 29th day of Novbr. 1790
J. Williams Ss CC

****

North Carolina State Archives
General Assembly Sessions Records
December, 1791- January, 1792, Box #2
Senate Resolutions

Resolution 10th January, 1792, No. Carol. & Pay Rolls

North Carolina
    In Senate 10th January, 1792
Resolved that the Comptroller be and he is hereby directed to issue Certificates to the Officers and Privates employed in the expedition carried on under the Command of General Joseph Martin against the Indians in the Western Country agreeable to Act of Assembly passed at Fayetteville in the year 1789 and that the Comptroller shall specify in the face of the Certificate so to be issued that they shall only be receivable in payment of taxes and arrearages Due this State from the Inhabitants of the Western Territory ceded to the Congress of the United States and on no other account whatever are they to be received or this State liable for the payment of any of them.
Wm. Lenoir, S.S.
By order, S. Haywood, Clk
In the House of Commons 11th Jany 1792, read & Concurred with
S. Cabarrus, Spkr H.C., By Order, Jno. Hunt, CHC

Chapter Two
General Assembly Sessions

A True Copy, J. Hunt, Clk-CHC

****

North Carolina State Archives
General Assembly Sessions Records
December, 1791- January, 1792, Box #2
House Resolutions

Resolutions

North Carolina
     In the House of Commons 11th January 1792. Whereas in consequence of an Act intitled "An Act for opening the Land Office for the redemption of specie and other Certificates, & discharging the arrears due to the Army." Many of the Citizens of this State entered large bodies of Land in the Office of John Armstrong, late entry taker; and by an Act passed at Fayetteville in 1789 intitled "An Act for the purpose of ceding to the United States of America, certain Western Lands therein described," the Legislature of this State ceded all the right, Title and claim of North Carolina to the sovereignty and territory of the lands situated West of a line therein described to the United States of America, which cession included all the Lands entered in the said Office of John Armstrong, which cession included all the Lands entered in the Office of John Armstrong; And whereas also by certain treaties entered into between the United States and certain Indian tribes, a large quantity of the said land has been ceded and guarranteed to the said Indian tribes by the United States whereby the claimants are prevented from completing their grants and the holders of grants from occupying the said lands purchased under the laws of this State, notwithstanding the United States are bound by the express terms and conditions of the said Act of Cession to suffer such person to complete their claims in as full and ample manner as if the cession had never been made; And whereas sundry Persons whose claims and lands are thus situated have Petitioned this General Assembly for relief.
     Resolved that it be recommended to such Persons to make application to the Congress of the United States for relief respecting the premises, and that the Senators and representatives of this State in the Congress of the United States be and they are hereby instructed to require of the Congress of the United States full and perfect compliance with the conditions of the said Act of Cession, and that they use their utmost

Chapter Two
General Assembly Sessions

endeavours to procure, compleat Justice to the claimants of Western Lands under entries made in the Office of John Armstrong, by virtue of the Act entitled "An Act for opening the Land Office for the redemption of specie and other Certificates, & discharging the arrears due to the Army," and the Clerk of this House is hereby required to forward to the Senators and representatives a Copy of the Petition of the claimants of Western Lands preferred to the present General Assembly.
S. Cabarrus, Spk H.C., By Order J. Hunt, CHC
In Senate 20th Jany 1792, read & Concurred with, Wm. Lenoir, S.S.

****

North Carolina State Archives
General Assembly Sessions Records
November, 1792-January, 1793, Box #1
House Bills

Petition of the District of Capt. Jas Wilson

To the Honble the Genll Assembly of the State of North Carolina at Newbern Assembled
The Petition of the Citizens Inhabitants of the Lower and Eastern End of the County of Rutherford Most Humbly, Sheweth, that the Court House of said County is at a distance to Inconvenient for the Attendance of your Petitioners on Every Public Session, it being from thirty five to fifteen miles from the Majority of us your Petitioners and the Water sometimes unpassable -- And whereas the Right of Election is the undoubted Previledge of Every Citizen and Where of Right he ought to attend give his Vote and discharge the duties he owes to himself and his Country, -- And Among Your Petitioners there is a Number whose Circumstances and Infirmities makes it nearly Impossible to attend at the Place Appointed by law, on days of Election.
We therefore pray as the Substance of this our Pettition that a Separate Place of Election be Allowed, Your Pettioners in the Lower & Eastern End of said County as it will promote the Interest, Ease & Convenience & be of Public utility to us your Pettioners - And your Pettioners as in duty bound shall Forever Pray.
October 1792

Chapter Two
General Assembly Sessions

James Wilson, Henrey Willis, Jos Chitwood, Henry Moss, Joseph Scott, Benjamin Bracket, Edward Francis, Frederic Cogdell, Christopher Wallerd, Senr., Christopher Wallerd, Peter Wake[?], William White, Daniel Mooney, Jesse McGlamery, Phillip More[?], Abraham McCarley, Benj. Beaver, Ezekiel Dowens, James Collis, Wm. Wells, Ezekiel Fortner, William Rogers, Robert Crauder, Joseph Wells, John Collis, Daniel Wortman, Jeremiah White, Thomas Garner, Thomas White, Joseph Carpenter, William York, John Wilkison, Benjamin Wilkison, Aarron Thomas, Benjamin Willis, Edward Upton, Benjamin Bracket, James Chapman, James White, Thomas Fortner, Peter Silar, David Roper, Samuel Carpenter, William Garner, James Garner, Charles Roper, John Johnson, John Miller, Aguston White, David Johnston, Stephan White, William Wellman, John White, Peter White, Thomas Upton, Edward Upton Junr., Howel Mays, William Killian, John Parker, Joshua Hucaby, John Hanes, Isaac White, Robert Cook, Tom Twig[?], Robert Oarr, Jo Brown, David Cloin, William Queen, Peter Woodward, Senr., Wm Willis, William Willis, Junr., David Roper, John Heldebrand, Hezekiah Davis, Samuell Young, David Harris, Jacob Lanerd, Andrew Mitchel, Philip Crowder, David Nowlen, Wm. Cesterson, Charles McDaniel, Daniel Johnson, Robert Chapman, Nathan Chapman, Josuway Chapman, William H. Currey, Thos. Faiman[?], Thomas Boyd, Robert Boyd, Thomas Willis, Jonas Bedford, Samuel Green, Jas. Pally, John Boyd, Joseph Willis, Jacob Dye, Henry Willis[?], Jacob Brillhart, John Anderson, Senr., John McEntire, Alexander McEntire, Elijah Hardin, Charles Durrum, Travis Hambrick, Siles Randall, John Harris, James Hardin, Edmon Hardin, John Person, Joseph Bradly, Benjamin Weaver, John Hambrick, Enoch Hambrick, William Putmon, Jacob Vinsant, Abraham Kuykindall, Samuel McMurray, Henry Hambrick, Jeremiah Hambrick, Joseph Lusk, William Lusk, John Thompson, William Elmore, William Tidley, Nathan Hamrick, Edward Constant, Frances Neals, John Wilson, Senr., John Wilson, Junr., Jeames Hamrick, Senr., Jeames Hamrick, Junr., John For[?], James Kuykendall, Dannel Camp, Charles Stier, Frances More, Junr., George More, Micajah Cornwell, Edward Cornwell, Jeremiah [?], Edmond Smith, William Smith, Jacob Smith, Abednigo Addams, Senr., Abednigo Addams, Junr., Frances Addams, William Addams, Samuel Farmer, John Farmer, John Sequir, John McEntire, Senr., John Collins, Jeames Bridges, John Bridges, Senr., John Bridges, Junr., Jeames Bridges, Senr., Edward Camp, Price Hamrick, Benjamin Putmon, Willis Putmon, Elias Putmon, Jonathan Fouch, William Mode, James Mode, William McEntire, David Hardin, Senr., Andrew Daughturdy, Henry Kurlock, James McEntire, John Parker,

Chapter Two
General Assembly Sessions

John Roberts, James Blackburn, Samuel Blackburn, Patrick Downey, Isaac Collins, Jese Kuykendall, Ellthon Davis, William Tate, William Hardin, Benjamin Hardin, Wilson Putmon, John Maroon, Peter Maroon, Jacob Maroon, William Constant, Jonathan Hardin, Junr., Jonathan Hardin, Senr., George Magness, Zacriah Smith, John Mode, Abner Camp, Samuel Hamrick, David Elmore, Frances Batey, Robert Magness, Achillis Durrum, William Bridges, Morris Roberts, Joseph Lusk, John Lusk, Edward Tippey **[Rippey]**, Jesse Tippey, Jeames Linsey, Jos Camp, Henrey Flannerie, William Camp, Abitha Camp, John Lattimore, Clay'n Condecy, John Stockton, John Green, James Buchanan, John Cornwell, Thos Stockton, Davis Stockton, Lemuel Moore **[Moose]**, **[Faded]**, Isaac Norman, David Gage, Thos. Hawkins, Samuel Gage, David Mordon, Absalom Greagory, Samuel Turner, Samel Barlet, Matthias Eg[?], Reuben Blanton, Peter X Willis, Edward X Ayers[?], Jessey Gibs, Henry X Lander, Henrey X Gren, Spencer X Wilson, Samuel X Turner, William X Salleng, Joseph X Collins, John X Southerling, John X Hill, William X Hill, Benjamin X Magness, Jonathan Johnson, Jesse X Clark, Christopher X Landers, William Humphries, James Gage, Burnwell Blanton, Isaac X Faber, Daniel X Shipman, William X Humphries, James Rawlins, Isaac X Burges, Isaac X Lee, Stephen X Philips, William Holland, John Haws, Thomas X Franklin, Delaney X Boling, Richard X McGinnis, Joseph X Smart, William X Ross, John X Wenbrown, John X Johnson, James Blan[?], Hampton Gen[?], Samuel X Bridges, Robert X Sweden, Aaron X Bridges, Charles X Darbey, William X Rooker, Robert X McMenn, John X Curkindall, Charles X Wilkins, Thomas Brigis, John Jones, Benjamin Williams, Jonas Williams, William Williams, Nathen Rendall, Daniel Riggs, Daniel Shipman, Shadrach X Green, Edward X Johnson, Jacob X Fleming, Alexander X Ross, Jacob X Gage, Robert X Lee, George X Lalles[?], Henerey X Franklin, Marten X Armstrong, Jeams X Blackburn, Moses X Saterfield, Thomas X Hockens, Daniel X Web, Thomas McSwane, John X Walker, William X Johnson, Thomas X Rowlins, Daniel Shipman

****

North Carolina State Archives
General Assembly Sessions Records
November, 1792-January, 1793, Box #2

Dec.-13, 1792

Chapter Two
General Assembly Sessions

To the Honourable the General Assembly
Gentlemen,
    I send you herewith a letter received from the Honble Mr. Johnston one of the Senators of this State in Congress: the observation he has been pleased to make on the Act of Assembly to prevent the stealing of Slaves calls for your particular attendance in having said Act revised and amended so as to secure our slaves from being carried off to those states where slavery is abolished.
    You have also a letter from the Honble Mr. Hawkins the other senator in Congress relative to the agency of our public accounts & together with a Joint communication from those Gentleman
                      Alex. Martin

Nov.-21, 1792

To The Honourable The General Assembly
Gentlemen,
    I do myself the Honour to lay before you for your Information, a letter from the President of the United States, enclosing his Proclamation issued in Consequence of some refractory Proceedings taken Place in particular parts of some of the States, tending to obstruct the Operation of the Laws of the United States, for raising a Revenue upon spirits distilled within the same. - As I have not heard of such, or any proceedings in this State, that tend to contravene the Laws of the Union in any Respect; I think the President may be respectfully answered, that due attention has been paid to his Proclamation by the same being published through the State by our Printer and others, and I am happy to inform him that no person or persons within the Description it contains are existing in this State to my Knowledge or Belief

    I also lay before you a letter from Governor Blount containing interesting Information of the hostile intentions of the Creek, and part of the Cherokee Indians, against the Inhabitants of the Western Territory with whom Our People on the Frontier of this State must be inevitably involved
Novr. 21st 1792   Alex: Martin
Enclosures: 1792. Sept. 15. By George Washington, President etc., a Proclamation

1792. Sept. 29. Washington to

Chapter Two
General Assembly Sessions

Martin. (See Executive Papers)

****

North Carolina State Archives
General Assembly Sessions Records
November, 1792-January, 1793, Box #2
Governors Messages

To the Honourable The General Assembly
Gentlemen,

  I do myself the Honour to lay before you for your Information, a letter from the President of the United States, enclosing his Proclamation issued in Consequence of some refractory Proceedings taken Place in particular parts of some of the States, tending to obstruct the Operation of the Laws of the United States, for raising a Revenue upon Spirits distilled within the same. As I have not heard of such, or any proceedings in this State, that tend to contravene the Law of the Union in any Respect; I think the President may be respectfully answered, that due Attention has been paid to his Proclamation by the same being published through the State by our Printers and others, and I am happy to inform him that no person or persons within the Description it contains are existing in this State to my knowledge or Belief.
  I also lay before you a Letter from Governor Blount containing interesting Information of the hostile Intentions of the Creek, and part of the Cherokee Indians, against the Inhabitants of the Western Territory with whom Our People on the Frontiers of this State may be initially involved.
Alex: Martin, Novr. 21st 1792

To the Honourable the General Assembly

Gentlemen,
  I have to inform you that Francis Child Esquire late Comptroller of the public Accounts of this State died in August last; and that the temporary Appointment of that Office by the Advice of the Council of State hath been made to John Craven Esquire. As this Appointment is to continue no longer than to the End of the present Session of the General Assembly should your Honourable Body think the Necessity and

Chapter Two
General Assembly Sessions

Importance of that Office still exist you will have it in your Power to take such Measures in filling the same with such person you may judge proper. Alex: Martin, Nov. 26th 1792.

****

North Carolina State Archives
General Assembly Sessions Records
December, 1793 - January, 1794, Box #2
Governor's Message

The Honorable the General Assembly of the State of North Carolina, Gentleman,

In the Month of January last I received a letter from the Secretary of War, in answer to one from Governor Martin to the President of the United States, respecting the probability of an Indian War, and calling on the general Government for some protection for our frontiers.

He enclosed me a copy of a letter from James Seagrove Esqr., Agent of the United States for Indian Affairs in the State of Georgia, to shew me that the Creek Nation were amicably disposed towards the United States. At the same time he informs me that the President Confided to me the power of calling into Service or not calling into Service as the necessity of the case might require, a certain number of Scouts or Patroles not exceeding six or eight for a Frontier of twelve miles in extent.

After receiving this letter, I wrote to Brigadier General McDowell of Burke County, and to the commanding Officers of the other Counties in Morgan District to give me the earliest intelligence of the movements of the Indians, or whether they apprehended an attack from them, or that any depredations would be committed by them upon the Citizens of this State, and intended to be governed in my conduct of calling or not calling into service the Patroles, by the information which I might receive from them.

At the same time I wrote to the Secretary of War, that it was my opinion that in order to derive any use from the Patroles the Militia should be so arranged, that a certain part of them might be called into Service at a moments warning, whenever an alarm was given - To this letter I have never received any information from the Westward respecting the Indians, till since my arrival at this place, a letter was handed me from Colo. D. Vance of Buncombe County.

Chapter Two
General Assembly Sessions

     From that letter, which I do myself the honor to lay before you it appears, that tho' no person has been killed by them, that they have become lately very troublesome, and have committed very considerable depredations, on the property of the Citizens of this State, and that it is probable that they may make an attack on our frontier.

     Should the Legislature think it advisable I would immediately give the necessary orders for calling the Scouts into Service and at the same time issue instructions to the Commanding Officer of the district of Morgan to have the Militia of that district, classed into three or four divisions as the case might require, with express instructions to the first class to hold themselves in readiness to march at a moments warning to such part of the frontier as may be attacked by the Indians. This measure would be attended with considerable advantages, give confidence to our fellow citizens in that quarter of the State, and insure their safety & will be attended with very little expence to the State, and cannot be deemed an infringement of the Constitution of the United States for tho' we have no right to make war, it will not be denied that we have a right to guard against any desultory attack that may be made upon us.

     I am with respect, Gentlemen
Your most Obedt. Servant
Richard Dobbs Spaight
Fayetteville 7th Decmr, 1793

Message from his Excellency the Governor
In the House of Commons 9th Decr. 1793 read & referred to the Committee on Public Bills
By order, J Hunt, CHC

In Senate 9th Decemr. 1793 read & referred as by the House of Commons.
By order, J Haywood

****

North Carolina State Archives
General Assembly Sessions Records
December, 1793 - January, 1794, Box #2
Governor's Message

North Carolina
     To the Honorable the General Assembly

Chapter Two
General Assembly Sessions

Gentlemen

    I received your message of the 21st instant informing me that I was re-elected Chief Magistrate of the State for the ensuing years, and requesting me to signify at what time I will attend in order to take the oaths of qualifications.

    I will wait on the two Houses tomorrow if they meet, if not the next day at twelve o'Clock to take the oaths prescribed by law for my qualifications.

    I have the honor to be with respect, Gentlemen
Your most Obedt. Servant
Richard Dobbs Spaight.
Fayetteville, Decr. 24th 1793

Governor's Message, In Senate 24th Decr. 1793, read & ordered to be sent to the House of Commons
By order, S Haywood

State of North Carolina
In the House of Representatives December 6th 1793

    The Committee to whom was referred the business of Examining into and ascertaining the truth of a Report that an Armed force is now levying within this State by Persons under a Foreign Authority without the permission and Contrary to the express prohibition of the Government of the United States and this State.
Report

    That they have made diligent Enquiry respecting the truth of this report and have collected such Evidence relating thereto as was immediately within their reach, That your Committee are perfectly satisfied from the information on the oaths of divers Credible Persons which they have received That William Tate, Jacob R. Brown, William Urby, Robert Tate, Richard Speke, Citizens of this State and other persons unknown to your Committee also Citizens of this State have received and accepted Military Commissions, from M Genet, Minister plenipotentiary from the Republic of France, to the United States of America authorizing them and instructions requiring them to raise or garrise train & Conduct Troops within the United States of America. That the avowed purpose for which these Troops are now raising is to rendevous in the State of Georgia & from thence to proceed to the Spanish Dominions with a view to Conquest or plunder as their strength might enable or opportunity might

Chapter Two
General Assembly Sessions

tempt them, That in the Event of a French Fleet approaching the Coasts of the Southern States a junction co-operation with it, is contemplated by the Persons above named: But that tho this was the Avowed Object of these Troops and their Leaders among themselves from their Junction to conceal the whole System from Persons not initiated and the Subordination established to M Genet, the Author of the plans and the Source of Authority to the Officers - It is probable that the Corps when raised must yield to any Change of destination which the Judgment or inclination of M Genet may point out to them

That several of the persons above named received together with their Commissions instructions by which they were to regulate their enrollments of Men stating the pay, rations, Cloathing plunder and division of Conquered Lands, to be allotted to the Officers and Men who should enter into this Service and marking the proportions of the Acquisitions to be reserved to the Republic of France -- That the Persons above named in pursuance of the powers vested in them by the said Commissions and in obedience to the instructions of M Genet and his Agents without any authority from the United States, or from this State to enroll numbers of the Citizens of this State whom they deluded with the hopes of plunder and the acquisition of riches in the Service of the Republic of France to be subject to the Orders of M Genet the Minister plenipotentiary of France.

That Stephen Drayton and John Hamilton also Citizens of this State have made application to the good Citizens thereof to engage in this Scheme of raising Men in this State for the Service of France to Act under the Orders of M Genet and to commit Acts of hostility against Nations at peace with the United States of America, and have avowed that they acted by the Authority of M Genet the Minister Plenipotentiary of the Republic of France, That upon the whole of the information which your Committee have been able to obtain This is a daring and dangerous attempt by a Foreign Minister to intermeddle in the affairs of the United States, to usurp the powers of Government and to levy Troops in the bosom of the Union without the Authority and contrary to the express sense of the Government of the United States and in violation of the laws of Nations & That the direct tendency of these measures of the Foreign Minister is to disturb the internal tranquility of the United States and to involve them in hostilities with Nations with whom they are now at peace, which sound policy requires should be preserved -- That in the opinion of your Committee this attempt is the more dangerous, and alarming as many Citizens of the United States have been thereby seduced from their duty by insidious acts practised on their kindred affection to the French Republic and have been

Chapter Two
General Assembly Sessions

drawn into a scheme in the execution of which they have usurped the Functions of Government and exercised the power of the sword which the wisdom of the Constitution hath vested exclusively in the Congress of the President of the United States -- That this Committee therefore recommend that the Governor of this State be requested to issue his Proclamation forbidding all persons from enrolling any of the Citizens of this State and prohibiting the Citizens from enlisting under any Officers or for any purposes not previously sanctioned by the Government of the United States or of this State And also forbidding all unlawful assemblages of Troops unauthorized by Government And that the Governor be requested to exert the whole public force to the utmost extent if necessary to insure Obedience to his Proclamation.

That in the opinion of this Committee the said William Tate, Jacob R. Brown, Robert Tate, Stephen Drayton, John Hambleton and Richard Speke have been guilty of high Crimes and misdemeanors and they recommend that the Attorney General and Solicitors be directed forthwith to institute or cause to be instituted and Conducted prosecutions in the proper Courts of Law against the said William Tate, Jacob R. Brown, Robert Tate, Stephen Drayton, John Hambleton and Richard Speke for accepting or engaging to accept Commissions from a Foreign power to raise Troops within the United States and for going about within the State levying or attempting to levy Troops and for seducing & endeavouring to seduce the Citizens of this State to enroll themselves for foreign Service to commit Acts of hostility against Nations with whom the United States are at peace without the permission of the Government and contrary to the Proclamation of the President of the United States declaring these States to be in a State of Neutrality and Peace -- That Copies of the Evidence collected by this Committee together with the proceedings of this House thereon be forwarded immediately to the President of the United States and to the Executives of the State of North Carolina **[Torn]**

Information
Resolved Unanimously that this House do concur in the said Report. Ordered that the Report and Resolution be sent to the Senate for the Concurrence. By Order of the House
John Sandford

Resolve Unanimously that this House do concur with the House of Representatives in the foregoing Report and Resolution. Ordered that the Report and Resolution be sent to the House of Representatives

Chapter Two
General Assembly Sessions

By Order of the Senate
Felix Warley, CS

A true Copy and which I Attest in Columbia this 13th December 1793
John Sandford Dart[?], Clerk of the House of Representatives

****

DukeUniversity
Perkins Library, Manuscript Room
Thomas Lenoir Papers

[Letter from Wm. Brittain to Wm. Lenoir, dated 6 August 1794]

Buncombe County [**Torn**   ]
1794, Aug. 6

Dear Sir
     I Fondly Imbrace the Oppertunity of Transmitting these few lines to you by which you will be informed that I arived home on the 3d day of this Instant but with great difficulty Occationed by high Waters on the fifteenth day from that on which I left Newbern and found all well the disposition of our Neighbors the Indians Seems to be inclinable for peace - about three days ago a Neighbor of Mine Came home from Green **[Faded]** [**Torn**   ] Who inform'd me that Capt. Ri[**Torn**   ] told him that about ten days [**Torn**   ] man near Knoxville who was [**Torn**   ] and Immediately Governor Blount went to the Towns and demanded of them the Murderer and it is Said they have actually given him up and it is further Said he is to be put to Death - Should this be truth the Circumstances appears favourable that their Chiefs are disposed for peace another Circumstance I Can State as a fact that is a Certain Wm Lewis Whose Family was murdered at the foot of the [**Torn**   ] last Faul near Chuckey [**Torn**   ] time take Captive a little Girl [**Torn**   ] family and without So[**Torn**   ] Brought her in to our Inhabitants and has given her up during my absence at Newbern - Dear Sir as you do frequently receive the public News papers in which is Contained the accounts of the Wars of Urope pleas to give me an account of what comes to hand respecting the Combined forces and the French Republickans when Ever you get later Inteligence than we Receive [**Torn**   ] Newbern [

Chapter Two
General Assembly Sessions

Torn] Then **[Torn]** offers Please to give my Compliments to Colonel Allen Colo. Herndon Capt. Jones

I am with great Respect yrs &c
    Wm Brittain

****

North Carolina State Archives
General Assembly Sessions Records
November-December, 1795, Box #2
Propositions and Grievances

    Memorial of David Vance of Buncombe County

In Senate 2nd Decembr 1795, read & referred to the Committee of Propo. & Grievances

J Haywood C

In House of Commons 4 December 1795 read & referred as by the Senate

By Order J Hunt C

The Honourable, the Genl. Assembly of the State of No. Carolina, now sitting at Rawleigh -

 The memorial of David Vance of Buncombe County, Most Humbly
         Sheweth

  That a day or two before your Memorialist discharged the Patroles on the frontiers of this County (in pursuance of Instructions from his Excellency the Governor of this State) some of the Citizens of the State of South Carolina pursued two Indians who had Stolen some Horses from them, into this County, overtook, Killed & Scalped them Very near to the frontier Settlers, and when the People found the patroles were Actually discharged, they were very much Alarmed indeed, Expecting that the Indians (as usual) would immediately retaliate.

Chapter Two
General Assembly Sessions

The frontier Settlers was so much Alarmed that they began to move their familys into the interior parts of the County, and some of them moved intirely off.

In order to Quiet the minds of the People, and keep them at their habitations your Memorialist pointed out twenty one Active Woods-men and placed them out as Spies on the frontier for a few days, to see how the Matter would terminate, whether the Indians were, or were not for mischief

A payroll for the Services performed by said Spyes, with the Number of days each was in Service, Accompanies this Memorial. Shou'd Your Honourabll Body take up the Matter and Grant the Spies pay for their Services, it would lay them, and Your Memorialist under lasting Obligations, And Your Memorialist as in Duty Bound will ever pray.
November 20th. 1795.   D. Vance

****

North Carolina State Archives
General Assembly Sessions Records
November-December, 1795, Box #2
Propositions and Grievances

Report of the Committee Propo: and Grievs. On the petition of David Vance

Resolved that the House do Concur with this Report

By Order - J Hunt CHC   J Leigh Spk H.C.

In Senate 7th Decr 1795 read and Concurred with

By Order   J Haywood C   Benja [?] Spk

The Committee propo: and Grievs. to whom was referred the petition of David Vance.

Report
        That the apprehension of incursions being made into the frontier settlements of Buncombe County, by the Indians, for the purpose of retaliating for the death of two of their tribe, there pursued and killed by Inhabitants of South Carolina, appears to your Committee to be sufficiently

Chapter Two
General Assembly Sessions

well grounded, to require the petitioner as an Officer, to raise the men contained in the payroll accompanying said petition Yet as said frontiers have for several Years been protected at the expense of the General Government. Your Committee at the same time they conceive said men ought to be paid for their Service. Yet are of opinion, that said payment ought to be made by the United States and not at the expense of this State alone, and until a refusal is there made, they are opposed to any allowance.

      Which is submitted
      Absalom Bostick Ck

****

North Carolina State Archives
General Assembly Sessions Records
November-December, 1797, Box #
Propositions and Grievances

        1797
      Joshua Prouts
       Petition

     The House of Commons
      8 Decr. 1797 read
    & ref'd to the Committee of
    propo. & Grievances No. 2
     By Order - J Hunt

In Senate 8th December 1797, read & referred by the House of Commons
    J Haywood C
    Sandford

State of North Carolina
Anson County

  To the Honourable the General Assembly Now sitting at Raleigh

The Humble Petition of Joshua Prout Sheweth that from the Year 1768 to the Year 1775 Colo. Thomas Wade deceased, the Father in Law of your Petitioner, carried on a Considerable Trade with a Certain Tribe or Nation

Chapter Two
General Assembly Sessions

of Indians Known by the Name of the Cherokees, by his Agent Thomas Price, and in the Year 1774 the Indians being considerably in Arrears, proposed to the said Price to purchase a Large Tract of Country of them in discharge of their Debt, about which time his Majesty King George the third, Issued his Proclamation prohibiting any private Companies from purchasing Lands of the Indian Tribes without a permit from the Governor of the State where such Land might be, whereupon the aforesaid Thomas Price conversed with Sir James Wright the then Governor of the State of Georgia (he being the nearest to whom he could with Convenience have access) respecting the matter who on the 10th January 1774 wrote to the said Price advising him to accept the Indians proposal of Land, and promised to do all in his power to obtain the Royal Assent to his Deed. Two other Men supposed to be in the same Circumstance with Price by the Names of Lewis & Wood, held a Treaty with the Indians at the Mouth of Swannanoah River on the 22d. November 1775 where the said Nation of Indians by their Agents Ettacullacula or Carpenter, Wooach or Little Pidgeon & Telicesky three overhill Warriors Counted of the Boundaries of the Land, Including all that Tract of Country lying & being on the East of French Broad River from the Head of Muddy Creek to the Waters of Toy River and all the Northern? Waters there of & to the Western Banks of French Broad River, Runing due West from the Head of Muddy Creek & from that Joining the Carolina line from that Joining the Wattaugah Line at which time they in behalf of their Nation, Sign'd a Deed & delivered the same by Twig & Turf in Consequence of which the said Price burned his Books, and all parties seemed perfectly satisfied the Indians Leaving the purchases in peaceable possession who Continued disposing of the same untill the year 1776, when the Tories & Indians made a descent on that part of the County and drove them off, they Returned & continued untill 1780, after which they fled & joined the United States against their Common Enemy. Price deeded one third of the aforesaid Tract of Country to the aforesaid Colo. Wade's Estate being much derang'd becoming Insolvent this Land was sold by his Executors to Asist in the discharge of a Considerable Ballance due Thomas Wade Junr. by said Estate agreeable to a Report of a Committee appointed by the County Court of Anson, to settle the Accounts of the Executors of the said Colo. Wade, with which Report the said Court concurred, and Thomas Wade Junr became the purchaser since which he is deceased, & his Executors Refusing to Act & your petitioner being his largest Creditor administered on his Estate with the Will Annexed, and agreeable to a Clause in the Last Will & Testament of said deceased, Authorizing & empowering his Executors to sell & Convey

Chapter Two
General Assembly Sessions

his Real Estate, your petitioner on the 20th June 1797 did proceed to sell at Public Vendue the Real Estate of the said Thomas Wade Junr., to discharge his just debts when your petitioner by his Friend became the purchaser of the said Tract, as upon Record in the proper Offices in Anson County. Now as the State of North Carolina has never paid any thing to the Indians for this Land, nor have they any Right thereto by any Treaty whatever, untill the Treaty concluded at Hopewell in 1785 at which time the Indians Received nothing for this Land, Knowing they had before sold it to Price, & the State of North Carolina having received into her Treasury perhaps to the Amount of 20,000 pounds, and is Yearly receiving large Sums for Taxes on said Land, & having made Richard Henderson & Co. compensation for a Tract of Country purchased of the said Indians about the same time, expressly in the Face of Government. Your Petitioner thinks in Justice that he ought to be allowed some compensation for Extinguishing the Indian Title as aforesaid, by way of Reimbursement from the Treasury of the State of North Carolina for his purchase money aforesaid, & the Interest arising thereon, or any other way your Honourable Body may think proper, & therefore prays your Honourable Body to take the matter into your Consideration, and Grant your Petitioner such Relief as in your wise Councils you may think Just & Right, and your Petitioner as in Duty Bound will ever pray
      Joshua Prout

****

North Carolina State Archives
General assembly Sessions Records
November-December, 1797

    Memorial of some of the Inhabitants of Buncombe County
         In House of Commons
          11th Decembr 1797
          Read & referred to
   Mastr Franklin, Brittain, Alexander, Skinner, & Gaither
           By order
           J Hunt CHC

        In Senate 10th Decr 1797
        read & referred to the
       Committee on public Bills

Chapter Two
General Assembly Sessions

The Honourable the General Assembly of the State of North Carolina now Setting at Raleigh

The Memorial of the Inhabitants of Buncombe County Humbly Sheweth

That General Pickens (one of the Commissioners appointed to run the line between the Whites and the Indians did, about ten days ago run a line thro' part of the South end of said County, which line is Said to be the Boundary between us and the Cherokee Indians

Your Memorialists conceive that said line is Verry far from agreeing with the Boundary pointed out in the Treaty. The treaty Says runing to the North Carolina Boundary, then North to a point from which a line &c - Now General Pickens came thro' the Mountains between Easlytows, and French Broad river and run down on the East side of French Broad river fifteen or twenty Miles thro' the Settlements in this County untill his Suppos'd North Carolina Boundary, Thence North one quarter of a Mile his Suppos'd point, thence North fourteen Degrees West Crossing to the West Side of French Broad and partly up the West Side of said river for a Considerable distance for from the place where the line Crossed the Mountains at the head of French Broad river to the Suppos'd North Carolina Boundary, which is upwards of twenty Miles, the two lines is in some places not more than two or three Miles apart, in other places four or five Miles, and at the greatest distance not more than twelve or fifteen Miles apart, in the before Mentioned distance.

Your Memorialists Consider themselves Verry much injured by said line and runing as it has done, and which we humbly conceive is Contrary to law, for to run down in such an Accute Angle and throu out the Flourishing young Settlement on the head of French Broad river to the Indians, we humbly presume must be absurd, The white people is dissatisfied with it, and the Indians full as much, for the Course the line is going will leave some of their towns on our Side. The Indians Say they do not want the Unacas[?] Plantations for say they you are the best Neighbors on all the frontiers.

Your Memorialists are disposed at all times to submit to the Laws of the Government under which they live, But think it a Verry hard case indeed, to be compelled to give their Lawful property to the Cherokee Indians or any other without a Compensation, So hard that at present we can't think of Submitting to it - We Legally Bought our Lands from the

183

Chapter Two
General Assembly Sessions

State of North Carolina and paid our Money for the same, has the States Grants, and hope to be protected.

    Your Memorialists conceive themselves in a Very disagreeable Situation, therefore hope your Honourable Body will take their case under Consideration, and appoint Commissioners to examine whether the line is run Agreeably to Law, or whether the North Carolina Boundary is fixed in the right place, Or any other way that you in Your Wisdom may devise to make your Memorialists Sensible they are not impos'd upon, and Your Memorialists will Ever pray   November 27th 1797

D. Vance	L. Clayton	Robt. Orr
Jas. Scott	Wm. Welsh	W Wilson
Benjamen Odle	G Odle	
Geo. Swain		
Moses Webster	John Patton	
Wm. Murphy		
Robt. Patton	Joseph Henry	
Jas. Rutherford		
John Bradley	William Sexton	
Stephen [?]iliken		
James Davidson	Benjm Davidson	
William Moore Sn		
Thomas Moore	Jna Carson	
James Wilson		
David Miller		

****

University of North Carolina
Southern Historical Collection
Preston Davie Papers
Collection # 3406
Box #4, Folder #274

    Letter from Timothy Pickering to The Reverend Doctor Green

Thursday Morning
Jany. 1. 1799

Dr. Sir

    Mr. Dinsmoor is recently come to town from the Cherokee Country and will dine with me to day at three o'clock. If you are not

Chapter Two
General Assembly Sessions

engaged it will give me great pleasure to have your company. An opportunity will be afforded to obtain more accurate information of that Indian Nation, and probably of the neighboring tribes, in relation to a religious mission, than is to be derived from any other Source.

I am respectfully yours
Timothy Pickering

Doctor Greene

Every lady in this land Hath ten fingers - on each hand Five, - & twenty nails on hands & feet, And this is true without deceit.

Chapter Three

Governor's Office

The Humble Address of Christ: Ths. Renfrew in behalf of the [?] residing in Wachovia to His Excellency the Govr. Of North Carolina, March 12, 1757

May it please Your Excellency

We His Majestys most Loyal and most dutifull Subjects the Brethren residing in Wachovia, humbly beg leave to lay before Your Excellency that,
Tho' we consientiously scruple to be engaged in Wars as Soldiers, to follow after our Enemies to take away their Lives &c. adhering to the very same Sentiments we have professed before the British Parliament where we obtained an Act securing us against being forced to bear Arms or to go to War &c.
Yet in this troublesome Time when every body thought himself in Danger of being fallen upon by the murdering Indians, we have kept strict Watch & have secured our Settlement with Stocades, which has been hitherto so Successful for us and our Neighbours that took shelter amongst us, as to prevent a Surprize & blood Shedding on both sides.
And now we think it might be good not only for ourselves but also for the Inhabitants round about us to continue the said Watch, and to prevent thereby many Evil Designs of such Unmercifull Creatures tho they should at present comit no Hostilities in our Province.
But being Sensible, that this can not be regularly done without the Governors Special Leave, or rather His Orders, we hereby request your Excelly. To authorize the said Watch under your Hand and Seal and to appoint Mr. Jacob Loesch to be chief overseer of this above mentioned

Chapter Three
Governor's Office

Watch. And we further wish Your Excelly. Would be pleased to put one of our Brethren in the Commission of the Peace for we humbly conceive it would greatly contribute to the Tranquillity of our Settlement & we beg leave to recommend the above mentioned Mr. Jacob Loesch for that Function, who if he should have Your Excellys. Approbation, would be acknowledged by us with particular Gratefuness towards Your Excelly.
And Your Petitioners will ever pray &c.

    Signed in the Name and in behalf of the Brethren residing in Dobbs Parish, Wachovia in North Carolina
Christ: Thos. Renfrew
Bethlehem in the Forcks of Delaware, March 12th 1757.

****

[Editor's note: Most of this document is missing.]

To His Excellency Arthur Dobbs Esqr., Capt. General and Governor in Chief in and over ye Province of North Carolina.

    The Humble Petn. of ye Inhabitants on ye Frontiers of Anson & Rowan Countys in this Province on ye South Fork of ye Catauba River Most Humbly ---- Sheweth

    Whereas many of Petitioners have been Robbed and Assaulted By Indians who Call themselves Shawanaws, at other times **[Torn]** themselves Mingoes, or Sinakers and at other times Cherekees which **[Torn]** of three our Cattle a Killing D**[Torn]** Horses & **[Torn]**

Enemy Indians **[Torn]**
We Yr. Petrs. Are almost at our wits end **[Torn]**
Plantations or our Necessary Business for **[Torn]**
May see some of **[?]** so full are ye woods of **[Torn]**
Of our Settlement that they had Several of ye **[Torn]**
But we yr. Petrs. Have **[?]** Consulted to **[Torn]**
Excellency, Therefore We Yr. Petrs. Most **[Torn]**
Distressed Condition into Prudent Consideration **[Torn]**
A Scout for our Safe Guard and ye Suppression **[Torn]**
Proper for ye Fort to be Erected at Warlicks Mill **[Torn]**
Bounds for ye Scouters to extend from Little **[Torn]**
Of ye Catauba River Between ye Settlement & ye **[Torn]**

Chapter Three
Governor's Office

Well Satisfied that Yr. Excellency Would be pleased [**Torn**]
Capt. Of ye Scouts over such Bounds we know [**Torn**]

[Editor's note: The rest of this document is torn and missing.]

****

Sept. 26th 1751

To the Honble the President & Council
The Petition of William Price, humbly Sheweth,
    That your Petr. Obtain'd the late Governors Warrt. For 400 Acres of Land in Anson County on the North side of the Catabo River being the Place your Petr. Lives on.
    That the said Land was duly survey'd by virtue of the said Warrant by Mr. Francis Mackilwean Deputy Surveyor.
    That the said Warrant thereupon was duly returned by the sd. Deputy Surveyor to the Surveyor Genl. As by doth appear.
    That your Petr hath by Mr Saml Young Depy. Surveyor caused diligent Search to be made in the Secretarys Office for the said Warrant & Survey in order to compleat his Title to the said Land but without effect, the sd. Warrant not being to be found in the sd. Office.
    Your Petr therefore humbly prays that your Honr. taking the premises into your Consideration will be pleased to order the said Land to be resurveyed that on the return thereof your Petr. May obtain a Patent Delay'd.

****

The Humble Petition of the Inhabitants of Anson County

To His Excellency Gabriel Johnston Esqr. Governour & Commander in Chief in & over the Province of North Carolina and his Majesties Most Honble. Council.

The humble petition of the Inhabitants of Anson County by we the Subscribers.

    That one John Eliss an Indian traidr. Hath taken upon himself Liberty to warn off the Inhabitants of ye Lands of above County and

Chapter Three
Governor's Office

swears if they do not Goe off it will be worse for them also Swears that the King has no Right to any Lands thereto to Send any Officers and that the Indians shall not be Cheated out of their Lands &c. Begs Yr. Advice what to do with this Guest[?]

Some Says after a White woman was Killed in her House the Acct: of wch. Murder Came to the County Court then setting who Imediately Sent a Message to the above Sd. Nation by some of the Members of Said Court Demanding Satisfaction for the above Crime which was then Supposed to be Committed by ye Calabas, they seemingly was under a Concorse and they promised if they Could upon Enquiry Discover that any of their people had Committed that barbarous Murder they should Suffer Accordingly upon which Sent Notice to their King then in So. Carolina Receiving presents also Sent Express for all their Out Hunters in Ordr. For a full Enquiry and with a resolution to make a Lasting peace with this Province which showes this Nation is not Inclining to War.

But it is generally believed for several Reasons since appearing that Either the Sinnicars or Tusks Murdered this Woman with Intention to Sett the white people & Calabas to War, Both Tusks & Sinnicars being now at War with the Catabas.

And further Begs Yr. Excellency & Honrs. Would not Permit the Tusks Nation to Goe to War with the Catabas without first obtaining from His Excellency a Certificate of their Number & Names by which means if any Damage is Done Among the back Inhabitants as has been lately; by the above Measurs it will be found out; Haps Yr. Excellency & Honrs. Will take all speedy Measures to procure our Safety; and Incoridge the Settlement which will be the Greatest Ever was made in these Sutheran parts if no War with the Indians Happens.
Jas. Mackilwean
Charles Robinson
Newbern Octr. 19th 1749

****

Read the Petn. of the Chowan Indians Complaining that James Brown, Rd Minshew & others to whom some years past Sold & convey'd several smal Parcels of Ye Lands formerly allotted them by Ye Govt. were not content to keep within their proper bounds but incroached upon the Indians lands not made over to [?] thereby defrauding his maty. Of his Quit Rents & them of their Property and defeating the Intention of the late Lords Proprs. In favour of the sd. poor Indians, they therefore pray'd that the said Jas

Chapter Three
Governor's Office

Brown, Rd. Minshew & Ye rest of ye Purchasers may be ordered to lay out their several and respective Parcels of Land (each and every of) that their true Quantity conveyed to them by their respective Deeds, in or for to ascertain their Bounds & prevent any future Incroachments on the Petrs. Lands wch Since Such Sale, so [?] remain to them in propriety.

That the parties Complain'd of have Notice Accordingly
Six Pence interlined over them in the Record B. Q. page 411

****

[Editor's Note: There is no date on this document. The date is possibly in 1754.]

Petition for a Patrol Company, Anson Co.
To His Excellency Arthur Dobbs, Esqr.

To His Excellency Arthur Dobbs Esqr. Comr. General & Governor in Chief in & over Ye Province of North Carolina

The Humble Petition of ye Inhabitants of ye Frunteers of Anson County in This Province Most Humbly Sheweth

Whereas Many of the Petitioners have been Robbed, & assaulted By Ye Indians who Calls themselves Shanaws, and Some times Sinakers & at other times Cherekees wch. We Doubt not but they are a Mixter of Ye Three; & By them our Calfs is Killed & Horses and Houshold Goods dayly are taken away from us, and our Houses By ym. Burning, and threatening to take Yr. Pettitioners Lives, and very often abusing our Women & Children So yt. Severals of Yr. Petrs. Was obliged to fly from our Livings, and Leave our Crops wch. Seem'd to be aplentiful appearance of a Large Harvest, wch. Is all Lost By ye Barbarous and Cruel Enemy which is Dailey Making Prays of yr. Petrs. And others. We yr. Petrs. Being at a loss, By not having authority from Yr. Excellency to Proceed against our Enemys, ye Shanaws, and their asociates, wch. Are Dailey amongst us, Discovering of our Defenceless & Naked Condition wch. Enemy we have Great Reason to fear is harboured, & Countenanced Both by ye Cherekee, & Catauba Indians, & Doubts not but the End will be Dangerous, if not prevented By Yr. Excelencies Wise & Prudent Judgments. Therefore We Yr. Petrs. Most Humbly Begs yt. Yr. Excellency will take yr. Petrs. Into

Chapter Three
Governor's Office

Yr. Wise and Prudent Consideration; And grant Yr. Destressed Petrs. Relief, by appointing us a Scout for our Safeguard & Defence and to be Stationed Between Enoree River & ye Head Waters of Thickety & **[Torn]** Petrs. Mutually Agree **[Torn]** Nominate Ye Bear[?] Capt Wm. Green to be Captain of Ye **[Editor's Note: The whole next line is torn and faded.]**

Conduct and Courage and well acquainted with ye Woods, also yr. Petrs. Does think it will be highly Convenient yt. A fort Should be forthwith Erected, in Such a Place in ye Bounds aforsd. As Yr. Excellency & ye Bearor Shall think Proper wch. Countenanced By Yr. Excellency will be a mean to Encourage yr. Petrs. To abide By the Rights and will be a very Great Encouragmt. To others to come & Settle, there being Large Bodies of Good Land to Settle in Yr. Excellencies Bounds, Therefore we Yr. Petrs. Most Humbly Pray Yr. Excellency would be pleased to take our Present Condition under Yr. Wise & Prudent Consideration & endeavour our Relief by such prudent Means as Yr. Excellency will think most Proper & with all ye Speed ye Nature of the Case will admit of, many of us almost Resolved to Leave our all & go where we may Most Reasonably Expect to Enjoy peace, But as we have purchased our Lands in yr. Govermt. We most Humbly Begg & pray Yr. Excellencies Protection & yr. Petrs. As in Duty Bound Shall Ever.
The Subscribers under neet Copied of by order.

Jas Maye, Alexr. McMillan, Jno. McMillan, George Kenedy, Wm. Kennedy, Tom, Jno. Stevenson, Jno.Kelse, Jas. Hughy, Henry Forster, Jas. McEwain, Robt. Dugan, Geo. Storey, Joseph Kelse, Jas. Means, Jas. Mitchel, Thos. Mitchel, David Mitchel, Jno. Brown, Alexr. Lokert, Hugh Donovin, Cormick McCaughrey, Bartley Brown, Geo. Brandon, Christopher Brandon, Jas Oterson, Jos. Jolly, Wm. Bogar, Anthony Park, Arthur Forster, Jas. Brandon, Andw. Forster, Jno. Withro, Robt. Tate, Thos Farrel, Jas. Patton, Wm. Patton, Jno. Latta, Alexr. Johnston, Saml. Gilkey, Robt. Miller Senr., Robt. Miller Junr., James Miller, Nathl. Miller, Jno. Kelsey, Wm. Dickinson, Thos. Young, Jos. Jones, Mat. Floid, Arthur McCluer, Edwd. Clenton, Jeremy Green, Jno. Burnsides, Wm. Sharp, Wm. Hugh, Nathan Nicholson, Michl. Sope, David Burch, David Parks, Jas. Wilson, Hugh Lawson, Roger Lawson.

****

Chapter Three
Governor's Office

Proceedings at a Treaty with the Overhill Cherokee Indians held at Fort Patrick Henry near the long Island on Holston River in June and July 1777

To the Commissioners appointed on behalf of the Commonwealth of Virginia to Treat with the Cherokee Indians the 26th Inst. June,
Gentlemen,
I received Your letter dated at Fort Patrick Henry and since that time Col. Christian has had before the Board of Council the proceedings of the Treaty held with the overhill Cherokee Indians, In transacting of which the Board are of opinion that You have Acted with propriety. I have sent by Express to the Govr. Of North Carolina Notifying him of the time proposed for the next meeting and desiring Sd to send Commissioners to Act on behalf of that State. I have had several Conferences with these Indians and have generally thrown out the same Ideas that You did, and moreover endeavoured to lead them into the light of our situation with Great Britain, and also that of our Commercial Connections. I have referred them to You and the Commissioners who I hope will attend to represent North Carolina in order to have a boundary line between them and the white people established, and told them that if such Commissioners do not or when met will not join in that business, You are then to agree with the Indians upon a line betwixt them and Virginia in the best manner You Can for the Interest of the frontier Inhabitants so that You at the same time do strick Justice to the Indians. It is a verry desirable object to obtain an alteration of our Boundary line run by Donelson. We cannot communicate with the Kentuckie with tolerable Convenience but through Cumberland Gap. If the Indians therefore will agree to an extension so as to take in that place it may be verry useful. But at all events it seems necessary to stipulate a right for our people to travel through that Gap unmolested. You are in all Your transactions to keep in View as much as possible the Interest of the United States as well as that of this particular one.
I have sent orders for Mr. Maddison and Mr. Shelby to supply You with what provisions You may want for the Indians which You are to supply them with as You think their necessity may acquire in order that they or their wives and Children may not suffer for want of Bread. The goods, Ammunition, Salt, Whiskey and Tobacco which I expect will be laid in You are to distribute as You may think best to give the Indians Satisfaction. You may promise them a further supply of goods as soon as our Commerce will enable us to furnish them. As a proper person residing amongst those people might render great service to the Country. You may

Chapter Three
Governor's Office

employ one for that purpose and inform this Board who You may appoint and on what terms. And if a proper person Cannot be engaged for the above purpose You may employ two Traders in whome You can Confide to give the earliest Inteligence of any occurrence that may be of Importance. As a Black Smith may be of great service in dressing their Guns and other suitable work for them You may employ one to reside among them to be had on reasonable terms. Several things may happen in which You are not particularly Instructed, in all such Cases You are impowered to Act for the good of the United States in the best manner You Can. Should the Treaty terminate in the manner this Board expects it will be necessary to continue many Troops in Washington County, You are therefore impowered and desired to discharge all the men on those Stations except such as You may think necessary to Continue.
I am Gentlemen
Your most Humble Servt.
P. Henry

To Col. William Christian
Col. William Preston and
Col. Evan Shelby or any two of them.

On the 28th Col. Gist and a party of Indians arrived, and in Consequence of this Inteligence the following Letter was written and sent by Express to Genl. Rutherford.
        Virginia Fort Patrick Henry on Holston River
June 28th 1777

Sir:
        Col. Nathaniel Gist has this hour arrived at this place from Chote, where he had been ordered by Government, to bring in a number of Cherokees to a Treaty to be held here; and informs that an Indian runner had come from Tallassa, a Creek Town about 12 or 13 days ago, when he saw all the Warriors of that Nation Convened at a great Council. That they then agreed to a man on going to War against the frontiers of Georgia and were to set out for that purpose in seven days from that time. The fellow that brings this Inteligence Col. Gist is well acquainted with and says it cannot be doubted of. He also informs that the English have landed four thousand Troops at Pensacola who intended to proceed up through the Creek Nation, and that a number of Highlanders were amongst them, this

Chapter Three
Governor's Office

account he had from an Indian who saw them and Came straight from Pensacola. The Indian also informs that the English Agents were buying great numbers of Pack Horses from the Choctaw Traders, for the purpose of Carrying a Campaign against some of the States perhaps Georgia. This interesting inteligence I have made free to send You by way of Col. Carter, that it may be forwarded with all Convenient speed to Col. Williamson; that the frontiers of Georgia may have Notice of their danger and if possible prevent the stroke intended against them by the Savages.
I am, Sir, tho unacquainted
Yr. Verry Humble Servt.
Wm. Preston

To Genl. Rutherford

The Commissioners from North Carolina were at Colo. Carters on their way to the Treaty when the above letter came open they immediately certified a true Copy thereof and sent it the nearest way to Col. Williamson and wrote an apology to Genl. Rutherford for taking the liberty.

30th June   Col. Christian with Oconostota and his party that were at Williamsburgh Came to the Fort. And a few minutes afterwards Waightstill Avery, William Sharpe, Robert Lanier & Joseph Winston Esqrs. The Commissioners from North Carolina arrived

---

State of North Carolina

To Waightstill Avery, William Sharpe, Robert Lanier and Joseph Winston Esqrs. Greeting;

     Out of the assurance we have of Your Integrity Abilities and Fidelity to the State, we do hereby appoint you the said Waightstill Avery, William Sharp, Robert Lanier and Joseph Winston Commissioners on the part and behalf of this State to Act in Conjunction with the Commissioners appointed by the States of Virginia and South Carolina or either of them in establishing a Peace and fixing a Boundary line bewteen the Cherokee Indians and the white people.
     You or any two or more of You are therefore to proceed to the Long Island on Holston, on the twenty sixth day of this Instant or at such

Chapter Three
Governor's Office

time and place as may be agreed upon by the Commissioners of the aforesaid States for the purpose aforesaid; And You or any two or more of You are hereby Invested with Competent power to Negociate the aforesaid Treaty; and any Acts by You or two or more of You in Conjunction with Commissioners of the other States or the Commissioners of the other States or the Commissioners of either of them done shall be obligatory on this State.

    Witness Richard Caswell Esqr. Governor Captain General and Commander in Chief of the said State under his hand and seal at arms at Newbern the 12th day of June Anno Dommini 1777. And in the first Year of our Independence.
By his Excellencys Command   Rd. Caswell
James Glasgow, Sec.

Wednesday 2d. July, an Indian Warrior named the Big Bullet was killed on the Great Island by some evil minded white man. A few of the Indian Chiefs were immediately Assembled when Oconostota made to the Commissioners of both States the following speech.

    My Brothers will hear what I have to say to them as I have Come from my Father below (meaning Govr. Henry) We are now talking in the House of Peace let both our Fathers hear of the accident that has happened. I remember the talk that was lately given at Wms. Burgh, and the Belt; I hold it still. The Govr. Told me that no man should break the Belt given me by him, whose talk I have now in my mind. He told me he had hold of one end of the Belt and myself the other; but the white people has given the first stroke and tried to break it; they have struck me and spilt Blood about the Chain unknown to my father. What they have done shall not spoil the good talks. Let my Brothers now talk and try to clear it up. The talk is like last night which I had with our Father, it shall not by a bad man. I shall think nothing of it as it was done by a bad man. Our Father took fifty of our women and children and sent them flour to support them when they were like to perish. If he speaks nothing about this accident - I shall not. But the good Talks between Your beloved men are hurt with Blood sprinkled about; I hope you'll try to clear it off. My Brother knows I have been with him and done all I could for Peace, as he was leading us by the hand for Peace this accident happened. I hope my Brothers will say nothing that bad as we are talking of peace. My people shall hear nothing that's bad as I believe it was done by a verry bad Man who has no way of

Chapter Three
Governor's Office

living. Cameron and Stuart will hear of this accident. They will laugh and be pleased at it; but I do nor care for what they Can say. I shall tell my own people not to mind Cameron & Stuarts Talks, I have told them I was done with him, and all the Talks they give me, my Brothers of Virginia shall hear.

I shall say the same to the Warriors who I expect every day; and desire them not to mind it as it was done by a bad man. I look upon it as an accident; My Brothers need not believe I think hard of it, for I am no ways angry on this occasion as it was done by a verry bad man. This is the second time such an accident has happened, but it shall not make us think the least hard of it.

To which the Commissioners returned the following answer:

We Your Brothers of Virginia and North Carolina are extremely sorry for the accident that has fallen out in the murder of one of your people by a wicked White man, while we are eating and drinking together and talking of Peace; A Peace which we hope we and our Children will enjoy to the mutual benefit of both Nations. We hope You are convinced that this horrid Action was done by some Devilish wit minded person who wants to destroy the good talks that are now between Your Brothers & You. We have lost people in Your Nation by bad men, and we forgave it as we knew the good men and Warriors were not concerned; as the great Being above knows that we are innocent of it; And that it will not be a means of hindering the peace so happily began between us. You know that forty four of your people traveled to see the Governor of Virginia, that they were well treated and returned in safety, which may Convince You of our regard for and care of Your beloved man and his friends as well as of all Your people.

We now promise You that we will use our utmost endeavours to have the Murderer taken and punished according to our Laws. We thank you for your good talks on this occasion, and are rejoiced that our sentiments are the same and that both parties are willing to wipe away the Blood off the great Chain of friendship, which binds us together as one people. In hopes you will overlook this accident for which we all heartily grieved, and that it will not spoil the good talks on either side, we give You this string of Wampum.

Chapter Three
Governor's Office

July 3rd   Began an enquiry in order to discover the murderer, Examined a number of persons on Oath, found the Gun that had been discharged at the Indian, took up the owner, who acquitted himself by introducing a number of Witnesses that proved his being in another place at that time.

In the afternoon the following Advertisement was posted on the Fort Gate and a number of Copies thereof made out and sent through the Country.

Six hundred Dollars Reward

Whereas some wicked and evil minded person unknown on the Second Instant did in a secret and cowardly manner, felloniously kill and murder a Cherokee Indian, Called the Big Bullet, while the said Indian was attending a Treaty of Peace, and by the Law of Nations was entitled to all the protection of a foreign Embassador.

And whereas the said Barbarous & Treacherous act of felony tends to destroy all confidence between the Indiand and white People, prevent Peace, prolong the Indian War and perpetuate the calamities thereof, without and on the frontiers of Virginia & North Carolina.

We the subscribers therefore in order to keep the way of Peace open, and bring the offender to Condign punishment, have thought fit to offer the above reward of Six hundred Dollars, to any person who will discover the murderer of the said Indian Called the Big Bullet; being a Barbarous, treacherous felony against the Law of Nations, and such as would disgrace the most faithless Savage. And we do hereby promise and engage that the above reward shall be paid on conviction of the offender. Fort Henry 3rd of July 1777.

Wm. Christian	} Commissioners
Wm. Preston	} from Virginia
Waightstill Avery	}
Wm. Sharpe	} Commissioners
Robt. Lanier	} from North Carolina
Joseph Winston	}

Chapter Three
Governor's Office

At a Treaty held at this place last April the Commissioners sent a Talk by Col. Gist to the Dragging Canoe who returned Colo. Gist the following answer.
Brother
    Tho' Your messenger is not come to me Yet I have heard your Talks and hold them fast as long as I live, for they have opened my Eyes and made me see clear, that Cameron and Stewart have been telling me lies, when we had any Talks with the Virginians he was always mad with us, and told us that all that the Virginians wanted was to get our Land and kill us, and that he had often told us we would not hear him till the Virginians would come and kill us all. Now Brother I plainly see that he made me quarrel with the greatest friends that we ever had, who took pity on us even in the greatest distress, when my old men, Women and Children is perrishing for something to live on, this makes it more plain to me that he cared not how many of us were killed on both sides so that we were dead, killed in Battle, or perrished with hunger, any way so we were dead.

    Brother, I heard you were taken prisoner and confined, my heart was Sorry as tho You had been my born Brother, when I thought of their bad treatment to you I expected never to see You. I thought they had killed You or sent You away as that I should never see You more. That made my heart Verry Cross and I went to War more for revenge for you than any other reason. But now Brother I am sorry for it, since I see that the great being above has sent You back to save me and my people. Now Brother the great Warrior and Your beloved men are sitting together, I am determined that I nor my people shall never spoil their good talks while I live, when I am dead there will be another man to take my place.

    Brother I am going to see the man that told me all those lieing Talks and return him his meddle and Beds and tell him for the future to keep all his lieing talks to himself. He sends me word that he is coming from Mobile with a great many Scotsmen and intends to offer You a peace; if You wont accept it he intends to kill and force You to it. Brother I shall make no stop on the road, but shall be back soon and come straight to You and tell You all the news. If I should not come in soon pray excuse me to the beloved men as You are better acquainted with me than they are, and You can talk better than I can, and You know Brother I will not do anything that will make you ashamed of me among Your People.
Test. Geo. Hart June 8th 1777.

Chapter Three
Governor's Office

Joseph Vann a half Indian who had formerly been employed by Mr. Cameron as an Interpreter came to the Fort at the request of the Commissioners by Col. Gist. He shewed a letter from Cameron as follows.

Little Tallassa June 6th 1777

Sir

I received the Virginia Talks which You sent me by Haley for which I thank You. It seems to be verry low with them indeed by the mean artifices they fall upon to deceive the Indians but their lies will not avail, as I fancy the present Campaign will open the eyes of all America and deter them in future from revolting from their Lawful King. Excuse my not enlarging as I have not time, so must refer You to Mr. McDonald for the news as I understand You live contiguous to him. I am surpized You do not come in as I have sent several messages for You. I have kept You in pay till the 31st of December last, and if you will be here before the last of this month, I will endeavour to retain You in pay longer; but if You should neglect to come it will not be in my power to serve You.
I am Your Verry Humble Servt.
Alexr. Cameron
To Mr. Joseph Vann

July 4th The aniversary of the Declaration of Independence was observed. The Soldiers belonging to the Garrison were paraded and fired two rounds, each in six platoons and for the 13th one general Voley. The Indian Chiefs were acquainted with the festivity in the following speech, and had a present of Whiskey delivered to them at the same time.

Brothers

Just one Year ago the 13 United States declared themselves free and Independent. And that they would no longer be in subjiction and Slavery to the King of Great Britain. The Americans have now for one Year since their freedom fought against their Enemies that came in the Ships over the Great water, and have beat them in many Battles, have killed some thousands of them and taken many prisoners and the great Being above hath made them Verry prosperous. We hope therefore that this day every Year hereafter will be a day of rejoicing and Gladness.

Chapter Three
Governor's Office

Brothers, as this is a day of general rejoicing throughout the 13 United Countries from Canada to Floridas we hope our Brothers the Cherokees will now rejoice and be merry with us.

The Young Warriors then closed the entertainment with a Dance. From this time till the 10th ; Sundry Chiefs with small parties came in, on that day the old Tassell came in and spoke to the Commissioners as follows.

My Brothers may be certain I will tell them the truth. It was but the other day we were talking together when we promised we would tell all we knew to each other. I will now tell all I know about the ten Norward Indians that lately Came to Chote, as their talk was to me. These Mingoes Came in after Vanns express arrived. They had met with the second man of Chilhoway on his way here, and he turned back with them, and next day I met them at Chote and spoke to them as follows.

Brothers, I am Glad to see You once more; we have been at War and making Peace several Years. Last Year You came here and told me lies from Your Council, which did me and my people great hurt. But I now make You welcome; but Your stay must be short. (I gave them a small string and told them this was the beloved Town where the Warriors speak together). I see by Your looks that Your hearts are bad, and that You have been doing mischief as You came here. I gave you this String that You may tell the truth. I am now going to the beloved men at the Island where our Talks with the white people are good, and not as they used to be. You are Come Now Contrary to my expectation. Some of Your people Came here last Year and told lies, and set me and my people at War with a people that I never intended to be at War with; and it looked as if my Nation were but like one House against them. It was but the other day I was at the Island making Peace with my elder Brothers and all Your bad Talks shall not again spoil it. I am now talking with You who I have called my elder Brothers. I find the days are dark between You and the white people; but that shall not Spoil my good Talks. You may kill a great many of them, even four, five, or six thousand and as many more will Come in their place; But the red men cannot destroy them. Your lies made me have the short trouble I had, but I am now carrying on good Talks and all You Can say shall not prevent them. And I hope You will soon be doing the same, as our elder Brothers are verry merciful to our women and Children.

They then answered

Chapter Three
Governor's Office

Brothers we are only come to see You and not to hold talks, When we left our Towns all the Northern Tribes were ready to strike the white People. Only one man who desired them to wait untill he would go to the Lakes and see the white people there. We have been forty days on our journey. Sixty of us set out together from our Towns and on our way attacked a Fort on Kentuckie where we lost one man and got two Scalps, we left that Fort and attacked another small one, but no damage was done on either side that we know of. We then parted and forty nine went home; and we came to see if the Cherokees were Cut off as had been reported. But we are now in haste to return to meet the Indians who are to invade the frontiers from this River to the Forks of Ohio. The Western Tribes have all been spoken too; and the Northern Tribes are all ready for War. The Nottowagoes had been spoken to by a great Town of white people far off, (perhaps Quebeck) who said "will you be always fools, will you never learn Sense? Don't you know there is a line fixed between you and the white people, that if they set their foot over it you might cut it off; and if they turn and set their heels over, You might Cut them off also? Now they have come over the line and encroached on Your lands and why will you Suffer it? Don't You understand this? These Indians then argued this was truth, and immediately sent runners through all their land amongst all their Tribes, who agreed to send a few of their Warriors to strike the Blow, and then the white people might follow if they please, and go amongst them, and try to cut them off as they have done the Cherokees. These Notawagoes instantly sent out some Warriors who killed two white men and then returned, and a large Body of them were about to set out a second time; but the white people at the great Falls (perhaps Niagara) said they should not go out untill they would give them a writing on paper to lay on every mans Breast they should kill, that the white people might know the reason of it. We were told by some Twightwes that a large Body of their people had set out to kill white people, and on our way here above the Falls of Ohio we saw signs of them returning with a vast number of Horses they had taken from the white people, and we don't doubt but they have done great Damages. The Nottawagoes said if the white people comes out against You they will be discovered as your men are always in the woods, then you must give us notice and we will come and fight them. There are three Towns of the Shawnees & Delawares where the Cornstalk and Captain White eyes lives, whom we have spoken to and told them it was verry well for them to Carry on their good Talks with the white people, for that these Towns & us had no Connections. Two Nottawagoe Warriors came to two Delaware Towns with Belts, and told them, "they had agreed

Chapter Three
Governor's Office

to go to War with the white people and desired that they might moove off, last in the War they might be trod down by them, or the white people. That they did not want them to join; but they must remove beyond the Mingoes, to be out of their way. And they might still Carry on their good Talks with the white people. They also spoke to Capt. White Eyes and told him he was a great and a Warrior. That they had given him the beloved Fire, and it gave them great trouble to ask him to remove, as he was dreadful amongst the red men; for fear something might come out of the ground which would put out that fire." This is all we can tell you which we can assure you is the truth.

In the last part of the Talk they said, "You are now making peace for the security and safety of your Nation. We do not want Your Assistance. If we suffer, we will bear the loss ourselves, for we are looking for it, and deserve it; as our Young men are determined to go to War and try the white men. It may be that we and our elder Brothers may yet talk together of Peace. And we will keep hold of the friendship we have with the Cherokees, but we desire no assistance from them, as we did not give them any when they were in trouble."

I told the road they must take which was down the Little River and through Cumberland Gap; and that they must not hurt any white men on this side of that Mountain, least it would destroy the good talks that were going on. But now I am Convinced that it was them that did the mischief the other day (Meaning the Captivating Cash Brooks about thirty miles from this place) and not my people, for as I came up, I looked where they should have Crossed the river as I directed them; but could not discover Sign of them.

11th July in the morning the Commissioners from North Carolina were informed by a letter that a number of people on Nolachuckie & Watauga appeared to have Hostile intentions against the Indians on the Island, In consequence of which Messrs. Avery and Winston rode out in order to Suppress all such outrages.

The same day the Raven & Willenewau came in. In the evening the Old Tasel on behalf of the other Warriors spoke as follows.

Now You shall hear what I have to say to my elder Brothers. It seems as fresh in my mind as if it was only two nights ago since we had our last Talk. Our beloved man has been to see Your beloved man of Virginia. Now I have seen You my elder Brothers which makes me glad

Chapter Three
Governor's Office

and its augmented by our beloved mans return to us. I have now fast hold of You by the hand and will not let loose my hold. I am now verry thankful to the powers above that the people of my elder Brother and my own people are now got here to this place; a place which I have come to with all my people to make all things Straight. My heart is good to all my Brothers, but I am sorry I have been a little short in coming here. There was so many days appointed for my beloved man to go and see our beloved elder Brother of Virginia and likewise to return in, which they did not according to the appointed time. But now we are here together in order to make all things Straight. Yesterday You and I had Talks together; You said it was what I would to bring on the business which I do not desire because You are the elder Brothers. All our principal men are now here and tomorrow morning if You please You may bring on the principal Talks. There are many of my people desirous to return home again, and I would be glad how soon the business might come on that they may go to work in their fields which are now Suffering for want of Labour.

A String of Beads

The Commissioners postponed the business near two days waiting the return of Messrs. Avery & Winston

13th July the Potclay Chief of Chilhowey and the Pidgeon of Notchy Creek being Deputed by the Chiefs of the Cherokees now on the Long Island to have a Conference with the Commissioners on the subject of the late Murder of the Big Bullett in order that the whole matter may be done away and the Blood washed off before the Treaty is Opened which is proposed to be tomorrow. To whom the Commissioners spoke as follows.

Brethren,
    We Your Brothers of Virginia and North Carolina are extremely sorry for the accident that happened in the murder of the Big Bullet by one of our wicked men. We have already declared to your beloved man, and we now declare to you that it was done Contrary to our intention; and that we were altogether strangers to it and we also assure You that we have done every thing on our power to discover the murderer and have him tried and punished by our Laws, for the Great Being above hath said that whosoever shedeth Mans Blood, by man shall his Blood be shed. We now take the Ball out of his Body and bury it deep in the ground, that no uneasiness or remembrance thereof may remain in Your minds, and that

Chapter Three
Governor's Office

Your hearts may beat rest while You sit at our Council Fire. With these few goods we Cover the ground when this unfortunate man fell, and the grave in which he is laid, that the places never more be known or remembered by his friends and relations, and that their Tears may be wiped away, and that no drops of his Blood may fall into our Council Fire, or on the chain of friendship that links us together, but that all may be washed off. And that we shall not drop our Enquiry after the murderer as we abhor both him and the crime he has done.
Three match Coats & three Shirts

These Deputies returned to their Camp on the Island and after some time spent, they with about twelve other Chiefs returned to the Fort; and after spreading the three match Coats on two Benches and seating the Commissioners and Oconostota & Attakullakulla thereon; The Potclay spoke as follows.

My elder Brothers
Are now going to hear what I have to say to them. These Warriors now sitting here have prepared to let you hear a particular Talk, because they did send the good Talks to Chota by the woman messenger, which all my beloved men and Warriors accepted, received gladly and thought verry good. On receiving the Talks at Chota, I rose up to go and make reply to it. The Doors were all shut, were dark, but I opened them, and made the path light for them to pass along. I found the seats that had been prepared, for our beloved men to have the good talks on, were lying here in the Grass. I lighted up the pipe of friendship from off them; opened all strong Gates in the way, and went to see the Governor of Virginia. I opened and made the way clear. One of the beloved men of Virginia took me by the hand, and led me and my great beloved man to the great beloved man of Virginia, who sit him down on his Great Seat of friendship & Justice. We found it a beloved place of friendship, which we never knew before; till we were placed on that seat. Now our beloved man has been led in the same manner back safe to this place. My Great friend and Brother hath led my Great beloved man safe to this place from the Great man of Virginia; Where he had been brightning the Great chain of friendship so bright that its brightness might reach the skies. When we had got to this place, the Chain happened to turn a little, and one of our men fell, but that shall make no odds; all the Warriors have agreed it shall not, and that they will hold the chain verry fast and Strong. I look upon it as permitted by the Great Being above that this accident happened.

Chapter Three
Governor's Office

A String of Beads

Then the Mankiller of Great Highwassee rose and spoke as follows.

    I am now going to speak to You my elder Brothers tis a desolate place where we first took hold of each other, and went to the Great seat of Justice. I now mean to return thanks for the kind treatment received on the journey. I am verry glad to see that my Great friend and Brother has taken such particular Care of my Great beloved man. I find that it was not by his desire or that of any of my elder Brothers people, the late accident happened; for we are still drawing the same breath of light, every day with you, and sitting on the same seats round the same Fire. We cannot blame the Great Supreme Being above for the accident that has happened. I've heard it said that this Great Being sent a beloved man to us to make mens minds peacible, and at the same time sent likewise a Bad man to the Earth, who I blame as the author of this mischief. But the first Great man is now clearing and taking it all away and turning it all to good. Now I'm convinced twas that bad man who was sent to Earth, who put it into the mind of the bad white man to do this Act; and pluck away the Great bright chain which bound us together. But now every drop of Blood is wiped from off this chain so that not a speck remains thereon, and I give you this in Confirmation thereof.

A String of Beads

I am now going to speak to my Brothers of North Carolina who were here likewise when this accident happened, and confirm to them what has been said to my Brothers of Virginia, and to assure them it is all done away, and shall no more be thought of, for I have thrown away all thoughts thereof into the Swift running water which must Carry it Clean away. I am convinced in my own Breast it is not the Great Being above, but the wicked one who put it into the heart of the wit minded White man to do this Act. The Good being is all sufficient all powerful and good, and is a lover of all Flesh; and would not do it. He let down a Great stake and fastened it deep in the Ground; it was a wood that would never rot but stand there always. This was for all good men to take hold of and hold fast by. But the bad man is frequently laying Stones and chunks in the way of bad men for them to stumble over.

A String of Beads

July 14th 1777 Present in Council
William Christian   }

Chapter Three
Governor's Office

William Preston   } Commissioners for Virginia

Waightstill Avery   }
William Sharp   }
Robert Lanier   } Commissioners for North Carolina
Joseph Winston   }

Col. Nathaniel Gist on business from General Washington

Oconostoto   }
   &   } of Chota
The Raven   }

Atta Kulla Kulla   }
Big White Owl   } of Notchey Creek
Pidgeon   }

The Old Tassel   }
Willanawaw   } of Toguse
To Tac Ka Ch   }

Pot Clay   }
Abram   } of Chilhowey

Utaseh or Norward Warrior}
Creek Killer   } of Tellicho and a new
Chesnut   } Town at its mouth
Raven   }

Mankiller   }
Queluca   } of Highwasaw
Tarapine   }

Sunnuah   }
Skeyuca   }of the Island Town
Skia Tu Ka   } & Cetico

In He Ke Hiyah   }
An Nu Chah   } of Tuskuga

Chapter Three
Governor's Office

Chow, We, Hah a messenger from the Valey Settlements
To hear what should be done.

Joseph Vann and Charles Murphy Interpreters.
Major Daniel Smith Clerk

Col. Christian opened the Conference with the following speech.
Friends and Brethren, Beloved man and Chiefs of the Warlike Nation of the Cherokees.

    We Your Brethren of Virginia are rejoiced to see You once more sitting round the Council Fire, which was kindled at this place last spring, and which burns brighter and Clearer by our frequent meetings before it and that we have the pleasure to see the Great Chain which binds us together made stronger and our friendship enlarged by the addition of our Brethren of No. Carolina who are now sitting in Council with us, and who we are assured Came heartily disposed to strengthen and brighten the Chain, to put an end to a short tho destructive War, and to confirm a Lasting, Just and Honorable Peace. We hope that our meetings will be frequent and friendly, and that our Children will sit round this fire when we shall be no more. We Your Brothers of Virginia flatter ourselves that the treatment that Your beloved man and his Warriors and friends met with from our Governor, and on their long Journey to and from Wms.burgh has given them the greatest satisfaction; and we hope You are pleased that we have led them by the hand in safety to this place, and that we have delivered them into the bosom of their friends without any violence or insult being offered them during more than sixty days they were under our immediate Care. We on our part are pleased that our Common friend Colo. Gist and the young Gentleman who went with him into Your Country are returned safe to their friends and that they were well treated while they were there. This mutual Confidence will convince our common enemies that the white people and Cherokees are one people fastened together by the strongest bands of friendship and interest.
    Brethren, we have taken every method in our power to supply You, and we have it in command from our Governor to assure You, that as soon as our trade which has been greatly interupted by the War with England is on a better footing, You may expect a farther and more ample supply of goods.

Chapter Three
Governor's Office

We have also endeavoured to relieve the distress of Your people by a timely supply of provisions, salt, powder, lead and other necessaries in a larger and fuller manner than we have done our own frontier people who were sufferers by the War. This War and these distresses You were unhappily involved in by the advice of the Norward Indians and bad men among Yourselves, who persuaded Your Young men to begin a War contrary to the advice of Your old wise beloved men and Warriors whose hearts was good towards the white people.

But we now hope Your Young men have seen their error, and that for the future they will listen to the advice of their fathers and the old wise men, and pay no more regard to any bad men who may be amongst You or to any who will send letters to You to engage Your Nation any more in a War with Your elder Brothers the white people. You may now be convinced by our whole conduct since the War and even when our Army part of which belonged to North Carolina was in Your Country, how desirous and ready we have been to renew our ancient friendship and to be at peace with the Cherokees. You remember the talks we had here last Spring when we laid the foundation of a peace between You and Your elder Brothers the white people. In Confirmation of what I have now said I give You this String of Wampum

Brothers
    We are now met in full Council to build up that peace and make it strong and lasting; so strong that our greatest enemies Cannot break it, and so lasting that our Children Yet unborn may mutually enjoy the blessings and benefits of it. This is our design in meeting You here; and we expect You are Come to this place with the same intentions. The Great Being above who made us all, and who gave understanding to men, hath put it into all our hearts to meet here this day to put and end to a destructive War, by a firm and honorable peace; and we hope he will look down upon us with pleasure while we are engaged in so desirable a work, for he is a God of peace and does not delight in War tho he often permits it. In order to bring about this happy event we once more invite You to open your whole hearts, let all your complaints and grievances be made known without reserve and hide nothing from us, and we will do the same with you. As this is the surest method to heal all differences that have subsisted or subsist amongst us. We are fully authorized by the Governor of Virginia to fix a Boundary between Your Country and the white people, and to settle a firm peace with Your Nation for the benefit of Your people as well as ours.

Chapter Three
Governor's Office

     Tho' we have been here some time we waited with patience as we know Your journey was long and that You Could not all be here at the day appointed. In the mean time we have had the pleasure of talking with your beloved men eating, drinking and dancing with our Young men like friends and Brothers.

     We are verry sorry that Judge friend, the draging Canoe, the lying Fish and Young Tassel are not come to the Treaty as we expected they might have been of use in Your Council; but as You assure us there are Warriors here to represent all Your Towns and that you are fully authorized by Your people to Confirm the peace, we shall go on with that important business.

     In Confirmation that our hearts are good towards the Cherokees and that what we have said is truth we give You this String of Wampum.

                            A String

Mr. Avery then delivered the following speech.

     Friends and Brethren beloved Man and Chiefs of the Warlike Nation of the Cherokees.

     We Your Brothers of North Carolina are appointed by the Governor and Council of that Country to meet You at this place to hear Your talks and if Your talks and hearts are good toward the white people, we have power to join with our Brothers of Virginia to make a firm and lasting peace with You for the benefit of Your people and our people.

     We rejoice to see You all at the Council fire and to hear of the friendly intercourse between You and Your Brothers of Virginia.

     We rejoice that Your beloved man and some of his people have made a visit to the beloved man of Virginia & have returned in safety.

     It was that Your hearts would last Year to make War with us, but we are now glad to hear that You want to make peace. Your Nation begun the War and made the path dark towards three Countries (Virginia, No. Carolina and South Carolina) You made the path dark and bloody; the Warriors of these three Countries have now traveled in the path which you made dark and bloody, but we are glad to hear that Your Nation and South Carolina have washed the blood out of the path and that your Nation and the Virginians are now washing the path bright and clear between Your Countries.

     If Your hearts are good we are willing that the paths every where between Your Country and North Carolina should be made light and clear also.

Chapter Three
Governor's Office

We are glad to hear that a chain of friendship is established one end in Your Nation and the other end in Charles Town & that another chain of friendship is fixed one end in Chote and the other end in Wms.burgh.

We have power and are willing to establish another chain the one end in Chote and the other end in Newbern. We have power to Carry one end to our Governor in Newbern and he is there ready to take hold and hold it fast. Your elder Brothers of North Carolina were not first to make peace, nor will they be first to break it, but will be steady and faithful friends.

Brothers, as we came from our beloved man below we desire to hear what our brothers the Cherokees have to say; as You struck first and made the path dark, it is necessary that You should begin to Clear it up. We desire You to open Your hearts and freely make known to us and our brothers of Virginia all Your Complaints and grievances, and we will listen and hear and will endeavour to redress them and do you Justice.

To convince You that our hearts are good and that we are willing to make peace with you, we give you this string of Wampum.

A String

July 15th 1777

Present as yesterday and Col. Shelby also, A letter from Col. Williamson of South Carolina a speech of the Commissioners for South Carolina and Georgia to the Creeks and their answer thereto, as also the articles of a Treaty between South Carolina & Georgia and the middle Valley and lower Towns of the Cherokees were read and interpreted to the Indians.

Colo. Williamsons answer to Colo. Prestons letter of the 28th June last is as follows:

White Hall July 5th 1777
Sir,

A Copy of your letter to Genl. Rutherford of the 28th June was just now delivered to me the contents of which is verry alarming. But from all the inteligence I Can Collect I have the greatest reason to believe the inteligence given by Colo. Gist is ill founded. What I think is a Cinvincing proof that the Creeks are not disposed to break with us so readily; was their

Chapter Three
Governor's Office

readiness to agree to and meet the Georgia Commissioners in Congress at Mr. Galphins Cowpen at Oguchy in that State, the 5th of last month a copy of the talks are herewith forwarded. Eleven of the principle head men of the Creeks are now on the road (with Mr. Galphen) to Charlestown to visit the president and settle some matters in regard to the trade opened with them from Sd. State; during their absence below I cannot imagine these people will adopt unfriendly measures, from all these considerations and letters just received from Charlestown, which gives not the least hint of troops being expected on the Coast, I think this news must have been fabricated by some Emisary of Stuart or his party merely with a View to disturb the frontier settlers of the Southern States. Altho times wear a promising aspect, we should be on our guard, and I heartily thank You for your early Communication of this matter. Mr. Gist mentioned it to me in a letter dated Chote the 9th of June but not so particularly, Copy of which with other advices I this day dispatched by express to Charlestown to his Excellency the President. Mr Galphin writes me a few days ago that the Big fellow with a small party of disaffected Creek Indians were just returned from an excursion down about Holston River & brought with them one Scalp; but the head men who attended the Congress said if he & his party did not immediately lay down the hatchet they would spoil the path to Pensacola.

    Herewith I send you the latest Gazette from Charlestown which contains the articles of the definitive Treaty of peace entered into by the Commissioners from this State and Georgia with the Cherokees Deputies at Dewits Corner where six hundred and three Indians attended of all denominations.

    I am with respect
        Sir your mo obt. Humbl. Servt.
        A. Williamson

Articles of the definitive Treaty of Peace Concluded on and signed at Dewits Corner the 20th day of May 1777 between the States of So. Carolina and Georgia and the Cherokee Indians.

Article 1st The Cherokee Nation acknowledge that the Troops that during the last Summer repeatedly defeated their forces, victoriously penetrated through their lower Towns middle Settlements and Vallies, and quietly and unopposed, built, held and continue to hold the Fort at Seneca, thereby did effect and maintain the Conquest of all the Cherokee lands, eastward of the Unacay Mountain; and to and for their people did acquire possess, and yet

Chapter Three
Governor's Office

Continue, to hold in and over the said lands all and singular the rights incidental to Conquest; and the Cherokee Nation in Consequence thereof do cede the said lands to the said people, the people of South Carolina.

Article 2nd South Carolina will immediately send a supply of goods into the Cherokee Nation and settlements for sale and permit the Cherokees during their good behaviour to inhabit the middle settlements and Valies westward of the highest part of the Occonnee Mountain; but they shall not beyond a line extended South West and North East a cross the highest part of the Occonnee Mountain, proceed or advance without permission from the commanding Officer at Fort Rutledge, to apply for which one runner may at any time be sent by the Cherokees: provided never the less that during this present Year the Cherokees may raise gather and remove the Corn they have planted on the East side of the Occonnee Mountain.

Article 3rd The Government of South Carolina will endeavour that the Cherokees be furnished with supplies of goods as usual; and that the trade will be put under the best regulations. Every person who, without a proper pass or licence shall arrive in the Cherokee Nation or Settlements the Cherokees shall immediately apprehend and deliver to the Commanding Officer at Fort Rutledge, and Seize to their own up all the cattle, Horses, goods, and effects conducted into their Settlement by every such person.

Article 4th Every white person who instigated or endeavoured to instigate the Cherokees to the late War or encouraged or aided them, or endeavoured to do so in the prosecution of it, and who now is or hereafter may be in their power shall without delay, by the Cherokees be apprehended and delivered to the Commanding Officer at Fort Rutledge; and the Cherokees shall take to their own use all the effects which in their Nation or Settlements they may find in the possession of or belonging to every such white person. And for every such white person so delivered, shall be paid five hundred pounds weight of dressed leather or the value thereof.

Article 5th Any Indian who in the Cherokee Nation or Settlements shall murder a white person shall be immediately apprehended and conveyed to Fort Rutledge by the Cherokees who in presence of the Commanding Officer at that fort, shall put the murderer to death; and if any white or other person belonging to South Carolina or Georgia, shall in the Cherokee Nation or any white or other person shall in South Carolina or Georgia murder a Cherokee Indian, every such person, duly convicted thereof shall

Chapter Three
Governor's Office

suffer death in presence of the Cherokee Indians, if any shall attend at the time and place of execution; and that they may have an opportunity of attending, due Notice of the time and place of such intended execution shall be sent to the Cherokees.

Article 6th All White and Indian persons shall be set at liberty as soon as possible; all Negroes taken during the late War and who now are or hereafter may be in the power of the Cherokees, shall as soon as possible be delivered up to the Commanding Officer at Fort Rutledge, together with the horses by any of their people before the late War stolen from South Carolina, Georgia, North Carolina or Virginia, and which now are or hereafter may be in the power of the Cherokees, to the end that restitution may be made to their true owners.

Article 7th For every runaway Negroe that shall be apprehended and delivered by the Cherokees to the Commanding Officer at Fort Rutledge shall be paid one hundred weight of leather, or the value thereof.

Article 8th The hatchet shall be forever buried and there shall be a universal peace and friendship reestablished between South Carolina including the Catawba and Georgia on one part and the Cherokee Nation on the other; there shall be a general oblivion of injuries; the Contracting parties shall use their utmost endeavours to maintain the peace and friendship now established, and the Cherokees shall at all times apprehend and deliver to the Commanding Officer at Fort Rutledge, every person white or red, who in their Nation or Settlements, shall by any means endeavour to instigate a War by the Cherokee Nation, or hostility, or roberry by any of their people, against or upon any of the American States, or subjects thereof.

    In Witness of all and every thing herein determined between South Carolina, Georgia and the Cherokee Nation, we their under written Commissioners and Deputies by virtue of our full powers, severally, and not one for the other, have signed this present definitive Treaty, in their respective Names, and have caused our Seals to be hereunto affixed.
    Done at Dewits Corner this twentieth day of May in the year of our Lord one thousand seven hundred and seventy Seven

Andrew Williamson   }
Leroy Hammond   }Commissioners for So. Carolina

Chapter Three
Governor's Office

William Henry Drayton }
D. Horry }

Jonathan Bryan }
Jonathan Cochran } Commissioners for Georgia
William Glascock }

Oustassittee }
Canaliskeeticowee }
Cleronakee }
Skullaluska }
Cloooketa } Cherokee Deputies
Choownatee }
Ooskuah }
Chinistiska }

Then Oconostoto informed the Commissioners that the Old Tassel and Old Raven were the Chief Speakers for him and the whole Nation that to them he had resigned his power on account of his age, but if they ever should speak contrary to his sentiments he would put them right.

   The Old Raven then rose and spoke as follows. Now my elder Brothers shall hear what I have to say. It has been several days since my elder Brother brought my beloved man here. I was pleased to hear the good talks Yesterday from all the beloved men who came here to meet us. It has been several days since You returned from the fatague and trouble of bringing my beloved man here, for which I am verry thankful, and also much pleased to see we all here are of one mind. I am come and I find every thing agreeable; I brought all the Young Warriors and many people belonging to my Nation to hear this good talk (here he handed one end of the belt which the old Warrior had got from the Governor, to Col Christian and held the other end himself) It has been a considerable time since my elder Brother took my beloved man and led him to this Great Seat of Justice and back again here ready to conclude all the good talks heretofore entered upon. I give You hold of one end of this Belt which I hold the other, an I never will let it go, but hold it fast forever. This is the bright chain of friendship which we have hold of, not only us but the Young ones on both sides, even the Children yet unborn have hold of it through us, and shall be fast linked together by it.

Chapter Three
Governor's Office

    This is the Great chain of friendship which the Great beloved man of Virginia ordered should be taken hold of by us his Children; it is a light for those Yet unborn what is done at this place; It was ordered by the Great beloved man of Virginia that it should be held fast by both of us everlastingly. The Great man above put it into his heart to do so, that it might be a light for both of our people to walk by; I join You all heart and hand. (here he withdrew the belt) yesterday You spoke to me that I should particularly open all my grievances, by which I understood You were taking pity on me, for which I am verry thankful, and as both Your Talks are good alike, You shall hear them. You said that You had my beloved man here some days, and that You waited patiently untill the rest of us come by passing the time away by seeing both our Young folks dancing and playing together. Now I have come myself and return you my thanks for the kind treatment given to my beloved man. This is the spot where we took hold of each other, on which the white seats of Justice were first placed and the peace fire kindled up. I am only the Younger Brother but yet I know how to keep these white seats of Justice fast here where they are set. And I will do it, as this is the place where the Seats of Friendship are; the place where each of us have taken hold of one another, it being put into all our hearts to do so by the Great man above. I am determined to keep this light of friendship always fresh in my mind even as now. Three beloved men are talking together Virginia, Carolina & Chote all talking the peace talks together; on my own part I never will neglect the least particular of this Peace, but observe every part thereof verry faithfully; each beloved man will confirm the same for the quiet and safety of all three parties. I have no more beloved men behind to tell every thing that is done to, but You have and I rely that You will make everything known that is done here to Your Great beloved men below. My elder Brothers of Carolina will open the doors of peace as well as Virginia, that we may see each other clearly, and that they may stand open everlastingly; You my elder Brothers was talking to me yesterday at this time of day, I listened attentively; You desired me to open my heart and make known my grievances; I should have been glad if they had reached your ears long ago, but I believe all talks that I ever made that way were spoiled; but now I believe you will do me Justice, for which I shall be verry thankful. I believe that long before my remembrance this land was first found out, the time you know as you have writings; but I do not know when the first settlements were made on these waters; but I believe they were before my remembrance, by the time these Meddles were given to us, (Shewing a Meddle) ever since these have been among us we have been more and

Chapter Three
Governor's Office

more distressed; my grievances have been for several years. The beloved man which I had in my land some time ago used to give us talks which I thought were verry good, but I believe now they were bad and never went to You or Your beloved men. We were kept in blindness by him and no grievances redressed which he frequently promised should be done. He told us that when he found any of Your people on our land to take their guns, Horses and every thing they had and said if we killed them no harm would Come of it, which advice I followed and it had like to have been my ruin. But I find that my elder Brothers know my poverty You are the beloved men, I ought to have applied to You before for I see You take pity on me; You desire me to open my heart, I'll hide nothing from you, which when I've done I'll leave You to consider on. You my elder Brothers took me by the hand and told me to sit still and not believe any of their lies. I believe, all Your talks were straight and good. There is another red people on the frontiers of Virginia who we are not at War with we talked together. They did not stay long with me, but went to the woods; I told them I was Coming here; perhaps some of my elder Brothers may suspect I encouraged them to hurt You; I have no private place about my body to hide any thing if I had done so. Tis my heart I am opening to You.

I shall make short my talks, for many words are not necessary to come to the truth, all my people knows this to be a truth & I hope yours do likewise.

A String

Now my elder Brothers are going to hear the last of the talk I shall deliver to day. The Great beloved man of Virginia spoke to mine who went to see him and said "Now my friend & Brother I take you by the hand here is my Friend who will lead you to the rest of your people; there the people of North Carolina will meet you likewise, and fix a hard and lasting Boundary between Your and their Countries for I find you have been much wronged" I hope this Boundary will be made so that it may not be crossed without consent being first had.

A String

I have now said all I can say to the purpose, I don't care how soon I could be going home for I have a bad enemy in my corn field, I want to go and turn him out. (meaning weeds) The peace and safety of both parties was made before we came here. We only come to shew You our good will and to meet our beloved man.

Chapter Three
Governor's Office

The Old Tassell then rose and adressing himself to the Commissioners of Virginia (after shaking hand) Spoke as follows:

    It is the third moon since we first took hold of each other by the hand, which was ordered by the Great man above, and You remember what talks we had together; I spoke freely from my heart that it might sink deeper into Yours; as we were making the peace when I was here before, my friends you said this was the bloody path, I have said that all the flesh wasted on both sides should be thought of no more, but as if they had been buried so long ago that a large tree had grown upon the grave. Twas You and me had this talk when we were concluding peace. It shall be an everlasting peace. It was so ordered by the great man above and for that reason we will be the last to break it, altho a wicked white man did spill a little blood which shall no more be thought of. Now all my elder Brothers have heard both beginning and end of our talks. I expect there will be no interuption for any of either people to go where they please, These beads are for Colo. Gist to take to the Norward

                                    A String to Colo. Gist

    I remember what you said Concerning the letters from Colo. Williamson who I know verry well, I heard all you said on this matter before, and also that Colo. Williamson had been through all our Country, and that he wanted the land as far as the Seneca. I remember all the talks which my people said they had with Colo. Williamson. When he said he wanted the land as far as the Unacay Mountain, our people said they would consider of it. I live in Toqua and my beloved people in Chote, we did not go far away and Came back again these middle Settlement people did so too, and I don't see how they can claim the land by that, for we drove the white people from their houses too. Many of them people have been to that treaty but chiefly women and children they returned from there naked as my hand and crying with hunger by which it appeared that they only wanted our land and not to make peace. The beloved men of Virginia now here I suppose are good men sent by their Great beloved man. I think the same of my Brothers of North Carolina. Now I hope Your Great beloved men will take pity on us and do us Justice, as our provisions is chiefly destroyed, and give us a little room, because Your people have encroached upon us verry close and scarcely given us room to turn round. I've been talking with the beloved men of Virginia, and I hope nothing will break the good talks we have had together. My Brothers of North Carolina were not

Chapter Three
Governor's Office

here before to hear the good talks, but these they hear and I hope all three of us will observe them.

Colo. Christian in behalf of the Commissioners then spoke as follows:

> Brethren, Our Governor the beloved men of Virginia and North Carolina have given us their Commissioners full power and authority to settle a peace and fix a boundary line between the Overhill Cherokees (as the middle and lower Settlements are not represented here) and their own Countries, in the same manner as if they were both present, this important part of the peace now making between us we ought to go fully and clearly into at this time, that nothing might be left to occasion disputes hereafter. But that every thing in our power may be now done and finished, to make the peace firm and the boundary lasting and that every obstacle thereto may be removed and thrown out of the way.
> We would now desire to be informed what people they were that have settled on your lands by whom you have been injured and at what time, that it may be in our power to give you an answer which we shall do tomorrow morning at which time we shall propose a boundary.

July 15th, in the evening, Present as before.
The Raven then spoke as follows.

> As you gave me the opportunity to consult all my people about the matter proposed, I have got all their opinions since we broke up a while ago, there is a great many of my people waiting at home to here what is to be done here. The Great beloved man of Virginia took pity of us and sent for us here to settle every thing well and clear. You shall hear what we have concluded on and shall leave Yourselves to judge of it till morning. As the beloved man of Virginia has taken pity of us from the greatest to the smallest; and the beloved men here from both States, who we are thankful to hear, and hope they will take upon themselves to do us Justice, We have been trespassed upon by bodies of people on our hunting grounds. The Great beloved man desired that a boundary line should be run between us and the white people, and said that Colo. Shelby lived near the line and was to see that each party kept on their own side of the line. Here is the Long Island where we are talking the peace talks and where we have the white Seats of Justice, and the beloved fire; let this place never be removed but kept for Justice, and the peace talks; let these Seats and this fire always remain fast here on this particular Spot of ground. If you fix upon a boundary and have it run I don't want Your people that have grain

Chapter Three
Governor's Office

in the ground to remove till their grain is ripe; let their grain first be ripe and then remove.

If the beloved men think fit let the West line be extended to the North fork and from thence to the great gap in Cumberland Mountain.

The proposal that I shall make to North Carolina shall be that the line where it struck the River above Colo. Shelbys shall run from thence a South course. The Nonachuckey people have extended much down that River and on several Creeks.

They are the people we want moved off, and some about the mouth of Watauga. There is Chilhowey and Cettico that have their Hunting grounds Chiefly up Nonachuckey that is the course they hunt and never down the River. If I can Carry home the news that these people are to be removed, they will be verry thankful.

Mr. Avery then interogated them as follows.

We take notice that the Indians complain of encroachments on Watauga & Nonachuckey, do You complain of all Watauga?

(The Raven) We complain only of the lower part as high up as Colo. Carters and Nonachuckee.

Mr. Avery) do you complain of all Nonachuckee?

Raven) We complain of above and below Browns and Tuskiga old Towns.

Mr. Avery) did not the white people settle there by Your consent?

Raven) They did, but fear only made us agree to it and we expected redress again, but the white people instead of stoping where they were; encroached still farther and father; fear only made us agree to a settlement at all, but we expected Government would again remedy us.

Mr. Avery) did You not afterwards agree to sell those lands and receive pay for them?

Oconostoto) I told the Watauga & Nonachuckie people that I would send talks to my Father over the water (it was then good times) I told these people that if he agreed to it, then they must stay, but that his consent must be had. They gave us guns, but as they made a great deal of grain raised

Chapter Three
Governor's Office

stock and destroyed our hunting. I told them that we could not take pay for the lands but the rent only.

A memorial of Colo. Richard Henderson and Company was presented to the Commissioners of Virginia & North Carolina relating to their purchase of land from the Indians which they have ordered to be entered on the Journal of their proceedings immediately after this; and they are unanimously of opinion that as they have no instructions from their respective Governments to enquire into the Validity of private purchases from the Cherokees, and as they are fully satisfied that if the Commissioners were now to interfere with the Indians to support the private Claims mentioned in the said memorial, it would at this critical time be attended with bad consequences to the Treaty of peace now carrying on with that Nation; And as the matter does not properly come before them, they ought not to take any notice of the memorial in any of their Conferences with these people

The Memorial.

To the Gentlemen Commissioners appointed by the States of Virginia, North Carolina & South Carolina, to negociate a peace and settle a boundary between the Cherokee Indians and the white people.

The memorial of Richard Henderson, Thomas Hart, Nathaniel Hart, John Williams, William Johnston, John Luttrell, James Hogg, David Hart, and Leo: Hen: Bullock, sheweth.

That Your memorialists did on the seventeenth day of March in the Year of our Lord one thousand seven hundred and seventy five purchase of the said Cherokee Indians in fair and open Treaty a large tract or territory of land lying on the Ohio and Branches thereof and immediately adjoining the line lately run by Colo. Donelson as a boundary between the Virginians and the said Cherokees, which was at that time Conveyed by two separate deeds from the said Cherokees to Your Memorialists; by which said purchase and deeds all the lands below or on the South East side of Kentuckie or Louisa River up the head thereof ot to where Colo. Donelsons line crosses or strikes the same, thence along said Donelsons line to Holston River six miles above the Long Island, thence down the said River to where the course of Powels Mountain strikes or intersects the same, thence North Eastwardly along Powels Mountain or the course thereof to a point from which a North West course will strike

Chapter Three
Governor's Office

the head of the most Southwardly Branch of Cumberland River, thence down the said River including all its waters to the Ohio, thence up the Ohio to the mouth of the said Kentuckie or Louisa River, were Granted and Conveyed to Your Memorialists with free liberty of forming immediate settlements thereon without the least disturbance or molestation of them the said Indians.

And whereas the settling and agreeing on a Boundary line between the said Indians and white people seems to be a principle object under Your Consideration, and what we suppose You have full power to perform. We hope regard will be had to our said purchase, so far as not to permit the Indians to reclaim the lands or any part thereof, which by consent of the whole Nation they so fairly sold and willingly gave up.

Your memorialists conceive with great difference to the Gentlemen Commissioners, that the Cherokees cannot nor in Justice ought not to enter on the lands, on the North side of Holston or hunt thereon above where the course of Powels Mountain intersects the said River, nor in any manner be permitted to enter on the land sold as aforesaid to your memorialists.

Your Memorialists acknowledge that some of the good people of Virginia have given out in speeches that the lands so bought of the Cherokees were not of the property of Your Memorialists, but belonged to that State or Commonwealth; that in Consequence of such claim the matter is to be heard on third Monday in their next Session of Assembly, at which time Your Memorialists have no doubt but that Assembly will disclaim all pretentions to the lands in dispute, and the title of Your Memorialists become firmly and indisputably established.

As the Treaty and purchase are matters of public notoriety and the depositions respecting that matter are now in possession of the Virginia Assembly so they cannot at this time be laid before the Commissioners for Treating and Settling a boundary between the Cherokees and white people.

Your Memorialists hope that the Commissioners will not proceed to run a line through their purchase, or Yield any part of the lands contained therein to the Indians as it will be a manifest injury to private property, and what no law or policy whatever can require, as the Indians Voluntarily and for a valuable Consideration gave them up, and after a most deliberate consultation agreed forever thereafter to restrain themselves from reclaiming or demanding the lands in question.
June 18th 1777
John Luttrell, James Hogg, David Hart, Leo: Hen: Bullock, Richard Henderson, Thomas Hart, Natl. Hart, John Williams & William Johnston.

Chapter Three
Governor's Office

July 16th 1777 Present as Yesterday
Colo. Christian spoke as follows:

Friends and Brethren
  We Your Brothers of Virginia could reddily give You reasons why the lands on this River were settled by white people, and shew that the good old King over the water granted these lands to us who were his subjects, and give us great encouragement from time to time to settle ourselves and families thereon, we could also shew You that this present King who has endeavoured to enslave his people, could find no other way to break these Grants than by ordering his servants Stewart and Cameron to tell You that the white people had settled these lands without his consent, and to desire You to drive them off or kill them, this was one reason why you went to War, by which you have been so much sufferers.
  But to convince you more and more that we want to do you the Strictest Justice as well as our own people who settled this River and planted corn last year; and go so low on the River as to take in these settlements and to run a straight line from the River to a point two or three miles below Cumberland gap, that our road to our settlements on the Kentuckie (a country we long ago bought of the No. ward Indians) may be open and that our people may travel to and from that country unmolested, and without doing You any damages. This boundary will fully satisfy your elder Brothers of Virginia; it is all he desired us to ask, and but a verry little more than you yourselves offered last night. The lands that will fall within the lines we have proposed, produce but little game to your Hunters and therefore cannot be of much service to your Nation, and this boundary will stand firm and unshaken through many generations; as our Governor will recommend it to the Great Council of Virginia to make laws to punish any white man who will settle below it within the limits of Virginia, or by any means attempt to injure You in the peaceable possession thereof. We shall also recommend it to our Governor to order the line from the River below the plantations to the Mountain three miles below Cumberland Gap to be run as soon as the season of the Year will admit, which we suppose will be in the fall, or it may be done now if you desire it. By abiding to this line a final end will be put to all our differences and the Cherokees & Virginia be lasting friends. We desire to inform You that we do not wish to oblige or force you to comply with this demand, for should you believe it unjust or hurtful to Your Nation, and therein differ in opinion from us we

Chapter Three
Governor's Office

would desire you to tell us freely and without reserve in the same manner as if we were sitting round your Council fire in Chote. You may be assured that we did not send for you to this place in order to take any advantages of your distance from home or weakness here. We consider you as a Great Nation met with us in free and open Treaty; and you may be assured that we will protect you from all harm and conduct you Safe to Your Country; and that altho we may differ in opinion we will do you all the Service we can: therefore whatever You do or say on this important article of our Treaty we hope you will do it from your heart and speak your sentiments without fear or reserve.

We desire in the name of Virginia if this line is agreed on that for the future You shall not consent that any white people shall settle on your side thereof on any account whatsoever within the limits of Virginia without the Concurrence of the Governor or his Commissioners appointed for that purpose: So that you ought not to sell, rent, or make any agreement whatsoever with private persons respecting the Lands aforesaid or give them the least encouragement to settle or hunt therein or even keep their stocks of Cattle or Horses within Your Country. And should any wicked white man attempt such a thing You are to give us notice thereof and we shall order a party to bring him off and punish him.

A Double String

The Warriors then withdrew for a short time to consult each other and after returning the old Raven spoke as follows:

Friends and Brothers

I am going to speak to you because it is a general talk. Yesterday you heard all the sentiments of my heart. I left you last night to consider what I said to you. You desired me to consider a proper Boundary; and you now propose another to go a little farther than I mentioned. As my friends and Brothers are talking together they are to declare every thing in truth to each other. I understand from my friend it was by the old Great Man over the water that my land was settled; but I know nothing of it. The time is fresh in both our memories when he was sitting on the Throne and if the land ever belonged to him its more than I knew of. You and I were talking last night together on the subject of the Boundary line and I told You what I thought a proper place. You propose a line that goes beyond what I mentioned and binds verry close upon me. My people have many minds about it and I cannot readily agree that the line You propose shall be established. One of the greatest grievances that I complained of was that

Chapter Three
Governor's Office

of encroachments on our lands. But let not this hurt our peace talks. It was the desire of the great beloved man of Virginia that a firm boundary should be made between the elder and Younger Brothers and altho there is a little odds in our opinions let it not spoil our peace. It is often times the case when one Brother wants a thing which another sets store by that the first desires hard to get it; but if they are affectionate Brothers it is no odds. I hope nothing will be carried to the Governor of Virginia but whats agreeable to him; altho I cant agree to the demand that is made. I own I was a little Surprized when I heard what my friend said just now. But I confess I ought not as he told me at the same time that both me and my people should be safe, which was not the case some years ago. This matter is a little misterious and I cannot give you a clear answer. But I hope you will reconsider the matter and reflect that it is one of my greatest grievances. I hope you will take no resentment at this my objection as from the talks we have just had, I have no reason to think you will. What I desire is that You would reconsider the matter and I will consult my people likewise.

Returned the String

      Down this River is the place that causes some of my Warriors to object; but it will not spoil our good talks. We want to fix a firm and lasting Boundary. When this is once done my people will know where it is and they shall not trespass upon you.

Mr. Avery then spoke as follows:
      Beloved man and Chiefs of the Cherokee Nation. Brothers you have complained to us that the people of North Carolina have encroached on your lands. Now listen and hear what your Brothers of North Carolina have to say to you.
      Many years ago the Governor of North Carolina, who you Called the Big Wolf (Governor Tryon) agreed with your Nation, and fixed a line between your and our people. And so long as both Nations lived in peace our Governor and Council did not order any settlement, to be made over that line. If any such had been made without your consent, you ought to have complained to our Governor and Council. When our Governor and Council heard of the settlements on Watauga being made without their consent, and that you had made bargins with those people about lands without consulting them, they were not well pleased with those people nor with you: that you should make bargins to place inhabitants, between your Country and our Country without their consent. However in time of peace

Chapter Three
Governor's Office

these inhabitants were not driven away or removed off. Neither were they taken under protection. But they were let alone; no Officers were appointed by Government; no beloved man sent to sit on the seats of Justice there. You did not complain to the Govr. And Council to have them removed. When You began the late War, you broke over the line between your Nation and our people on the head waters of the Catawba & Broad Rivers, And after you had broke over the line and made the path dark and Bloody between our two Countries we traveled in the path of War to your Country. Our Governor and Council sent out an Army against Your Nation. And at the same time, by the desire of the settlers on the waters of Watauga & Nolachucky, took them under the protection of the State, and supplied them with money, ammunitions & salt &c. And they were taken in, & admitted in time of the War, as our people. We promised to support them in that place; & by the assistance & a little of the power of North Carolina, they have lived there in time of War. Before the War this power was restrained & kept back beyond the line fixed by the Big Wolf. But now by making War You have been the occasion of bringing this power to Watauga & Nolachucky. And Now some of our beloved men may come & sit on the seats of Justice there. You have requested that those people should be removed quite away; and the power of North Carolina is great enough to remove them. But you made a War & we then took these people for our own people. You have made it verry troublesome for us to remove them; and it would be more agreeable to our Governor and great Council, for them to stay. We desire in behalf of the State of North Carolina, that if a line should now be agreed upon between your Country & our Country, that You for the future, shall not consent that any white people shall settle on Your side the line, on any account whatever, without the consent of our Governor and Great Council or Commissioners by them appointed for that purpose, and we desire that you will now faithfully promise that You will not hereafter sell rent or make any agreement whatsoever, with private persons respecting the Lands on Your side the line, as aforesaid; or the range or priviledge of Hunting thereon, lest such bargins should ocassion Disputes bewteen You and your Brothers of North Carolina.

  Brothers; We are about to fix a line that is to remain through all generations, and be kept by our Childrens Children; and we hope that both Nations will hereafter never have any more disputes. We shall recommend it to our Governor & Great Council of North Carolina, to make Laws to punish any white man, who shall settle or encroach on your lands or in any manner injure or disturb you. By fixing a line and abiding by the same, we

Chapter Three
Governor's Office

may be lasting friends. We desire to inform you that we do not wish to oblige or force you to comply with our proposals now to be made: for if you should believe them to be unjust and hurtful to your Nation, & therein differ in opinion from us, we desire you to tell us freely and without reserve, in the same manner as you would tell Your own people in Chote. And Whatever you say on this important article of our Treaty, we hope you will Speak freely from Your hearts. We desire to know your opinion whether you think it would be Just to remove the inhabitants of Watauga & Nolachuckey; or whether You do not think it would be better for both Nations for your beloved man & Chiefs to fix a boundary, below our inhabitants, beginning at the ford on Holston, where the path crosses at the lower end of Valley, running thence a course towards a point about three miles below Cumberland Gap untill it intersects the line hereafter to be extended between the States of Virginia & North Carolina; and from the said ford, a straight line towards Nolachuckey River five Miles West of the Mouth of McKamies Creek thence South, crossing Nolachuckey to the Southern bank thereof & from thence South East into the mountains, which divide the Hunting grounds of the Overhill Towns from those of Middle Settlements.

A String

To which the Old Tassell replied,

I look upon it the line You ask is much too nigh to my Nation it takes in all your settlers on Nolachuckey River, which are themselves too nigh; but this shall not spoil our good talks, I want liberty to raise my Children and have an open Country. I speak freely because I have a right to speak in my own behalf. This line I cannot agree to, as it is too near my Nation; nearer I believe than you think for, for I look upon it you would not make an unreasonable demand. I am verry thankful for the many good talks between us for the Safety and security of my people: but did not expect you would talk of boundaries so near my Towns. It seems as if my elder Brothers speak with a stranger mouth than I can; but this argument seems weak when set against what I say, for that line is too near me. I believe my elder Brothers want to know my principles; I thought they had known them before. I never was guilty of telling lies, all my people depend upon my word; and I tell you none of them have a bad heart against my Elder Brothers at this time. This is all I have to say this evening upon the subject; tomorrow I will speak again.

Chapter Three
Governor's Office

I want to talk about Colo. Gist going to General Washington & I want the Commissioners to write a letter for Colo. Gist to carry to that great Warrior in behalf of my Nation.

17th July Present as on the 15th
The Old Tassell spoke as follows:

Now the beloved men of North Carolina shall hear my reply to what they said to me last night. The talks you gave me came from the Governor to make a path from your Country to mine and was verry good till you came to talk of the boundary line. My beloved man and the beloved man of Virginia have taken hold of each other fast high up the arm.

It may be the same by my Brothers of North Carolina. But by their asking so much land it seems as if they want to see what we would say, that we might refuse something; And the might catch us in a trap for an excuse. I left people both at home and in the Woods far beyond there, who are waiting and listening to hear what I do. As you are talking of much land I don't know how they would like that part of your proposal. As I said before the beloved men are here together. My beloved Man has been to see the Great beloved man of Virginia who I suppose wrote to Your Great beloved man to send you here, and talk about making Peace. I want to know whether he wrote anything to him to require so much land as you seem to do. I am talking to my Brothers so I call you all, as to land I did not expect any thing on that subject; but only concerning peace. The man above hath ordered it so that the white benches shall be set down for us, and I hope nothing will enter either of our hearts but good thoughts. I would leave it to the beloved man of Virginia to settle all things about lands between us. I am talking with my elder Brothers on a subject I cannot clearly comprehend. I did not expect it would have been put to me at this time; for my elder Brothers have imposed much on me in the land way, if this and another house was packed full of goods they would not make satisfaction.

But I will leave the difference between us to the great Warrior of all America. It seems misterious to me why you should ask so much land and so near me. I am sensible that if we give up these lands they will bring you more a great deal than hundreds of pounds. It spoils our hunting ground; but always remains good to you to raise families and Stocks, when the goods we receive of you are rotten and gone to nothing.

Chapter Three
Governor's Office

    Your Stocks are tame and marked; but we don't know ours they are wild. Hunting is our principle way of living. I hope you will consider this and pity me. Here is my old friend the Elk (meaning Colo. Preston) and two particular from Virginia hearing the answer I make to my brothers of North Carolina. You require a thing I cannot do, for which reason I return You this String of Beads to consider upon again.

    In my talks at Chote Town house there shall be nothing bad towards my elder Brothers. I will hold them fast and strong. I have been often told that my elder Brothers were naked and had nothing. I said if so I will be naked also. I looked for nothing but to raise my children in peace and safety. My former friend who is now my Brothers enemy told me if I listened to you I should wear hickory bark Skirts; but that Talk I do not mind.

Returned the String

Then the Old Tassell spoke to the Virginia Commissioners as follows:

    I am going to speak to my friends and elder Brothers who I hope will remember what I am going to say. Ever since winter the good talks have been going on between us. Here is the Raven who first came to us with the good talks. Your Second Messenger happened to be killed by some of our bad people, who were not at that time well to my elder Brothers, and it was a great grievance to me. Even the Raven Came here last winter it was proposed to him by my elder Brothers, that a great and good Warrior should go with him into the Nation; but this he rejected to for fear some bad people should accidently meet with him, and kill him, In that case the Raven said "he must die also." Then another man was sent with him, for which I am verry thankful to my elder Brothers, in that they left the good Warrior with his own people. Now I have got this good Warrior fast by the hand, and will lead him to the beloved Seats in Chote, where he shall sit down and keep the beloved talks, between me and my Elder Brothers. I'll take him and lead him through all the Towns in Safety. He shall sit and smoke with my beloved man, and hold the chain of friendship hard and fast, that nobody shall pluck it from him, as I have him by the hand and determine never to let him go. I hope my elder Brother will never be sorry that he is gone with me, As he is a good man to you he will be the same to us. Any News that comes to us there of any kind, and from any place he shall send it here to this Seat of Justice, that my elder Brothers may know it.

Colo. Christian then spoke as follows:

Chapter Three
Governor's Office

Friends and Brethren

At our last meeting at this place, a letter from our Great Warrior Genl. Washington was delivered to his Brother Oconostoto, by one of his War Captains and Your friend Colo. Gist. By this letter you were invited to send some of Your young Warriors to our Genls. Camp where they will meet with a hearty welcome, be treated as friends and be at liberty to return in safety to their Country whenever they desire it; and also they shall be under the care of Colo. Gist and be paid and well cloathed during their stay. He likewise mentioned to You the success of his Battles and engagements on many occasions.

We can now assure you from the best inteligence we have been able to procure that his success continues and that his army is increased to a great number. You are sensible that Colo. Gist went all the way to see that Army and the Great Council of thirteen United Countries last winter, and brought inteligence and good talks from thence. You know the pains and trouble he has been at, and how careful he has been to you in bringing about a happy peace, betwixt you and your Brethren the white people. And that he has long been a friend to your Nation. From these reasons we would earnestly recommend it to you, to let some of your Warriors and young men accompany him to the Northward, as they can safely trust themselves with him. They will then have an opportunity of traveling through an extensive, rich, and populous Country. They will see the Grand Council of thirteen United Countries, in the Great City of Philadelphia; and at the Generals Camp they will see the finest and largest Army that was ever was in America, drawn into the field to fight for the liberty of all the good people therein, and to keep them from being enslaved. They may also if they choose it learn the white peoples art of War, under that Great and experienced General, who will be a father and friend to your Nation. When they return, they can bring back all the News. We do not want them to fight our Battles, but to see the riches and grandeur of our Army and Country. This invitation has been given to many tribes of Indians in friendship with the white people; and some parties of the Warriors as we have been informed have joined the General. For the same purpose he has desired some of your Young men, which is to show our enemies, that we have many Nations of Indians in friendship with us.

To which the Tassell replied as follows:

Here is my friend and Brother (pointing to Col. Gist) whom I look upon as one of my own people. He is going to leave me and travel into a far Country, but I hope he'll return. Here is one of my people the Pidgeon

Chapter Three
Governor's Offfice

that will accompany him but I do not know of many more that will. He will think no trouble of the journey it is all by land and will seem light to him. He once went over the Great Water where he could not see which way he was going; but this journey will be all by land and he will think nothing of Fatague. I am verry thankful that such a man as the pidgeon has undertaken this journey; because we think much of him, and I rely that my friend will take care of him. I cannot be accountable how many men will go with the Pidgeon and my friend; I know of only three or four there may be more but will see at night. Now this is the last talk I have to give. We have been long here and some of my people are desirous to go to their Corn fields which may be on Sufferance for want of labour.

      Tomorrow I am verry sensible some of them will set out. I want the talks over myself as soon as possible; but I know matters of great consequence Cannot be hurried on. I hope the business will get so far done that I may go in three days.

      But we will see one another often times at this place where the beloved fire is left.

A String to Colo. Gist

The Tassell continued his speech as follows:
      The beloved man who is pitched upon to hold the good talks (meaning Capt, Jo Martin) fast with me; my beloved man the Raven shall take him fast by the Hand and lead him to the beloved seats in Chote, there to hold each other forever. I had a beloved man once in my land, which was Cameron, who was always talking in my house, in behalf of the white Traders, who brought us supplies of goods. It has been but a little while dark. Here is Ellis Harland who lives in the beloved Town; when we get home, shall go to Seneca and bring us goods as usual. There is George Lowry, my Trader in Toquo; him and Colo. Gist took hold of each other, and hold the peace Talk, and my friend here knows it; I determine to send him with Ellis Harland likewise. Joseph Vann is inclined to supply us with goods; He will be living again with us verry shortly in friendship, and I hope will be agreeable to you. When I have this your Warrior and my friend sitting on the seat of Justice in Chote; every small thing that is heard (as often times it is from the Creek Nation) shall be sent and explained by him to my elder Brothers; and I will always assist him in this good work. The Warriors that go to the great and Noble Warrior, will let him know that I have this good man with me in my towns. It may be some satisfaction for him to hear, of one of his Young Warriors being to well received in our beloved Town. I hope your great and noble Warrior of

Chapter Three
Governor's Office

America, will consider my condition, because it is poor and low with me; because I think the people of South Carolina are seeking too much land from me. I hope these my friends here do not take this amiss. My desire is that this powerful Warrior will give me some redress, for the great injury of taking from me one of my principal Towns.

This day Colo. Christian delivered to the Commissioners of North Carolina the following proposals (Viz.)

July 17th 1777
The Virginia Commissioners propose to join with the Commissioners of North Carolina, in recommending to the Governors of the two States, an extension of the Boundary line between the States as far West as can be obtained of the Indians; if possible beyond the present inhabitants who planted and were actual settlers in 1776. That then the Virginia Commissioners will propose to the Indians to run a line from that point, to a point in the mountain three miles below Cumberland Gap; and that they will give the Indians a specific Sum for the lands North of that line; and that the North Carolina Commissioners should propose to the Indians, from where the extension of the Boundary, between the two States terminates, to turn such courses as will secure their inhabitants as far as the line of the hunting Grounds, between the middle & Overhill Settlements.

    Colo. Christian having intimated that an immediate answer in writing was expected, the following was prepared and delivered (Viz.)

    We the Commissioners of North Carolina do agree with the Commissioners of Virginia, to recommend to the General Assemblies of the two States, to extend the line between them as far West, as the Indians shall agree to give up at this Treaty. But we think that the Proposals made yesterday respecting the boundary line between our State and the Indians, ought not to be altered. We think it would be verry unjust to give up to the Indians any part of the Settlements, that our State took under protection during the War. We are of opinion that the proposal of yesterday, will no more than secure us a regular boundary tolerably straight so as to include our inhabitants on both sides of Holston River, as many on the North side will probably fall into our State. As we expect that no Settlements will be permitted to be made within five miles of the Indian line on our side; we think it will be so much the more necessary that this line should be regular & straight; and that it would be verry inconvenient to have it irregular with many angles.

Chapter Three
Governor's Office

We have no intentions to purchase any lands from the Indians; neither can we imagine that the General Assembly of our State will think it Just to pay large sums of money for lands and settlements, which they have at a great expence, protected during the War.

July 18th Present as in the 15th
Colo. Christian spoke as follows:
Friends & Brethren
    Our business at this place was to make peace with our ancient allies the Cherokees; a peace that cannot be broken by the artifice or injustice of our enemies & yours and which we hope will be settled on such a good foundation as to continue unbroken through many succeeding generations; and under which Your Nation may live in Safety, flourish and become more powerful than ever. In order thereto we desired you to make your complaints & grievances all know without reserve; and we should do the same with you. This we have both done; and find you have been greatly imposed upon, and abused by bad men amongst Yourselves, who persuaded you from time to time to rob the white people, and at length to go to War with them, before you made your complaints known to our Governor; by which means you involved yourselves & us in trouble. But as all this is done away, and we are once more become friends and Allies; We thought the surest way to continue that friendship and strengthen that Alliance, would be to fix a boundary between You & Your brothers of Virginia that may stand firm & unbroken thro' ages yet to come. The boundary we propose is to take in all the inhabitants on this side the River, to the Second Creek below the Warriors ford at the lower end of Carters Valley, being about three miles below the fording; then a straight line in Cumberland Mountain, three Miles below the great gap, thro' which the path goes to the Kentuckie.

    Brethren consider that the difference between this line, and that run by Colo. Donelson, by consent of your Nation; and you will find it is not so great as you imagined. You are sensible that if we had desired or wanted Your land, we should have left an Army in Your Country and not have invited you to treat with us, or support you in your greatest distress & promised to assist in protecting you against your enemies, all this was done to you as friends, without requiring any other return than your friendship and confidence. Nor do we now mean to ask the above lands from you, for any favour you have already received or is about to receive from us at this Treaty. So far from it that we propose to give you two hundred head

Chapter Three
Governor's Office

of breeding Cows and one hundred head of Sheep for it, by the fall to be delivered at this place when the line is run, at which we desire some of Your Warriors to be present that Your people may have stocks of their own. This Stock we give as a Compensation for the land that falls within our State when the boundary line between Virginia and North Carolina is run; which may be of great use in cloathing and supporting your people. In short, on your agreeing to this boundary, our peace will be confirmed and you may rest assured of the friendship of Virginia on all future occasions, and that we will become one people linked together by the strongest chain of friendship, interest and mutual defence. This is the earnest desire of our Governor and his great men who desired us to do you the strictest Justice, as we expect it is of Your beloved man and his Warriors. It will then be in our power to prevent our people from breaking over the line or other wise injuring You, which will not be in our power if there is no boundary fixed between us. We will also send a beloved Warrior with the interpreter to reside in Chote to write your letters, and deliver our talks to you from time to time and to transact Your business while he continues there; and we will also send a person down with you now, to repair your Arms, when they are out of order, at the expence of Virginia.

Brethren we have now endeavoured to show you some of the many benefits that will arise to your people, by fixing on and settling a boundary between Your Country and Virginia, in the manner we have proposed; from which You may readily conclude the many inconveniences that must follow on a refusal tho' we are at Peace.

We hope You will calmly and attentively consider these things, and be assured that we don't want to take least advantage of Your situation, but to do every thing with You on Just and generous terms.
A Double String

The Commissioners then withdrew, and left the Indians alone to consult. After a short time being met again, the Raven spoke as follows,

Now my elder Brothers shall hear what I have to say which is the certain truth without wavering. You and me have each other fast by the hand and we will forever keep our hold; altho' some difference may arise in our opinion, while we are talking the friendly talks together. The bright Chain of friendship is laid aside till we can settle the bounds of our Countries. I find that my elder Brothers pities me, and is not willing to share me of my land, which makes me take consideration of the matter. Here is my friends, Brothers and beloved man on both sides, holding verry agreeable talks together which I hope will never be interupted. The path

Chapter Three
Governor's Office

shall last forever and I shall sit at home safe, and confide that my elder Brothers will put it out of the power of all people to cros it, as if it was a wall that reached up to the skies. I shall sit at home and believe that this path now going to be made is such as no man may cross. My elder Brothers may be assured that I will prevent all my young men in the same manner. I trust to Your beloved man to take care that none of Your people breaks over this line. As all the good talks have been ended and we are making the path good between us we will always be Brothers and this path shall forever be observed; as our Children after us are here represented and we are Acting for future generations. My elder Brothers desired me to mention a boundary, and after that You proposed another. But I tell You now we will begin our line at the mouth of a big Creek just below Robisons Fort, and run from thence a straight line three miles to the left of Cumberland Gap. As for the path towards Kentuckie, I don't know exactly where it is; but the Gap I speak of is a verry remarkable one, and there is a verry high nobb to the left of it which the line may run to. And let the path go where it will I don't mind, for You are welcome to a path, through our land any where. From the mouth of this Creek to the top of that mountain, is the boundary fixed in my mind, and I give it up freely; tho' it is or used to be a considerable part of our hunting ground; by reason you talk verry good, and has pity on me. My Young people have not all got guns. My stock is all wild, and as You have pitied me, I hope you will give me a few, out of the abundance you have. I should not have spoke on this head, but a number of my young men are quite without, and our stock is getting verry wild. Many of my people are at home and some that are counted particular Warriors; to them I shall endeavour to make all things straight and prevent all evil. Tho' from the talks sent to me I have no right to think any attempt, to break our chain of friendship. I have taken hold of a Warrior of my elder Brother to carry home with me, that nothing shall be hid. He shall sit down with me at home on the seat of Justice, and give You every inteligence that comes to my Nation. He is the same man first proposed last winter, and I am glad the reasons I then gave weighed with you for not sending him, but the unfortunate one (meaning Saml. Newel) Now as we have fixed on a boundary which when it is run, as the Warrior will ever be with us, if any of my people trespass on you through him you shall know it and the same will be done if your people encroach on me, I'll hold the bright clear string of friendship in the front of my breast, as a mark that he shall be noticed through all my Nation. This Warrior I'm going to receive, shall never receive any damage. I always will suppress any plot (if any should be) that may be to his hurt. I have done talking now. I understood

Chapter Three
Governor's Office

there was a quantity of ammunition here to be given us; I should be glad it might be given to us this evening that we may be done. This String I give that it may be confirmed to You that what I have said is the truth; and that I expect to take Your Warrior home with me and make him a great Warrior in my Nation.

A String

Colo. Christian then spoke as follows:
Friends and Brethren,
    We are sorry to give You or ourselves any farther trouble about a boundary between You and Your Brethren of Virginia, as the time is passing, that both parties longs to get to their homes and families. We agree with you that the line shall be like a wall, high and strong that none can pass over or break down. But all that we asked at first was to keep our settlers within that wall, and that we could travel to the Kentuckie without doing you any injury for which we have offered You a reasonable reward or consideration. But we hope you will consider the matter again; and tho' from the mouth of the Creek you mention, to that we proposed, the line to begin at, is but a verry little way; it will leave out near twenty of our people, who have planted corn there, and can be of little use to you. Therefore we expect you will allow the line to begin at the mouth of the Second Creek below the ford and extend to the place you point out in Cumberland Mountain. Then these people who settled there will be pleased as well as all your Brothers and the line will be strong. You know our beloved man the Governor has not strained you in any thing, for which reason we expect you will not stand out about that small point of land; but small as it is, several families must be ruined if they should be moved off; and it cannot be of any real benefit to you.

The Raven spoke as follows:
    I depend on You to let the Governor of Virginia know that I had fixed a boundary, but that at your request I suffered it to go to the place you propose upon my land.

Colo. Christian spoke as follows:
Brothers,
    We have settled the boundary between You & Your Brothers of Virginia and you may be assured our Governor and great Council will make it verry strong. What we have promised You shall be delivered when we run the line, of which you shall have due notice. We will inform our

Chapter Three
Governor's Office

Governor, of your friendly behaviour at the treaty and shew him Your good talks. We will send a proper person to reside in Chote to hear your talks and do your business and ours while he stays there. And we promise You he shall be a good man and a Warrior.

That all we have done or may do here may be remembered by us and our Children yet unborn, we will write the whole on a large paper; and your beloved man and Warriors sign it on behalf of all the Overhill Cherokees, and we shall do the same on behalf of our Governor and his Council. And that you may have it, when you please, to shew it to all your people and know all that it contains; we will give you a fair Copy of it. While we are preparing this paper, in the mean time we would in the name of our Governor, earnestly recommend it to you to agree with our Brothers the Commissioners from North Carolina, & fix a strong wall between your people and that Country, by which the peace, safety and happiness of your Nation will be fully secured and you will have the great chain that begins in Chote held fast by the Governors of three Great Countries, which border on yours. And there is no doubt but these Governors will on all occasions, shew you their friendship, and do your people all the service they can; by which these three great Countries and the Cherokees will become one people. In confirmation

A String

July 19th present as on the 15th }
Mr. Avery spoke as follows   }

Beloved man and Chiefs of the Cherokee Nation
    Brothers We (North Carolina and Chota) have for some days past, been speaking the talks of peace. We have listened attentively to what You said, and hope we remember all. What you say about peace is verry good and friendly.

Brothers now listen and hear what we are going to say, we come from the Governor & Council of North Carolina, to speak for them and all that Country. They must all hear the peace talks that you and we shall speak this day, and will all observe the peace that shall be made, and we must do Justice to all. Brothers listen well to what I am going to say.

In former times you had little intercourse with your Brothers of North Carolina. We considered you as neighbours friends & Brothers. Your Young men and ours have had time to grow up in the last peace. After the Big Wolf (Govr. Tryon) had settled a line with your Nation; our Governor and Great Council sent you no talks all that time, that we know

Chapter Three
Governor's Office

of, or received any from you. Thus matters continued untill last fall was a year, our Great Council appointed a beloved man to deliver you a talk; you were then our friends. They gave this beloved Man a thousand pounds, out of their Treasury, which was sufficient to buy 3 or 4000 of gun powder. With this money he was to purchase such goods as would best suit You and to give them to You as a present. Mr. Wilkinson at Keowee was to give you notice. Our beloved man went last april or may was a Year; few or none of You came to hear our good talks & receive our presents. We then thought to send you good talks frequently, to Cultivate a good friendship with you, and hear good talks from You as friends. We hope this will be the case when we live in friendship hereafter.

We propose that a beloved man shall reside at Chote in behalf of our State to deliver the talks of our Great beloved man to your Great beloved man and all your Warriors: Also to write Your talks to him, that the good talks may go from the everlasting doors of friendship, that shall always stand open at Newbern to the doors of friendship at Chota; and the good talks also go from Chota to Newbern; and that by this means the path of Peace may be kept Clear, and Brothers on both sides see one another clearly. Your Complaints if you shall hereafter have any will surely come to the ears of one great beloved man & the great Council, which You told us you long ago wished for.

In your talks to us, day before yesterday, you seemed to doubt whether Your Brothers of North Carolina, were sincerely willing to make peace with you. Brothers we were sorry to hear this. We appeal to the great being above who knows all our hearts. He knows all our hearts are sincere, and that we are willing to have peace with you, if you will make peace with us on Just and honorable terms; A peace that will be lasting. We do not desire to make a short Peace; but a firm and ever lasting peace. If you will not settle a boundary line with us the peace cannot be lasting; for we cannot tell our people how far to go, and this will make disputes between us hereafter. You propose to delay this matter and refer it to the Governor of Virginia; but he has nothing to do with it, both States having distinct separate interests (and powers) like two Brothers. You said that you did not expect it, did not come prepared for this necessary part of the Treaty, which is verry strange & misterious to us.

You also seem to suspect that we want to entrap you for an excuse, but in order to convince you that your suspicions are wrong, we would observe to you that when your Nation had began this War, that no provocation & excuse enough; if your Brothers of North Carolina had been averse to peace, they needed no other excuse to carry on the War. But our

Chapter Three
Governor's Office

armies returned & left the whole Country to Your Nation, as before the War. This may convince You that our State are not desirous to drive you away; but to let you live there in Peace as friends, & neighbours, if you will remain peacible and be friends. This may also convince You that our State did not covet Your lands in as much as one Army, did not stay in the middle settlements, where they had possession, and might have built forts and kept the Country. We desired you to speak your mind freely and believe you have done it; we thank you for it. We also have spoken our minds freely, and this is the way to know one anothers Sentiments freely.

  Now Brothers listen to what we shall say. Our Great beloved man and Great Council of North Carolina, are desirous not to suffer any bad men to live between Your Country, and Your Brothers of that Country; and they want to establish a Seat of Justice at Watauga, and to send a beloved man to sit therein; that this beloved man may keep all bad people in order, and cause those that are verry bad to be hanged up by the neck; and suffer none to injure you or make mischief between us. You have proposed that all the people of Watauga & Nolachuckie, should be removed quite away, and we have told you in what manner during the War which you made; North Carolina took them under protection for their own people and supported them there in War; And that you by making this War had caused this protection to come. That having now become friends and promised to support them, we desire to be always friends. We now tell you that we think it unjust and unreasonable, for you to ask us to drive them away. You mention Your distress. You allow it good and right to pity those in distress, during the War, You distressed the inhabitants of Watauga and Nolachuckie. You were stronger, and endeavoured to destroy their substance and kill them all, in their distress North Carolina pitied and gave them help & support; this we hope you allow was right and good, their substance which you destroyed and the damage you did them was verry great. They are still in distress & still entitled the pity & assistance of North Carolina & must have it; which you will also allow is right. The Horses which You took from the people, Your beloved man promised last fall should be brought in and returned and the stock made good we are Sorry that this has not been complied with on your part.

  Brothers listen. The Great Being above hath said that the man who would have friends must himself friendly. Now as Calamity is the common lot of mankind, you may in the course of things see great trouble, & want our assistance as friends & allies now Brothers, if you are good and friendly on this Occasion, who knows but the Great Being above who lives to reward friendly actions, may put into the Heart of the Great

Chapter Three
Governor's Office

beloved man of North Carolina & the Great Council to help you at some future day when your necessities may require it. He no doubt, put it into their hearts to make you the present we spoke of, and he can send down all good thoughts into the hearts of man. Lastly to convince You that we are sincerely disposed for peace, & willing to be as easy with you as we possibly can, in Justice to our own inhabitants; We have reconsidered the matter of the boundary line; and now propose one which we understand will be more agreeable to Your Warriors (Viz.) Beginning on the North bank of Holston River, at the mouth of Clouds Creek being the second Creek, below the lower end of Carters Valey, running thence a straight line between the two States, hereafter to be extended; and running from the mouth of Clouds Creek aforesaid a straight line to the highest point of a mountain called the High Rock or Chimney Top, and from thence a straight line to the mouth of Camp Creek otherwise called McKamies **[McNamies?]** Creek on the South bank of Nolachuckie River, and from the mouth of Camp Creek a South East course into the mountains that divide the Hunting grounds, of the Over Hill Towns from those of the middle settlements.

In confirmation, a String

The Warriors being consulted for a short time, the Chiefs resumed their Seats, then the Old Tassell arose and replied as follows:

The beloved men of Carolina shall now hear what I have to say, now I will let you know what I have to Say; And I hope you'll remember, That the Island You see there belongs to Colo. Gist. It is to keep the beloved fire on, to bring the Cherokees to talk by. No man shall hold any right thereto but Colo. Gist. Your beloved fire was on this Side the River, last War your beloved fire was on this Side, and ours on the Island, so that it must be reserved for him. I am the man that speaks to my elder Brothers, I speak to my elder Brothers nothing but truth as I always do. Don't stop your ears, but hear and remember well. Don't forget, as people sometimes do. Here was my elder Brother talking just now. I shall remember what was said. I shall send my great Talk to the Great Warrior of America, for him to consider what has been doing. He is the head of all, he ought to hear and consider the talks; likewise the Governor of Virginia that nothing may be hid that has been done. You have asked me for the ground I walk upon; You have asked me for my land; the dividing line to begin on the River where the Virginia people left it, running thence to the Chimney Top; thence across Nonachucky to the Creek you mentioned. Let this be

Chapter Three
Governor's Office

the line untill Colo. Gist returns and brings word from the Great Warrior of America, and then the line can be marked. As you are the beloved men of Carolina, I listened to Your talks they went through my heart. The land I give up will ever hold good; it will ever be as good as it is new; and when we are all dead and gone it will continue to produce. Therefore I expect when you come to run the line, that You will bring some acknowledgement for land, which will afford bread to those yet unborn, when goods will be rotten and gone. You come here from the Governor of North Carolina to talk peace talks & make a line; but you'll tell your beloved man of the value of the land. Now I am done; I give up the land you asked; I shall say no more. If you ask for more, I will not give it. In confirmation I give you a String

A String

About this time it rained; The Commissioners, Indian Chiefs and some of the Warriors retired to a house in the Fort where Mr. Sharp spoke as follows:
  Brothers, we have now heard your talk about the Boundary line and want to understand it clearly. We would be glad that the Great Warrior of America should hear all the good talks that hath been between us at this place. But we think it absolutely necessary to have the line agreed to and established between Your Country and ours immediately. We think it is not necessary to delay that matter untill we hear from the Warrior of America; because our present controversy is a matter that only respects your Country and ours, and the sooner it is done the better, and what we agree to no man will alter. Remember now that we don't promise, nor flatter You with the hopes of any reward but our friendship which we hope you will merit and thereby may be as lasting as Your Nation. Therefore we hope you will now agree with us on a boundary, and meet some of our beloved men, sometime this fall (of which You shall have due notice) and have the path marked clear and make it high and strong; thereby our peace may be lasting and tend to the happiness of both Nations.
  N.B. The paragraph contained in the last five lines of the above talk was objected against, as improper to be delivered at this time, and the reasons given by Mr. Avery.

The Raven replied Sitting
  I do not know how to answer. I am agreeable to the last talk. I hope the great beloved man of Carolina will take pity on us and consider us for the land which I think he ought to do, but I do not demand it. But it

Chapter Three
Governor's Office

was always a custom when lines were run to get something. I hope pity will be taken on me but the line shall be made firm and lasting as I give up the land.

Articles of a Treaty of Peace made and Concluded at Fort Patrick Henry near the Long Island on Holston July 20th 1777 between the Commissioners from the Commonwealth of Virginia in behalf of that State; and the Subscribing Chiefs of that part of the Cherokee Nation called the Overhill Indians.

Article 1st That hostilities shall forever cease between the said Cherokees and the people of Virginia from this time; and that Peace, friendship, and Mutual Confidence ensue. And if either party is attacted by any Nation of Indians whatsoever, the other party is to give such assistance as may be required, as soon as men can be raised for that purpose, after the requisition is made; without pay or reward.

Article 2nd That all white or negroe prisoners belonging to any of the United States, among the said Indians, if any there be; Shall be given up immediately to the person who shall be appointed to reside at Chota as agent for the State of Virginia; to whom also the said Cherokees are to deliver all Horses Cattle or other property belonging to the people of Virginia; which they have taken since the beginning of the late War that can possibly be discovered and procured.

Article 3rd That no white man shall be suffered to reside in or pass thro' the Over Hill Towns without a proper Certificate signed by three magistrates in the County of Washington in Virginia, or in the County of Watauga in North Carolina to be produced to & approved of, by said Agent. Any person failing or neglecting to comply herewith is to be apprehended by the Cherokees and delivered to the said Agent, whom they are to assist in Conducting such person to the Commanding Officer at Fort Henry. And the said Cherokees may apply to their own use, all the effects such persons may be in possession of at the time they are taken in the Nation. And should any runaway Negroes get into the Overhill Towns, the Cherokees are to secure such Slaves untill the Agent can give Notice to the owners, who on receiving them are to pay such reward as the Agent may Judge reasonable.

Chapter Three
Governor's Office

Article 4th   That all white men residing in or passing thro' the Overhill Country properly authorized or certified as aforesaid, are to be protected in their persons and property, and to be at Liberty to remove in Safety when they desire it. If any white man shall murder an Indian he is to be delivered up to a magistrate in Washington County to be tried & put to death according to the Laws of the State. And if any Indian shall murder a white man the said Indian is to be put to death by the Cherokees, in the presence of the Agent at Chota or two Magistrates in the County of Washington.

Article 5th   That as many white people have settled on lands, below the boundary between Virginia and the Cherokees, commonly called Donaldsons line, (which lands they have repeatedly claimed in the course of this Treaty) & which makes it necessary to extend and fix a new boundary; and just and equitable to purchase the lands contained therein. It is therefore agreed by & between the said Commissioners in behalf of the Commonwealth of Virginia of the one part; and the Subscribing Chiefs in behalf of the said Cherokees, on the other part, in free & open Treaty, without restraint fear reserve or compulsion of either party that a boundary line between the people of Virginia & the Cherokees be established, and the lands within the same be sold and made over to the said Commonwealth, which line is to begin at the lower corner of Donaldson line on the North side of the River Holston and to run down that River according to the Meanders thereof, and binding thereon including the great Island to the mouth of Clouds Creek, being the second Creek below the Warriors ford at the mouth of Carters Valey; thence running a straight line to a high point on Cumberland Mountain, between three and five miles below or westward of the great gap, which leads to the Settlements on the Kentuckie this last mentioned line is to be considered as the boundary between Virginia and the Cherokees. And all the land between the said line, and that run by Colo. Donelson, and between the said River and Cumberland Mountain as low as the new Boundary, is to be the present purchase. For which tract of land or so much thereof as may be within the limits of Virginia, when the boundary between the States of Virginia & Carolina is extended, the said Commissioners agree in behalf of the Commonwealth, to give the said Cherokees two hundred cows and One hundred Sheep, to be delivered at the Great Island when the said line shall be run from the River to Cumberland Mountain, to which the said Cherokees promise to send deputies and twenty Young men, on due Notice of the time being given them. And for and in consideration of the said

Chapter Three
Governor's Office

Stocks of Cattle and Sheep, the said Chiefs do for themselves and their Nation sell make over & convey to the said Commonwealth all the lands contained within the above described Bounds, and do hereby forever quit and relinquish all their right title Claim or interest in and to the said lands or any part thereof and they agree that the same may be held enjoyed & ocupied by the purchasers, and that they have a Just right and are fully able to sell and convey the said lands in as full clear and ample a manner, as any lands can possibly be or ever have been sold made over or conveyed by any Indian whatever.

Article 6th And to prevent as far as possible any cause or pretence on either side to break and infringe on the peace so hapily established between Virginia and the Cherokees, it is agreed by the Commissioners and Indian Chiefs aforesaid, that no white man on any pretence whatsoever shall build plant improve settle hunt or drive any stock below the said boundary, on pain of being drove off by the Indians, and his property of every kind being taken from him. But all persons who are or may hereafter settle above said line are quietly and peacibly to reside therein without being molested disturbed or hindered by any Cherokee Indian or Indians, and should the stock of those who settle near above the line, range over the same into the Indian Land, they are not to be Claimed by any Indians, nor the Owner or any person for him to be prevented from hunting them, provided such person do not carry a gun, otherwise the Gun & Stock are both forfeited to the Indians, or any other person, who on due proof can make it appear; nor is any Indian to hunt or carry a Gun within the said purchase without license first obtained from two Justices; nor to travel from any of the Towns over the Hill to any part within the said Boundary, without a pass from the Agent. This Article to be in force untill a proper Law is made to prevent encroachments on the Indian Lands & no longer.

Article 7th That all Goods of every kind given by the Commonwealth of Virginia to the said Cherokees are to be delivered them; and that one of the Commissioners with a party of men go some distance to escort them out of the Settlements.
Signed by the Virga. Comrs. & 20 Chiefs & Warriors

Colo. Christian Spoke as follows:
Friends and Brethren, Warriors and Chiefs
      Last Spring we Your Brothers of Virginia met you at this place, and kindled the Council fore. We then Smoked the pipe of Peace shaked

Chapter Three
Governor's Office

the hand of friendship and brightened the Great chain that linked our fathers together, which unhappily had contracted some rust. We opened the path from Chote to Williamsburgh, washed the Blood away that darkened it and made it so clear and light, that Your beloved man and a number of his friends walked therein without stumbling, and shaked hands with our beloved man the Governor and his great Council and had many good talks with them. We have met a second time to confirm the Peace we then began and have been many days speaking together like friends, round the same Council fire. All our talks have been good as they were intended to strengthen and brighten the chain of friendship.

Our alliance has been made stronger by our Brethren of North Carolina who sit before this Council fire with us. They have taken hold of the Great chain to put it into the hands of their Governor at Newbern who we make no doubt will receive it with pleasure and hold it fast. We have burried the War hatchet and the black belts deep in the ground, and planted a tree over them, that they may forever be hid and forgotten by us; and in their place we have taken fast hold of the Great chain and the white Belts which we will never more let loose, we have made a firm, lasting and as we believe an honorable Peace; and established a boundary between Your Country and ours, which we hope will last till time shall be no more, future generations will see it and enjoy the happy effects of it when all present shall be in the dust and forgotten.

The cry and the noise of War will no more be heard in our land, by which so many brave Warriors fell, nor will your Warriors faces be any more blacked, to meet us in the field of battle nor their hands stained with the blood of lonely people traveling in the path. On Contrary we will every man return in peace and safety, to our own houses and employ ourselves in the most delightful business of life, that of raising and taking Care of our Children. Then our thoughts will be easy and our minds at rest: and we will not be so ready to listen to the talks of bad men, nor so easily imposed upon by them. The Great & Good being who rules and governs this world in wisdom, hath put into all our hearts to make this Peace. We hope he hath Smiled with pleasure upon us while we have been employed in it: and that the Peace we have now made will be a blessing to our posterity while that Great light shines, or this water Continues to run in this Stream. After giving our Warrior and friends who are going with You into Your particular care and delivering such presents as our Governor has sent to this place, nothing more remains for us to do, but to assure You of the friendship of Virginia; and that we will truly represent Your good conduct to our Governor; and to shake You our Brothers by the arm, wish

Chapter Three
Governor's Office

You a safe journey to Your Country, a happy meeting with Your families and friends and peace and prosperity to Your whole Nation.

A String.

Articles of a Treaty of peace made and Concluded at Fort Henry on Holston River near the Long Island July 20th 1777 between the Commissioners from the State of North Carolina in behalf of the said State of the one part and the Subscribing Chiefs of that pert of the Cherokee Nation Called the Overhill Indians of the other part.

Article 1st That Hostilities shall forever cease between the said Cherokees and the White people of North Carolina from this time forward; and that peace, friendship & mutual Confidence shall ensue.

Art: 2nd That all white or Negroe prisoners among the said Cherokees (if any there be) belonging to said State shall be given up immediately to the person who shall be appointed to reside among the said Cherokees as Agent for said State; to whom also the said Cherokees are to deliver all the Horses Cattle and other property belonging to the people of the said State, which they have taken away since the beginning of the late War, that can possibly be discovered and produced.

Art: 3rd That no white man shall be suffered to reside in or pass through the said Overhill Towns without a sufficient Certificate signed by three Justices of the Peace of some County of North Carolina or Washington County in Virginia or higher authority of any of the United States to be produced to, and approved of by the said Agent. Any person failing to Comply herewith shall be apprehended by the Cherokees and delivered to the Agent, whom they are to assist in Conducting such person to the nearest Justice of the Peace to be punished for the Violation of this Article; and the said Cherokees may apply to their own use all the effects such person shall then and there be possessed of at the time he is taken in said Towns or Country thereunto belonging, and should any runaway Negroes get into the Overhill Towns the Cherokees are to secure such Slaves unrill the Agent can give Notice to the owners, who on receiving them shall pay such reward as the Agent may judge reasonable.

Art: 4th That all white men residibg in or passing through the Overhill Country, authorized or Certified as aforesaid are to be protected in their

Chapter Three
Governor's Office

persons and property, and to be at liberty to remove in safety. And the said State of North Carolina shall have liberty to send one or more Traders with goods into any part of the said Overhill Country or towns for the purpose of furnishing the said Cherokees with necessarys. If any white man shall murder an Indian he is to be delivered up to a Justice of the Peace in the nearest County to be tried and put to death according to the Laws of the State. And if any Indian shall murder a white man, the said Indian shall be put to death by the Cherokees in the presence of the Agent at Chote or two Justices of the Peace of the nearest County.

Art: 5th That the Boundary line between the State of North Carolina and the said Overhill Cherokees shall forever hereafter be and remain as follows (To wit) Beginning at a point in the dividing line which during this treaty hath been agreed upon between the said Over hill Cherokees and the State of Virginia, where the line between that State and North Carolina (hereafter to be extended) shall cross or intersect the same; running thence a right line to the North bank of Holston River at the mouth of Clouds Creek, being the second Creek below the Warriors ford at the mouth of Carters Valey; thence a right line to the highest point of a mountain Called the High Rock or Chimney Top; from thence a right line to the mouth of Camp Creek otherwise called McNamies Creek on the South bank of Nonachuckie River, about ten miles or thereabouts below the mouth of Great Limestone, be the same more or less; and from the Mouth of Camp Creek aforesaid a South East course into the Mountains, which divide the Hunting grounds of the middle Settlements from those of the Overhill Cherokees. And the said Overhill Cherokees in behalf of themselves their heirs and successors do hereby freely in open Treaty, acknowledge and confess that all the lands to the East, North East & South East of the said line and lying South of the said line of Virginia at any time heretofore Claimed by the said Overhill Cherokees do of right now belong to the State of North Carolina; and the said Subscribing Chiefs in behalf of the said Overhill Cherokees their heirs and successors do hereby in open Treaty now and forever relinquish and give up to the said State and forever quit claim all right, title, claim and demand of in and to the Lands comprehended in the State of North Carolina by the lines aforesaid.

Art: 6th And to prevent as far as possible any cause or pretence on either side to break and infringe on the peace so happily established between North Carolina and the said Cherokees, it is agreed by the Commissioners and Indian Chiefs aforesaid, that no white man on any pretence

Chapter Three
Governor's Office

whatsoever, shall build, plant, improve, settle, hunt, or drive Stock below the said Boundary line on pain of being drove off by the Indians, and further punished according to Law. Nor shall any man who may go over the line in search of any Stray Creature be permitted on any pretence to carry a Gun on pain of forfeiting the same to the informer.

In testimony of all and singular the above Articles & agreements the parties aforesaid have hereunto set their hands and seals in open Treaty the day and Year above written.

   Read interpreted signed and ratified on the Great Island opposite to the Fort.

Memorandum before signing, that the Tassell yesterday objected against giving up the Great Island opposite Fort Henry to any person or country whatever except Colo. Nathaniel Gist for whom and themselves it was reserved by the Cherokees.

The Raven did the same this day in behalf of the Indians and desired that Colo. Gist might Sit down upon it when he pleased, as it belonged to him, and them to hold good talks on.

Waightstill Avery	(Seal)
William Sharp	(Seal)
Robert Lanier	(Seal)
Joseph Winston	(Seal)

Witnesses: Jacob Womack, James Robison, John Reed, Isaac Bledsoe, Brice Martin, John Redd & John kearns

      his mark
Oconostoto   (Seal)
(of Chote)

      his mark
Kay eta ch   (Seal)
(or the old Tassell
of Toquoe)

      his mark

Chapter Three
Governor's Office

Savanukeh   (Seal)
(or the Raven
of Chote)

         his mark
Willanawaw   (Seal)
(of Toquoe)

         his mark
Ootossetch   (Seal)
(of Highwassa)

         his mark
Attus ah   (Seal)
(or the No.
ward warrior
of the mouth of
Tellico River)

         his mark
Oos ku' ah   (Seal)
(or Abram of
Chilhowey)

         his mark
Tholloweh   (Seal)
(or the Raven
from the mouth
of Tellico River)

         his mark
Toos tooh   (Seal)
(from the
mouth of Tellico
River)

         his mark
Awo Yah   (Seal)
(or the Pidgeon
of Natchey Creek)

Chapter Three
Governor's Office

Oostosse' the   his mark   (Seal)
(or the mankiller
of highwassa)

Tille' hau' ch   his mark   (Seal)
(or the Chesnut
of Tellico)

Quu lu kah   his mark   (Seal)
(of Highwassa)

Anna ke hu jah   his mark   (Seal)
(or the Girl of
Tuskega)

Annee chah   his mark   (Seal)
(of Tuskega)

Ske' aktu kah   his mark   (Seal)
(of Cetico)

Atta kulula' kulla   his mark   (Seal)
(or the little
Carpenter of
Natchey Creek)

Oo koo ne kah   his mark   (Seal)
(or the White
Owl of Natchey
Creek)

Chapter Three
Governor's Office

Tha ta qulla
(or the Potclay
of Chilhowey)
      his mark   (Seal)

Tus ka sah
(or the Tarapin
of chiles tooch)
      his mark   (Seal)

his mark
Sun ne waut   (Seal)
(of Big Island
Town)

In the Island July the 20th before signing the fifth article of the Peace with the Virginians, when Colo. Christian came to that part which mentioned the Great Island; The old Tassell made an objection saying " I told you yesterday so plain that no one could misunderstand. We will not dispose of this Island but reserve it to hold our Great talks on. Even the grass is for our creatures and the wood to kindle our beloved fire with. People may settle around it but not on it. As Colo. Gist is our friend and Brother, it is his ground as well as ours; and he may sit down and settle upon it. When the old Tassell was Called upon to sign the Articles after they had been all fairly Interpreted, he said "ever since I signed a paper for Colo. Henderson I am afraid of signing papers. He told me many lies and deceived us. He never shewed to me but one paper and I hear he has eight or nine. But on being told by the Commissioners that this was a public agreement between two Nations, and as they would have a copy of the Articles, there could be no danger of deception.
He then signed verry readily.

Immediately after signing the North Carolina Articles;
Mr. Avery spoke as follows,
Friends and Brothers Chiefs and Warriors of the Cherokee Nation,
    We have now kindled the beloved fire, Smoked the pipe of Peace and joined the hand of friendship which is much augmented by your Brothers of Virginia. We have now made a firm and as we hope a lasting peace that will tend to the prosperity and happiness of both Nations. We

Chapter Three
Governor's Office

now assure You of a firm and steady friendship of North Carolina. We expect that Your Great beloved Man and some other Chiefs and Warriors will make a Visit this fall to our Governor and Great Council; and we promise they shall be treated kindly as friends and Brethren, conducted there and returned safe to the bosom of their own Country and people. We do also assure You that we will make known to our Governor Great Council and all our people, all the good Talks we have had together since we came to this place; and they will all rejoice to hear them. We hope that your people and our people will remember and keep the Peace inviolate.

The beloved man that we send to Your Towns to do your business and ours we expect you will treat as a friend & Brother and assist him in the recovery of the property that You took from the white people during the late War, and which you have now promised to deliver.

As You are in a great hurry, we shall not detain you longer than to observe that the great being above hath put it into all our hearts, and we have burried the hatchet deep in the ground never to be taken up again, and wiped away all the blood out of the path: it is all wholy done away, that our Children yet unborn to the latest ages may sit around this beloved fire. We now take You by the Arm high up, wish you a hearty farewell, and the happiness and prosperity of Your Nation. We shall carry the Chain of Friendship to our Great beloved man who will receive it willingly to his heart, hold it fast and keep it bright forever.

                                          A String

The Old Tassell then spoke as follows,

I was apprised of the matter Yesterday taking hold of an Agent. I think one is not Sufficient for both States, I will take hold of one of the North Carolina Warriors, and take him home. A great number of my people at home will hear all the good Talks, and when I bring a Warrior from each State, and preserve their peace and safety, then my people will see Clearly. Now I have taken hold of my Brother from North Carolina by the hand. Some of my people that are Ungovernable, may say something when I go home, but I will have the two beloved Warriors from both States by the hand. They can do business better than me.

As to the trade and Commerce, it lies in the breast of the Seat of Government, and my two beloved men will be there to see that all things will be done right and taken care of. I have had a little trade from Pensacola, things were dear, the first peace Talks of South Carolina and Georgia said "We see how your father took pity on you and supplied You

Chapter Three
Governor's Offfice

with Goods, but they were so dear You could not buy a rag to cover You, we will let You have them cheaper."

  We the Subscribers, Commissioners appointed in behalf of the State of North Carolina to negociate a Treaty of Peace and settle a boundary line with the Cherokees; having happily accomplished these desirable purposes with the Over hill Towns; in order to recover the Horses & other property belonging to the inhabitants of said State and have the same sent to their respective owners, & other purposes.
  We do therefore appoint Captain James Robison a temporary Agent for said State for the purposes hereafter mentioned.
  In consequence of this appointment, You the said Agent shall immediately repair to Chote in Company with the Warriors returning from this Treaty; at which place You are to reside while You continue in this business untill You receive further orders from the Governor of said State.
  When You arrive there or as soon afterwards as it is prudent You are to endeavour to find out the temper of the Draging Canoe and whether or how far he or his people approve of the present peace with North Carolina; as also Judge Friend the Lying Fish & other Chiefs who did not appear at the Treaty and if they do not full accede to the peace and boundary, whether there is any danger of one or more of those Chiefs renewing Hostilities against this or any other State. You will also endeavour to find out any talks that pass between the Cherokees, the Southern, Western and Northern Tribes of Indians.
  You are to make the strictest enquiry among all the Towns for persons who are enemies or unfriendly to the American cause, and have them convened before some Justice of the Peace to take an Oath of fidelity to the United States and on their refusal to be dealt with according to the Laws of this State.
  You will examine all travellers who pass through that Country, which You can meet with, and such as have not proper papers must be secured agreeable to the third article of the Treaty. You are immediately to use your utmost endeavours to have in your possession all the horses, cattle and other property belonging to the inhabitants of our State and cause the same to be conveyed safely and immediately to their respective owners, You will miss no opportunity of informing Government of the things worthy of notice. In all your transactions in that department you are to conduct Yourself with the utmost prudence; and by that means obtain the favour and confidence of the Chiefs..

Chapter Three
Governor's Office

As many things may occur which we cannot foresee and Consequently cannot instruct you, in these cases you must exercise Your own Judgment, having the strictest eye to the honor and interest of the United States in general and this in particular; as also to the articles of our Treaty.

Your close attention to the business to which You are now appointed, and your Canderer and uprightness in the performances thereof, will put in Your power to render essential Services to Your Country.

      Sir
      Your Humble Servts.

Waightstill Avery
William Sharp
Robert Lanier
Joseph Winston

Fort Henry 20th July 1777

July 21st 1777
To the Beloved men and Warriors of the middle, lower and Valley towns of the Cherokees
Friends and Brethren
  We the Commissioners from Virginia and North Carolina have the pleasure to inform You that we have kindled the Great Council fire at this place, that the beloved man of Chote with a number of his Warriors and about four hundred of his people are Sitting round it; and that we have been here several days delivering good talks to each other. we have brightened the chain of friendship that had contracted some rust; and the beloved man of Chote and our Governors have taken fast hold of it. We have washed the blood out of the path from Chote to this place; and from here to the Great Towns where our Governors live, so that the Cherokees may walk therein with safety. We have established a boundary between the Overhill Country and the two Countries of Virginia & North Carolina. A boundary so strong that it cannot be broken down, and so high that our Enemies cannot get over it. We and the Chiefs & Warriors have signed our names to the Articles of our peace and are about to part in peace tomorrow and return to our homes in safety and think of nothing but raising our Children.
  As the chain of friendship between North Carolina and Your Country has been broken, and the path made dark and bloody; we wish the

Chapter Three
Governor's Office

whole Cherokee Nation to be at peace with all the neighbouring Countries, that all the paths may be made upon & Clear; the great chain of friendship brightened and the Great Council fire once more kindled. We Your Brothers of North Carolina will recommend it to our Governor to hold a treaty of peace with you and to give you due Notice of the time and place where it shall be held, that all our differences may be made up and peace, friendship and mutual Confidence once more restored between North Carolina and your Country. And we do, in behalf of the powers of that Government promise protection & safety to all such of your Chiefs, Warriors and people who shall attend, & they shall be supplied with provisions during the Treaty.

    In the mean time hostilities shall cease and no more be committed by our Warriors on your people; and we expect on Your part that Your Warriors will not commit hostilities on our people; and that when we send a messenger to your Towns with good talks, you will permit him to perform his business and return in safety, and that you will protect him from insult.

    We your Brothers of Virginia earnestly wish & advise You to be at peace & in friendship with all your Neighbours. You know the evils of War as you have Suffered greatly by it; and you are no strangers to the blessings and benefits of peace. Therefore, there is no doubt but you will readily meet in Treaty with your Brethren and settle all differences. We desire you to have this talk read in your towns that all Your people may hear it. In confirmation we send you a String of White Beads.

William Christian   }
William Preston   } Comrs. From Virginia
Evan Shelby   }

Waightstill Avery   }
William Sharpe   } Comrs. From No. Carolina
Robert Lanier   }
Joseph Winston   }

    After the foregoing Talk had been interpreted to the Messenger from the Valey, one of the Chiefs of Cowee and a few other Middle Settlement Indians, that came to see the Treaty,
    Clana nah one of the Chiefs of Cowee spoke as follows,
I have listened to all your good talks and hope I shall remember all; and my people shall hear all. I look upon Chote to be the beloved Town of the whole Nation, and that it has been the means of saving all my people.

Chapter Three
Governor's Office

When my people hear all the good talks that have passed at this place they will be verry thankful. When I shall be coming at a great distance from Cowee my people will see the light of good news, like the day springing from afar. The beloved man of Cowee sent me to this place to hear all the talks that shall pass. I have found them all good and for the safety of my Nation. The chain of friendship is brightened, which will last during all ages and my people will be verry glad to hear it. All the beloved talks are equal to the talks of the beloved town of Chote; it is all one Seat of Justice.

It was by the consent of the beloved man of Chote to have a Seat of Justice at Cowee: I will be a day of rejoicing there to hear all the good talks at this place. I am verry thankful to have it in my power to receive Your good talks & Carry them to my people. It is not only I that rejoice but when they shall hear it it will open the hearts and breasts of all my people, with rejoicing at the good news. It will be an everlasting peace and safety to both sides, both me and my elder Brothers. I am glad to see that a beloved man of North Carolina is here to carry my talks to the great beloved Man of that Country. In Confirmation.

A String.

Thalhoona Koo a messenger from Cheeweyeh in the Valley then arose and spoke as follows,

I listened to all the talks, & am glad to hear them all good, and will carry them all to my people. I am the more proud for what You have told me this morning, that my own people shall hear all the good Talks as well as Chote and that part of the Nation; especially as you are a beloved man of North Carolina and I am only a messenger. I have received Your good Talks verry gladly and shall carry them home where my people are waiting and will receive them gladly as I have done. There are a great many beloved men in the Valley, Listening and waiting until I come home to hear Your good Talks, & they will receive them with a great deal of joy.

You the beloved men of North Carolina have spoke to me, that You will send for me to a Treaty. I will keep myself always prepared and my people will be in readiness whenever the Messenger Comes for to attend and meet you at that Treaty. You the beloved mwn from North Carolina have given good talks which I shall carry home. We our People & Yours are Strangers now, but I hope we shall not be so long; but be acquaintances & friends.

In confirmation, A String

Chapter Three
Governor's Office

Mr. Commisary

  You are to deliver to Capt. Isaac Shelby at Fort Patrick six hundred weight of flour & one bag in lieu of so much borrowed for the North Carolina Agent; and charge the same to the Public Account. Yours &c.

21st July 1777	} Waightstill Avery
To Mr. Andw. Grier	} William Sharpe
Commisary for Washington District	} Robert Lanier
	} Joseph Winston

It having been found during the course of the Treaty that it would be impossible to obtain Hostages; the Commissioners of North Carolina requested that some of the Indian Chiefs and Warriors would go down and make a visit to the Governor of that State, thinking that those visitors would for the present and during the journey answer the same purpose as Hostages. After the Articles were signed five Indians offered to go down into Rowan County to see three of their friends who were captivated during the War, and stay there untill the intended treaty with the Middle Settlements.

  For the above reason their proposal was excepted, & the said five Indians were delivered, (in form, in presence of the head Warriors) to the care of Major Womack; & the following protection and instructions for their safe conduct were given him.

Fort Patrick Henry
22nd July 1777.

  Whereas the Treaty of Peace between the State of North Carolina and the Over Hill Cherokees, hath been held and the Articles of said Peace agreed to, signed & ratified in open Treaty five Cherokee Indians have been delivered into Your Custody and charge (to wit) Anee chah one of the Chiefs of Tuskega, Willey of the same Town & three from Cowee of the Middle Settlements.

  You are hereby directed to Conduct them in safety to the Quaker Meadows, and there deliver them to Colo. Charles McDowel who will have them safely conveyed to the house of William Sharpe in Rowan County. The said Indians are recommended to the protection of several Officers both Civil and Military in this State, and to the kind treatment of all the good people thereof. As they will while among us be a great

Chapter Three
Governor's Office

security for the peacible behaviour of their Nation; And as the good treatment these may receive from our people be the means of inducing others to Come, who when the like measure shall be necessary, may answer the same Valuable purpose: We therefore request and hope that every person will endeavour to protect them from insult, and give them good usage that they may go home Satisfied.

      Sir
      Your Humble Servts.
Waightstill Avery
Wm. Sharpe

  The Commissioners wrote to the persons who had the three prisoners in their Custody, to send them to the house of William Sharpe that they might all be collected at one place & remain there until farther orders from his Excellency the Governor.

Chapter Four

North Carolina Laws

LAWS OF THE STATE OF NORTH CAROLINA REVISED, UNDER THE AUTHORITY OF THE GENERAL ASSEMBLY, VOLUME II
HENRY POTTER
RALEIGH: PRINTED AND SOLD BY J. GALES, 1821
CHAP. 774.
1809. An act to prevent speculations in obtaining lands which may hereafter accrue to this state, by purchase from the Indians. (Page 1161).

Whereas, from the several acts of Assembly establishing a boundary between this state and the Cherokee Indians, (See 1783, c. 185, s. 5.) and the several treaties between the said Indians and the United States, and the several lines run pursuant thereto, it is rendered doubtful where the present boundary extends, and whether the penalties for entering or surveying lands beyond the same, are in full force: And whereas speculators, regardless of the friendship and good faith which ought to be supported with the said Indians, are making entries on their lands; and it is suspected a great speculation is on foot to appropriate most of the valuable lands of the said Indians which lie within this state, so soon as their title shall have been extinguished by treaty, and thereby deprive the honest citizens, who regard the laws of their country, from appropriating lands when permitted by law, without much litigation and expense:

1. Be it therefore enacted, &c. That the land lying west of the line run by Meigs and Freeman, within the bounds of this state, shall not be subject to be entered under the entry laws of this state; but that the same, when the Indian title shall be extinct, shall remain and insure to the sole

Chapter Four
North Carolina Laws

use and benefit of the state; any law to the contrary notwithstanding. (See **1817, c. 950.).**

2. And be it further enacted, That all entries made, or grants obtained, or which may hereafter be made or obtained, shall be null and void.

****

***ACTS PASSED BY THE GENERAL ASSEMBLY OF THE STATE OF NORTH CAROLINA AT THE SESSION OF 1831-1832*
RALEIGH: PRINTED BY LAWRENCE & LEMAY
PRINTERS TO THE STATE. 1832**

**RESOLUTIONS.
1831-1832.**
Whereas it appears that much confusion exists in the accounts of the purchasers of Cherokee lands, on the books of the Public Treasurer, and that many discrepancies exist between the bonds given for the purchases of Cherokee lands and the entries made on those books; and it also appears that some errors occurred in making out the lists of those bonds in December, 1830, for the purpose of transferring them to the present Public Treasurer: Therefore,

Be it resolved, That the Public Treasurer be, and he is hereby directed to have a new set of books opened in his office, in which he shall cause to be entered a true and accurate statement, and account of all the bonds for the purchase of Cherokee lands which came to his possession on the twenty ninth December, eighteen hundred and thirty, so that it may clearly appear what was the total amount due, and what was due on each bond on that day; and that he enter on these books all sums which may have been since paid to him, or which may hereafter be paid, so as to exhibit at all times the true amount due on these bonds.

Resolved further, That the Public Treasurer make out and sign a correct list of these bonds, as they existed at the time he came into office, and deposit the same in the office of the Comptroller, for the examination and action of the committee of Finance at the next session of the General Assembly; and it shall be the duty of the Comptroller to receive and preserve said list; but he shall not be required to open accounts with the several purchasers of Cherokee lands as heretofore required.

Chapter Four
North Carolina Laws

Resolved lastly, That the Public Treasurer pay out of the Treasury the sum necessary to carry the object of the foregoing resolutions into effect: Provided, the same should not exceed one hundred dollars.

****

ACTS PASSED BY THE GENERAL ASSEMBLY OF THE STATE OF NORTH CAROLINA, AT THE SESSION OF 1833-34
RALEIGH: PRINTED BY LAWRENCE & LEMAY
PRINTERS TO THE STATE, 1834

CHAPTER XIII.
1833-1834. An act directing the sale of the lands remaining unsold, acquired by treaty from the Cherokee Indians. (Pages 34-35).

Be it enacted by the General Assembly of the State of North Carolina, and it is hereby the authority of the same, That the Governor be, and he is hereby authorised to direct the sale of so much of the lands lately acquired by treaty from the Cherokee Indians as have been surveyed and remain unsold, at such time and place as he may deem proper, under the direction of a commissioner to be by him appointed for that purpose, after having advertised the same for at least three months in the public newspapers of this city, the Western Carolinian of Salisbury, and such other papers as he may think proper; which sale shall be kept open one week, and no longer.

II. Be it further enacted, That if, during the sale, any section of land noticed to be of the first quality, shall not command in the market one dollar and fifty cents per acre, and in like manner, lands of the second quality not commanding seventy five cents per acre, and lands of a third quality not commanding twenty five cents per acre, the commissioner shall postpone the sale of such lands; and when the commissioner discovers that any section of land is likely to bring less than its value, either for want of competition or from combination among the bidders, he shall bid off the same for the State.

III. Be it further enacted, That the provisions of the second section of an act, passed in the year one thousand eight hundred and twenty one, entitled "an act concerning the lands lately acquired by treaty from the Cherokee Indians;" and the provisions of the seventh, twelfth, thirteenth, sixteenth and eighteenth sections of an act, passed in the year one thousand eight hundred and nineteen, entitled "an act prescribing the mode of

Chapter Four
North Carolina Laws

surveying and selling the lands lately acquired by treaty from the Cherokee Indians," be, and the same are hereby continued in force.

IV. Be it further enacted, That the Governor be, and he is hereby authorised to cause twelve additional lots to be surveyed in the town of Franklin, out of the four hundred acres reserved for the State, which may, together with those already surveyed, be exposed to sale under like rules and regulations as is prescribed in the before recited acts: Provided always, that the said commissioner be authorised, if in his opinion the interest of the State require it, to purchase in the same for the State.

V. Be it further enacted, That nothing in this act shall be so construed as to authorise the sale of any lands, the title of the State to which may be regarded as doubtful.

VI. Be it further enacted, That in case the said lands should be sold, that nothing in this act shall be so construed as to prevent persons who may have crops growing on the said lands, from gathering the same.

****

ACTS PASSED BY THE GENERAL ASSEMBLY OF THE STATE OF NORTH CAROLINA AT THE SESSION OF 1834-1835
RALEIGH: PHILO WHITE, PRINTER TO THE STATE, 1835

TREASURER'S REPORT

DATE	From Whom Recd		Bonds Paid		Principal		InterestT		TotalL	
1833			D	C	D	C	D	C	D	C
Nov. 23										
	Thomas Rogers	full 4th			13	37			13	37
	John Hooper	do 2nd	15	49	8			78	24	27
	Do do	part 3rd	25	73					25	73
	Goldman Ingram	full 4th	14	17	10			37	24	54
	Thomas Gribble	do 3rd	24	84.5	22		36.5		47	21
	Do do	part 4th	7	79					7	79
	Lincoln Fullam	do 3rd			90	00			90	00
	James Brimer	full 4th	15	21	6		14		21	35
	Amos Brown	part 3rd	51	50					51	50
	James Ruddell	do 4th	10	00					10	00
	Zachariah Cabe	part 4th	11	09	39	00			50	00
	Henry Dryman	full 2nd			4		52		4	52
	Do do	part 3rd			28	88			28	88
Dec. 2										
	Eli Ritchy	full 2nd	1	6.25	12		72.75		13	79
	Do do	part 3rd	12	87.5	13		33.5		26	21

Chapter Four
North Carolina Laws

James Murray	full 3rd	29	53	23	41	52	94	
Edward Chastain	do 4th	6	00	16	65	22	51	
Milton Brown do	3rd, 4th	38	27	17	41	55	68	
Zachariah Cabe	do 4th			126	40	126	40	
William M'Connell	do 4th	28	2.5	52	19.5	80	22	
1834 Jan.								
Michael Wikle	part 4th		20	00		20	00	
David Rogers	do 4th		16	32		16	32	
Mch. 11								
R. Love, Jr. & J. Moore	do 2nd	500	00			500	00	
Do do	do 3rd	420	00			420	00	
		1366	69.75	366	53.2	1733	23	

****

LAWS OF THE STATE OF NORTH CAROLINA PASSED BY THE GENERAL ASSEMBLY AT THE SESSION OF 1836-1837 **RALEIGH: THOMAS J. LEMAY, PRINTER, 1837.**

CHAP. VII. CHEROKEE LANDS.
1836-1837. An Act to amend an Act, entitled "an act authorising the entering of the unsurveyed lands acquired by treaty from the Cherokee Indians, A.D. 1817 and 1819, in the counties of Haywood and Macon." (Page 29).
Be it enacted by the General Assembly of the State of North Carolina, and it is hereby enacted by the authority of the same, That nothing in the aforesaid act contained shall be so construed as to authorize or allow the entry of any portion of the said lands, which were reserved or allotted to any Indian or Indians under said treaties, which the State has since acquired by purchase; and that the Secretary of State be, and he is hereby directed to issue no grant for any portion of the lands of the latter description, until the General Assembly shall otherwise order and direct. **[Ratified 10th January, 1837.].**

CHAP. VIII.
1836-1837. An Act to prevent frauds on Cherokee Indians, residing in this State. (Page 30).
Be it enacted by the General Assembly of the State of North Carolina, and it is hereby enacted by the authority of the same, That all contracts and agreements of every description, made after the eighteenth day of May one thousand eight hundred and thirty eight, with any

Chapter Four
North Carolina Laws

Cherokee Indian, or any person of Cherokee Indian Blood, within the second degree, for an amount equall to ten dollars or more, shall be null and void, unless some note or memorandum thereof be made in writing and signed by such Indian or person of Indian blood, or some other person by him authorised, in the presence of two creditable witnesses, who shall also subscribe the same. [Ratified 21st January, 1837.]

****

LAWS OF THE STATE OF NORTH CAROLINA PASSED BY THE GENERAL ASSEMBLY AT THE SESSION OF 1836-1837
RALEIGH: THOMAS J. LEMAY, PRINTER, 1837.

CHAP. LXXIII.
1836-1837. An Act for the relief of John Timson, a native Cherokee Indian, and his family. (Page 333).

Be it enacted by the General Assembly of the State of North Carolina, and it is hereby enacted by the authority of the same, That John Timson, a native Cherokee Indian, now residing in the county of Macon, his wife Lucy, their children, John C. Timson, Henry C. Timson, Sarah Ann Eliza Timson, Margaret Jane Timson, and such other children as may hereafter be born to the said John Timson, of the body of his present wife Lucy, be, and are hereby invested with full power and authority to enter, purchase and hold land and personal property in this State, and to take the same by gift, devise or descent: Provided, that before any of the aforesaid Indians shall be allowed to acquire lands, or shall be considered and recognized as freeholders, he or she shall first take the oaths of allegiance to the State of North Carolina and the United States of America, in open court, before the Court of Pleas and Quarter Sessions of Macon County.

Sec. 2. Be it further enacted, That the said John Timson and his family aforesaid, shall be, and they are hereby allowed to prosecute and defend suits, and to give evidence, in any court of justice in this State, in all causes, whether civil or criminal, which may be pending therein, under the same rules, regulations and restrictions which now apply to white persons; any law, usage or custom to the contrary notwithstanding. [Ratified 30th December, 1836.].

****

Chapter Four
North Carolina Laws

REVISED STATUTES OF NORTH CAROLINA PASSED BY THE GENERAL ASSEMBLY AT THE SESSION OF 1836-7 REVISED UNDER AN ACT OF THE GENERAL ASSEMBLY, PASSED AT THE SESSION OF 1833-4, VOLUME I.
RALEIGH: PUBLISHED BY TURNER AND HUGHES, 1837

CHAPTER L. FRAUDS. (Pages 290-291).

8. All contracts to convey or sell land, tenements, or hereditaments, or any interest in or concerning them, or any slave or slaves, shall be void and of no effect, unless such contract, or some memorandum or note thereof, shall be put in writing, signed by the party to be charged therewith, or by some other person, by him thereto lawfully authorized, except nevertheless contracts for leases not exceeding in duration the term of three years. **(1819, c. 1016.).**

11. All contracts and agreements of every description, made after the eighteenth day of May one thousand eight hundred and thirty eight, with any Cherokee Indian, or any person of Cherokee Indian blood, within the second degree, for an amount equal to ten dollars or more, shall be null and void, unless some note or memorandum thereof be made in writing and signed by such Indian or person of Indian blood, or some other person by him authorized, in the presence of two credible witnesses, who shall also subscribe the same. **(1836, c. 8.).**

****

LAWS OF THE STATE OF NORTH CAROLINA PASSED BY THE GENERAL ASSEMBLY AT THE SESSION OF 1838-1839
RALEIGH: PRINTED BY J. GALES AND SON
OFFICE OF THE RALEIGH REGISTER, 1839

CHAPTER X. COUNTIES.
1839. An Act to erect that Territory of this State lately acquired by Treaty from the Cherokee Indians, into a separate and distinct County, by the name of Cherokee. (Page 18).
Be it enacted by the General Assembly of the State of North Carolina, and it is hereby enacted by the authority of the same, That all that part of Macon County bounded as follows, viz: beginning at the junction of the Tennessee and Tuckaseegee Rivers; thence down the main channel of the Tennessee River to the State line of Tennessee; thence with the said Tennessee line, to where it intersects the Georgia line; thence with the

Chapter Four
North Carolina Laws

dividing line this State from Georgia, Eastwardly, to the Mountain dividing the waters of Hiwassee and Valley Rivers, from those of the Nantahala River; thence along with the highest summit, and the various courses of the said Mountain, to the point of beginning, be, and the same is hereby erected into a separate and distinct County, by the name of Cherokee, with all the rights, privileges, and immunities of the other Counties of this State. **[Ratified 4th January, 1839].**

RESOLUTION directing the Secretary of State to issue Grants for Lands sold at the late sale of the Cherokee Lands, in certain cases. (Pages 184-185).
Whereas, by the twelfth section of the Act of Assembly, passed at the last session, authorizing the sale of the Cherokee Lands, the Commissioners who superintended the same were authorized to receive payments in advance, either in whole or in part; and whereas, in several instances, the purchasers of said lands paid in full for them at the time of purchase, and obtained the Commissioners' receipt; and whereas, by the ninth section of the Act aforesaid, the Secretary of State is authorized to issue grants for said lands, only upon proof made to him of payment therefor, by the production of the Treasurer's receipt; and whereas, in the cases referred to, the Treasurer can give no receipt: For remedy whereof, be it
Resolved, That the Secretary of State shall be authorized to issue grants in the cases above referred to, for the lands sold at the late sale of the Cherokee lands, upon the production of the purchaser of a certificate from the Public Treasurer, certifying that it appears from the returns made to him by the Commissioners of sale, that any particular tract of land was paid for in full, to the said Commissioners, at the time of the sale - which certificate the Public Treasurer is hereby empowered to make. **[Ratified 28th December, 1838].**

****

LAWS OF THE STATE OF NORTH CAROLINA PASSED BY THE GENERAL ASSEMBLY AT THE SESSION OF 1840-41
RALEIGH: PRINTED BY W.R. GALES
OFFICE OF THE RALEIGH REGISTER, 1841

CHAPTER IV. CHEROKEE AGENCY.

Chapter Four
North Carolina Laws

1840-41. An Act authorising the Governor to appoint an Agent in the County of Macon or Cherokee. (Pages 7-9).

I. Be it enacted by the General Assembly of the State of North Carolina, and it is hereby enacted by the authority of the same, That the Governor of this State be, and he is hereby authorised, after the first day of March, one thousand eight hundred and forty one, to appoint an Agent, who shall, after his appointment, reside in the County of Macon or Cherokee, whose duty it shall be to receive payment, from time to time, of all purchasers of Cherokee Lands, of all or any part of the money due on their several bonds; to ascertain and report to the Treasury Department, once every three months, the condition of the debtors, as solvent, whether sold or unsold.

II. Be it further enacted, That the Agent so appointed shall be authorised to receive from the Public Treasurer, such of the bonds given for Cherokee Lands as the Public Treasurer, with the advice of the Governor, shall deem proper, for which said Agent shall execute to the Treasurer his receipt. Provided, that at no time shall the said Agent hold in his hands bonds and monies received thereupon, to an amount beyond the penalty of his bond; he shall take the bonds to the County of his residence, and there receive all such payments as may be voluntarily made, and institute suits in all cases, when he shall be directed to do so by the Public Treasurer, or when the interest of the State shall in the least seem to require it.

III. Be it further enacted, That the Agent thus appointed, shall receive in payment gold and silver coin, and the notes of all specie paying Banks in this State and South Carolina, and in addition to which the Agent may, and he is hereby required to receive from all debtors of Cherokee Lands, whose permanent residence may be West of the Blue Ridge, the notes of the specie paying Banks of Georgia, payable at Augusta and Savannah; he shall on the first Monday in every month, transmit to the Public Treasurer an accurate statement of his receipts during the month; and he shall be required to pay over to the Public Treasurer, or deposite to the credit of the Treasurer in such Bank as the Public Treasurer may designate, on the first Monday of the months of June, September, December and March, in each and every year, all monies by him received during the three preceding months.

IV. Be it further enacted, That the Agent thus appointed, shall, before entering on the duties of his office, take before the Governor, an oath for the faithful performance of all the duties enjoined by this Act, and shall enter into bond, with sufficient securities, in the sum of one hundred

Chapter Four
North Carolina Laws

thousand dollars, to secure the honest and faithful discharge of the several requisitions of this Act; which bond shall be made payable to the State of North Carolina, and upon breach of the conditions thereof, or any of them, the Treasurer shall cause the bond to be put in suit in the Superior Court of Wake County, and such bond shall not become void upon the first recovery, or if judgment shall be given for the Defendant, but may be put in suit, and prosecuted from time to time until the whole penalty shall be recovered.

V. And be it further enacted, That the Agent aforesaid shall receive, as a fair compensation for all the services required of him, three per centum on the amount of all sums received and collected; and he may be dismissed from office and a successor appointed at any time that the Governor may believe that his duties are not honestly and correctly discharged, and upon his dismissal from office, it shall be his duty to deliver over to the Treasurer, or to such person as the Governor shall appoint to succeed him, such bonds as may be in his hands and remain uncollected, and shall immediately account with the Public Treasurer for all monies by him received upon said bonds.[**Ratified the 30th day of December, A.D. 1840.**]

CHAPTER V. CHEROKEE AGENCY.
1840-41. An Act supplemental to an Act passed at the present Session of the General Assembly, authorising the Governor to appoint an Agent to collect the Cherokee Bonds. (Pages 9-10).

Be it enacted by the General Assembly of the State of North Carolina, and it is hereby enacted by the authority of the same, That it shall be the duty of the Treasurer whenever he shall deliver to the Agent appointed by the Act to which this is a supplement, any Cherokee Bonds, to take from the said Agent a memorandum or receipt, specifying the names of the obligors in said Bonds; the amount for which they were given, and the time when they become due, and also the payments made on them severally, and in the event of any of said bonds being lost or destroyed before they may be collected, a copy of the said memorandum or receipt, certified to be accurate by the Treasurer, whose hand writing may be proven by the oath of any person knowing it, shall be received as evidence in the same manner as the original bonds, and a recovery shall be had on them, without the production of the said bonds, any law, usage or custom to the contrary notwithstanding; Provided, however, as preparatory to the introduction of such receipts as evidence in the cases above specified, the loss of the bonds shall be proved in the manner usual in other

Chapter Four
North Carolina Laws

cases when secondary evidences is offered in lieu of evidence of the first degree. [Ratified the 11th day of January, 1841.]

****

LAWS OF THE STATE OF NORTH CAROLINA PASSED BY THE GENERAL ASSEMBLY AT THE SESSION OF 1844-45
RALEIGH: THOMAS J. LEMAY, PRINTER, 1845

CHAPTER XLVI. MISCELLANEOUS.
1844-45. An Act to encourage the culture and manufacture of silk and sugar among the Cherokee Indians in this State. (Pages 71-72)
Whereas a small portion of the Cherokee tribe of Indians are remaining in this State, who are represented by their white neighbors as conducting themselves in a peaceable and orderly manner, and who, under the influence of temperance and religious societies, are fast improving in the knowledge of the mechanic arts, agriculture and civilization; and whereas the Cherokees referred to, who belong to the towns of Qualla and Yuansan, Cheoih, have already commenced the culture and manufacture of silk; and for the encouragement thereof,

Be it enacted by the General Assembly of the State of North Carolina, and it is hereby enacted by the authority of the same, That the provisions of the act, entitled an act to encourage the culture and manufacture of silk and sugar in this State, passed in the year 1836, be, and the same are hereby extended to the said Cherokee Indians now belonging to said towns: Provided, that the provisions of this act not extend to any Indians who are not remaining in said towns by the permission of the Government of the United States, under treaty stipulations. [**Ratified the 10th day of January, 1845.**]

****

LAWS OF THE STATE OF NORTH CAROLINA PASSED BY THE GENERAL ASSEMBLY AT THE SESSION OF 1846-1847
RALEIGH: THOMAS J. LEMAY, PRINTER, 1847

Published agreeably to the ninety-fifth Chapter of the Revised Statutes.

Chapter V., Bonds, Cherokee.

Chapter Four
North Carolina Laws

1846-47. An Act to amend an act, passed at the last Session of the General Assembly, entitled "an act more effectually to secure debts due for the Cherokee lands, and to facilitate the collection of the same." (Page 19).

Sec. 1. Be it enacted by the General Assembly of the State of North Carolina, and it is hereby enacted by the authority of the same, That the provisions of the said act be extended to the securities of insolvent purchasers, whenever it is ascertained to the Governor by the agent of the State, the principals are so insolvent and have removed beyond the limits of the State, so that releases from them cannot be had, then and in that case, whenever the said securities, as aforesaid, shall release in manner prescribed, for the principals in said act, the Governor shall be, and he is hereby authorized to deliver up such bonds, to be cancelled in the same manner as if such releases were made by the principals; any thing in that law, to which this is an amendment, to the contrary notwithstanding.
[Ratified 18th January, 1847.]

Chapter VIII. Bonds, &c Transfer of.
1846-1847. An Act to provide for the Transfer of certain funds from the Internal Improvement Fund to the Public Treasury, and for other purposes. (Pages 25-26).

Sec. 1. Be it enacted by the General Assembly of the State of North Carolina, and it is hereby enacted by the authority of the same, That all the bonds due to the board of Internal Improvement, and secured in whole or in part by mortgage to the amount of fifteen thousand six hundred and thirteen dollars, as appears from the report of said Board of Internal Improvement, made to this General Assembly, be, and the same are hereby transferred to the Public Treasury.

Sec. 2. Be it further enacted, That the Public Treasurer, upon the receipt of the bonds as aforesaid, shall proceed to collect the same, as speedily as may be; and when so collected, or any part thereof, he shall deposit the same in the Public Treasury, to be used as other public funds.

Sec. 3. Be it further enacted, That the dividends of profits arising on one hundred and twelve shares of stock owned by the internal improvement fund, in the Bank of Cape Fear, be, and the same are hereby transferred to the public fund, until otherwise ordered by the General Assembly.

Sec. 4. Be it further enacted, That all monies received on account of Cherokee bonds, whether principal or interest, for lands heretofore sold, which shall be received at the Public Treasury until the first day of January, 1849, be, and the same are hereby directed to be placed in the

Chapter Four
North Carolina Laws

Public Treasury, and used as other public funds; and that the Public Treasurer be, and he is hereby directed to carry to the credit of the internal improvement fund, on the books of the Treasury, from time to time, all such sums as may be received under his section; and that he also credit the same fund, for all such amounts as he may receive under the first and third sections of this act, so as to shew at all times the true amount which the public fund is indebted to internal improvement fund.**[Ratified 18th day of January 1847.]**

Chapter XII. Cherokee Lands.
1846-47. An Act to amend an act, entitled "an act for the relief of purchasers of the Cherokee lands, passed 1830, chapter 34." (Pages 30-31).
Whereas, it appears that some tracts of land were materially intefered with by Indian Reservations, for which payments have been made into the Public Treasury, and to which the provisions of the present law do not extend, according to the opinion of the Attorney General, under said act: for remedy whereof,
Be it enacted by the General Assembly of the State of North Carolina, and it is hereby enacted by the authority of the same, That the provisions of said act shall extend to all cases where the purchase money has been paid into the Public Treasury, as well as where the bonds are held by the Public Treasurer; and in case the interest or any portion of the principal should under the provisions of said act be remitted, then and in that case the Public Treasurer is hereby authorized to refund to the person or persons paying the same, such sum as may be adjudged to them under the provisions of said statute.**[Ratified 18th January, 1847.]**

Chapter XIII. Cherokee Lands.
1846-47. An Act concerning the duties of the Cherokee Land Agent. (Page 31).
Be it enacted by the General Assembly of the State of North Carolina, and it is hereby enacted by the authority of the same, That it shall be the duty of the agent appointed to receive payment for Cherokee lands, to attend at the town of Murphy, in the county of Cherokee, on the first three days of each Superior Court for said county, for the purpose of receiving payments upon all bonds entrusted to his care by virtue of such agency.**[Ratified 18th January, 1847.]**

Chapter XIV. Cherokee Lands.

Chapter Four
North Carolina Laws

1846-47. An Act to provide for the sale of certain lands, in Cherokee and Macon counties, which have been surrendered to the State. (Pages 31-36).

Whereas, under the Act of the last General Assembly, entitled "an act more effectually to secure the debts due for Cherokee lands, and to facilitate the collection of the same," several tracts of land, commonly known as the Cherokee lands, were surrendered to the State, and ought to be again sold, as well as to secure homes to the first purchasers, as for the benefit of the State, no revenue whatever being derived by the State from said lands at present: for remedy whereof,

Be it enacted by the General Assembly of the State of North Carolina, and it is hereby enacted by the authority of the same, That all the lands surrendered by insolvents, under the provisions of said act, shall be again sold, under the following rules and restrictions, that is to say, the county court of Cherokee, (a majority of the Justices of said county being present) shall appoint one discreet person, residing in Cherokee county, and the Governor shall appoint two others, not residents of Cherokee county, who shall constitute a board of valuation, whose duty it shall be to value the lands so surrendered to the State, at a fair cash valuation, in the following manner: 1st, at their present worth, including the improvements placed upon them, by the former purchasers, or their assigns: 2nd, the worth of said lands when sold by the State in September, 1838, including such improvements as were on them at that time; taking into consideration in both cases the locality of said lands, and the facilities the purchasers may have in the transportation of their produce to market; and the said board of valuation shall make out duplicate lists of each class of valuation, as soon as may be, one copy of each class of such lists to be filed in the clerk's office of the county court of Cherokee, and the other they shall transmit to the Governor; and such copy filed in the clerk's office, as by this act directed, shall be kept by the clerk among the records of said court: Provided, that in no case shall the board of valuation hereby authorised place a less valuation upon the aforesaid land, than the rate fixed by the Act of Assembly of 1836, for the respective classes.

Sec. 2. Be it firther enacted, That the first purchasers who have surrendered said lands, their heirs, devisees, or assignees, respectively, shall have a pre-emption right to purchase the lands they, or either of them, have so surrendered, at the second valuation by said board: Provided, the right of pre-emption aforesaid, shall extend to no assignee, who may have become such since the surrender aforesaid; the said purchasers first paying one fourth of the purchase money, and giving bond with two or more

Chapter Four
North Carolina Laws

approved securities, (each of whom shall be considered good in his individual capacity for the whole debt,) to the agent of the State heretofore appointed under the act passed at the session of the General Assembly, held on the 3rd Monday of November, A.D. 1840, entitled "an act authorising the Governor to appoint an agent, in the county of Macon or Cherokee;" and such bonds, for the residue of the payment of the purchaser money, shall be made payable, in four equal annual instalments, bearing interest from date; and upon such bonds, when due and unpaid, suit shall be brought as upon the other bonds given for Cherokee lands, under the laws now in force concerning Cherokee bonds: Provided, nevertheless, that no suit shall be instituted in any Court of the State, when the amount due is within the jurisdiction of a Justice of the Peace; and in all such cases, the agent is hereby required to warrant for the same before some Justice of the Peace: And provided further, that in all cases where it may be necessary to bring a suit in Court, on any of the Cherokee bonds, the amount due and owing by the same parties, (although the same may be on several bonds) shall be consolidated in one action.

Sec. 3. Be it further enacted, That if the person or persons, who surrendered said lands, his, her, or their heirs, devisees, or assigns, should fail to comply with the requisitions of the second section of this act within three months after the valuations by the said board, then and in that case, the said agent for the State is hereby authorised and required to sell and dispose of any tract or tracts so surrendered, to any other person or persons desirous of purchasing the same, at the price of improved lands, upon such purchaser or purchasers first paying one fourth of the purchase money and giving the necessary bonds as required in said second section: Provided however, that if the agent of the State shall not be able to sell or dispose of the said lands at the price of improved lands, as herein provided, within six months from the expiration of the three months mentioned in this section, then, and in that case it shall be his duty to report that fact forthwith to the Governor of the State, accompanied by a list of all such lands, so remaining unsold; and the Governor, if he shall deem the same expedient, shall appoint one or two commissioners, as in his judjment may be deemed necessary, to superintend the sale of the said lands, at public auction, who, before entering on the discharge of their duty, shall execute to the Governor, for the use of the State, bond with approved security, in the sum of ten thousand dollars each, conditioned for the faithful performance of their duty, and accounting for all monies coming into their hands by virtue of their appointment as commissioners aforesaid.

Chapter Four
North Carolina Laws

Sec. 4. Be it further enacted, That in the event of a public sale being directed by the Governor, as aforesaid, it shall be his duty to advertise the same, for at least six weeks in not than less three newspapers of this State, setting forth the time and place of sale, which shall be held at the town of Murphy, in the county of Cherokee, and at such time as the Governor may appoint; and he shall also set forth, in the said advertisement, the terms and conditions of the said sale, which shall be the same as those mentioned in the second section of this act; and the Commissioners appointed as aforesaid, shall make a full report of their proceedings, together with an account of the cash by them received, to the Governor, within two months from the close of the said sales, and shall pay over, at the same time, to the Public Treasurer, all sums of money by them received on account of said sales; for which services they shall be allowed such sum as the Governor may deem just and reasonable, not exceeding three dollars per day, for every day that they may be engaged in travelling to the place and superintending the said sales, and making the necessary returns to the seat of Government: Provided however, that the public sale hereby authorised, shall not continue for a longer time than two weeks.

Sec. 5. Be it further enacted, That whenever it shall appear to said agent, that a part of any tract of land surrendered under the act of 1844, had been previously sold by the purchaser from the State to any other person or persons, then and in that case, it shall be the duty of the agent to have due regard to the interests of such subpurchaser at the time of surrender, and to resell to each, under the provisions of this act, according to the interest he or she may have had at the time of such surrender.

Sec. 6. Be it further enacted, That the pre-emption right, granted by the second section of this act, shall not extend to any person or persons who are not actual settlers on the lands, or who do not desire to become permanent residents in said counties of Cherokee and Macon: Provided, that nothing in this act contained, shall interfere with any right which any person or persons may have acquired under any existing law of the State.

Sec. 7. Be it further enacted, That each and every purchaser of any section or sections of said land, having obtained a certificate from the board constituted by this act, shall have full power and authority to institute an action of ejectment in the name of the State of North Carolina, against any person or persons, who may be in possession of such section of land, and shall, on application, refuse to deliver up quiet and peaceable possession thereof, or who shall intrude upon said purchasers, after they enter into possession, or who may hold over after their tenancy shall have expired. And the certificate of the board, to such purchaser, or his

Chapter Four
North Carolina Laws

assignee, shall be in evidence of title and right to sustain said action: Provided nevertheless, the said purchaser shall give bond and security for the payment of all costs accruing in said action, in case of his failure to recover.

Sec. 8. Be it further enacted, That as a full compensation for the performance by them of the duties herein required, the said board shall be allowed the sum of three dollars, each, for every day they may be necessarily engaged in the discharge of the duties herein imposed, to be paid by the agent of the Cherokee lands, out [of] monies in his hand, upon the affidavits of each of [the] members of said board, setting forth the number of days each may have so served; the receipt of the members of which board shall be received by the Public Treasurer, from the said Cherokee agent as cash, in any future settlement with him; and the said agent shall be allowed such compensation for the services required of him by this act, as the Governor, Treasurer and Comptroller may allow, upon satisfactory proof made to them, of the number of days which the said agent may have served, or such other evidence of the amount of service performed by him under this act; which compensation shall in no case amount to more than two dollars per day, for each whole day, the said agent may have been so employed.[**Ratified 18th of January, 1847.**]

CHAPTER LIX. Miscellaneous.
1846-47. An Act in favor of the Cherokee Chief, Junoluskee. (Page 128).

Whereas the Cherokee Chief Junoluskee, who distinguished himself in the service of the United States at the battle of the "Horses-Shoe," as commander of a body of Cherokees, as well as on divers other occasions during the last war with Great Britain, has, since his removal west of the Mississippi, returned to this State, and expressed a wish to remain and become a citizen thereof:

Sec. 1. Be it enacted by the General assembly of the State of North Carolina, and it is hereby enacted by the authority of the same, That the said Junoluskee be, and he is hereby declared a citizen of the State of North Carolina, and entitled to all the rights, priveleges and immunities consequent thereon.

Sec. 2. Be it further enacted, That the Secretary of State be, and he is hereby authorised and directed to convey unto the said Junoluskee, in fee simple, the tract of land in Cherokee county, in district 9, tract No. 19, containing three hundred and thirty seven acres; which said land the said Junoluskee shall be empowered to hold and enjoy, without the power to

Chapter Four
North Carolina Laws

see or convey the same, except for the term of two years from time to time: Provided nevertheless, that he shall have full power to dispose of the same by devise only.

Sec. 3. Be it further enacted, That the Public Treasurer be directed to pay unto the said Junoluskee the sum of one hundred dollars, out of any monies in the treasury not otherwise appropriated.

Sec. 4. Be it further enacted, That this act shall be in force from and after its passage. **[Ratified the 2nd day of January, 1847.]**

RESOLUTIONS.
1846-47. Resolution in relation to the bonds given for rent of Cherokee lands, surrendered to the State. (Page 250).

Resolved, That the obligors, their heirs, Executors and Administrators, in the bonds, heretofore given to the State, for rents of Cherokee lands surrendered to the State, under the act passed at the last session of the General Assembly, be, and they are hereby absolved and discharged from the payment of one half of the monies mentioned in said bonds: Provided, that this resolution shall in no wise affect the covenants contained in said bonds relative to the preservation and subsequent surrender of said lands, as therein stipulated. **[Ratified 16th of January, 1847.]**

RESOLUTIONS.
1846-47. Resolution in relation to the accounts of the purchasers of the Cherokee lands. (Page 251).

Resolved, That the Comptroller of public accounts be required, from the returns made by the agent for the collection of the Cherokee bonds, to the Treasury Department, to make the necessary and proper entries, on the accounts of the purchasers of Cherokee lands, on the books of his office, so that the said accounts shall show all payments made thereon, whether of principal or interest; and that the said Comptroller be required to continue to make similar entries on said accounts from the returns made by the said agent to the Comptroller's office, from time to time, so that the books and accounts of the said office shall at all times show the actual condition of the accounts of the purchasers of Cherokee Lands.

Resolved further, That the Comptroller shall be allowed for bringing up the aforesaid accounts, to the period when the Cherokee agent is directed to make a duplicate of his returns to the Comptroller's office, the sum of three hundred dollars, to be paid by the Public Treasurer, whenever

Chapter Four
North Carolina Laws

the said accounts on the Comptroller's books are brought up to the period aforesaid. **[Ratified 18th of January, 1847.]**

RESOLUTIONS
1846-47. Resolution in favor of James Wiggins and Alexander Nichols. (Page 378).
    Resolved, That the Governor of the State be, and he is hereby authorized and directed to accept a deed of release from James H. Wiggins, for Tract No. 1, Panther's Reservation, Macon County, and also a deed of release from Alexander Nichols, for Tract No. 75, District 8, Macon County, and to cancel the bonds of the said Wiggins and Nichols, given for the land aforesaid, in pursuance of an act passed by the General Assembly, at the session of 1844-45, entitled "an act more effectually to secure the debts due for Cherokee Lands, and to facilitate the collection of the same."
[Ratified the 2nd day of January, 1847.]

RESOLUTIONS
1846-47. Resolution in favor of William Morrison and Samuel Bryson. (Page 380).
    Resolved, That the Secretary of State be authorized and directed to issue a grant or grants to William Morrison and Samuel Bryson, for Tracts No. 31 and 32, in District No. 9, in the county of Macon, purchased by James Truitt, at the Cherokee land sales of 1836.
[Ratified 18th of January, 1847.]

RESOLUTIONS
1846-47. Resolution in favor of Ezekiel Dowdle and West Truitt. (Page 380).
    Resolved, That the Governor of the State be, and he is hereby authorized and directed to accept a deed of release from Samuel Bryson and William Morrison, assignees of James Truitt, for Tract No. 29, in District No. 9, purchased at Cherokee land sale of 1836, in Macon County, and that he cancel the bonds given for said land by said James Truitt, with Ezekiel Dowdle and West Truitt, his securities, in pursuance of an act passed by the General Assembly, at the session of 1844-45, entitled "an act more effectually to secure the debts due for Cherokee lands, and to facilitate the collection of the same."
[Ratified 12th day of January, 1847.]

RESOLUTIONS

Chapter Four
North Carolina Laws

1846-47. Resolution in favor of William Alexander. (Page 381).
Resolved, That the Secretary of State be, and he is hereby authorized to issue a grant to William Alexander for a tract of land in District third, Tract No. 118, Cherokee land sale of 1838.
[Ratified the 5th day of January, 1847.]

RESOLUTION
1846-47. Resolution in favor of Jacob Siler and Joseph Cathey. (Page 382).
Resolved, That the Public Treasurer be authorized and directed to pay to Jacob Siler ninety dollars for time and expenses of himself and Clerk in renting out Cherokee lands surrendered to the State, under an act of the last General Assembly, for expenses in travelling to and from Beattie's Ford, in the county of Lincoln, at the request of the late Treasurer of the State; and for time occupied in travelling to and from Raleigh, to cancel bonds for Cherokee lands surrendered to the State: also that the Treasurer be directed to pay Joseph Cathey the sum of ($16,) sixteen dollars, under the act of 1844-45, entitled "an act more effectually to secure debts due for Cherokee lands, and to facilitate the collection of the same."
[Ratified 8th day of January, 1847,]

RESOLUTION
1846-47. Resolution in favor of Thomas M. Angel. (Page 386).
Resolved, That the Secretary of State be authorized and directed to issue a grant or grants to Thomas M. Angel, of the County of Macon, for Tracts Nos. 92, 93, 94, 95, 101, 102, 103, in District No. 11, in said county, purchased by Henry Hogen, at the Cherokee land sales of 1836: Provided that said grant or grants shall not issue until the whole of the purchase money has been paid.
[Ratified the 5th day of January, 1847,]

RESOLUTION
1846-47. Resolution for the relief of Mary D. Moore. (Page 388).
Resolved, That the Governor be authorized to direct the agent of the State for the collection of bonds for purchase of Cherokee lands, to sell to Mary D. Moore, of Macon county, Tract No. 94, in District No. 16; and that he be directed to take her bond, with good security, for the amount due for said land at the time of the surrender of the same to the State by the said Mary D. Moore; and that the said Mary D. Moore shall have all the benefits of the act of 1844-45, entitled "an act more effectually to secure

Chapter Four
North Carolina Laws

the debts due for Cherokee lands, and to facilitate the collections of the same.
[Ratified 12th day of January, 1847.]

****

REPORT OF THE PUBLIC TREASURER
1846-47. Cherokee Bonds.

Received of Jacob Siler, agent,	16,357.25
Thomas L. Clingman, atto.	220.00
Edmond Jones,	874.67
N.S. Jarret,	24.36
James W. Guinn,	43.00
J.L. Dillard & others,	1,496.96
John Sudderth,	350.00
James Calloway,	50.00
M. Francis, atto. for A. Enloe,	125.00
S. Enloe, and others,	36.85
	19,578.09

****

LAWS OF THE STATE OF NORTH CAROLINA, PASSED BY THE GENERAL ASSEMBLY, AT THE SESSION OF 1848-49 PUBLISHED AGREEABLY TO THE NINETY FIFTH CHAPTER OF THE REVISED STATUTES.
RALEIGH: THOMAS J. LEMAY, PRINTER, 1849.

CHAPTER XLVII. Lands---Cherokee.
1848-49. An Act to facilitate the collection of certain debts given for Cherokee lands, and for other purposes. (Pages 95-97).
    Whereas at the different sales of the Cherokee lands, several tracts or parcels of land were sold separately to the same purchaser, and a bond for the whole amount of the purchase money, instead of separate bonds for each tract, was given; and whereas the original purchasers of such lands have, in many cases, sold and assigned the said lands to different persons; and whereas said assignees cannot pay for the tract or tracts so assigned to them and procure grants for the same, without first paying off the whole bond of the original purchaser, and therefore will not, and, in many cases,

Chapter Four
North Carolina Laws

cannot, pay off said bonds; and whereas the original purchasers have, in many cases, become insolvent, and the amount of their bonds cannot be collected; and whereas in some instances the sureties to the bonds of the original purchasers have satisfied said bonds, and have the agent's receipt in full for the same: Therefore,

Sec. 1. Be it enacted by the General Assembly of the State of North Carolina, and it is hereby enacted by the authority of the same, That in all cases where the original purchasers or their surety or sureties, of Cherokee lands, have failed to pay for the same, it should be the duty of the agent of the State for the collection of debts due for said Cherokee lands, to receive payment from any assignee of said original purchaser or purchasers, his heir, devisee or assignee, for any tract so assigned, and to give said assignee, his heir, devisee or assignee a receipt for the same, particularly specifying and describing the tract or parcel so assigned and paid for. And it shall be the duty of the Secretary of State, upon presentation of said Agent's receipt, to issue a grant for the tract or tracts of land, specified in said receipt, to the person or persons so paying for the same.

Sec. 2. Be it further enacted, That whenever in any case, the purchase money for Cherokee lands has been paid by or collected from the sureties to the original purchaser to the full amount of the bond or bonds given by them, it shall be the duty of the Secretary of State, whenever the fact of such payment has been satisfactorily certified to him by the said agent of the State, to issue a grant or grants for the lands so paid for to the person or persons paying for the same.

Sec. 3. Be it firther enacted, That nothing in this act contained shall authorize the agent to receipt for, or the Secretary of State to issue grants for any tract of land to the original purchasers or their sureties, unless the whole amount of the bond in which the price of said tract is included shall have been fully satisfied and paid off.

Sec. 4. Be it further enacted, That this act shall be in force from and after its ratification.
[Ratified 29th day of January, 1849.]

CHAPTER XLIX. Lands---Cherokee.
1848-49. An Act to amend an act, passed at the last session, entitled "An Act to provide for the sale of certain lands in Cherokee and Macon Counties, which have been surrendered to the State." (Pages 97-98).

Chapter Four
North Carolina Laws

Whereas no provision was made by the above recited act to require the agent of the State to return to the Comptroller's office an account of the lands resold under the provisions of said act: For remedy whereof,

Sec. 1. Be it enacted by the General Assembly of the State of North Carolina, and it is hereby enacted by the authority of the same, That the Cherokee land agent shall, on or before the first day of May next, return to the Comptroller's office a full and complete statement of all the surrendered lands, valued and resold under the above recited act, setting forth the names of the purchasers, the amount of each purchase, the amount paid, and the amount due, and when due. And in all cases where the bonds of the original purchasers have been cancelled, he shall return a statement thereof to the Comptroller, who shall credit the respective accounts of said purchasers, with the amount of said bonds.

Sec. 2. Be it further enacted, That upon the return of the statement of the agent to the Comptroller' office, shewing the account of sales as aforesaid, the Comptroller shall charge the obligors respectively in his books with amount of each bond; and when payments are made thereon, either to the Public Treasurer or the agent aforesaid, the Comptroller, on being furnished with the evidence of such payment, shall enter the proper credit for the same.
[Ratified 29th day of January, 1849.]

CHAPTER L. Lands---Cherokee.
1848-49. An Act for the relief of James Stewart of Cherokee County. (Pages 98-99).

Whereas Andrew J. Russell became the purchaser of two lots of Cherokee lands, at the land sale in 1838, number (112) one hundred and twelve, and (113) one hundred and thirteen, in district number six, lying in Cherokee county; and whereas the said Andrew J. Russell sold and assigned his interest in said lots to E.R. Scott, and the said E.R. Scott sold and assigned his interest in said lots to James Stewart, of Cherokee county; and whereas the said James Stewart has paid the purchase money for said lots into the Treasury of North Carolina, and the Secretary of State has issued grants for said lots in the name of the said E.R. Scott, and the said Scott has removed from the county, and resides in parts unknown: Therefore,

Sec. 1. Be it enacted by the General Assembly of the State of North Carolina, and it is hereby enacted by the authority of the same, That the Secretary of State be, and he is hereby directed to cancel the grants

Chapter Four
North Carolina Laws

issued in the name of E.R. Scott for lots numbered 112 and 113, in district number (6) six, of Cherokee lands, lying in Cherokee county, and issue grants to, and in the name of James Stewart for said lots of lands, any law to the contrary notwithstanding; and that this act shall take effect from and after the ratification thereof.
[Ratified 27th day of January, 1849.]

RESOLUTIONS
1848-49. Resolution concerning the improvement of the Indian Tribes. (Pages 227-228).

Whereas the condition of the various Indian tribes upon the Western frontiers of the United States, appeals to the humanity and justice of the General Government, to devise some plan by which a permanent home may be secured to them, by which their existence as a people may be secured and perpetuated; by which their moral, intellectual and social condition may be improved, and the blessings of civilization and civil liberty at length secured to them:

1. Be it therefore resolved, &c., That we recommend this to the serious consideration of the Congress of the United States, that, in the exercise of their wisdom, they may mature a plan by which the Indian tribes inhabiting our Western Territories may be placed more directly under the paternal care of the General Government; by which a specific region of country may be set apart for their permanent abode, secured to them forever against further encroachment, and undisturbed by the great current of Western emigration; by which their moral, intellectual and social condition may be improved and elevated; by which the blessings of education, civilization and christianity may be imparted to them; by which they may all be brought together and united in one grand confederation, and thus prepared for the enjoyment of civil and religious liberty; and if found practicable, they may be ultimately admitted into our Federal Union.

2. Resolved, That his Excellency the Governor of the State be requested to transmit a copy of these resolutions to each one of our Senators and Representatives in the Congre of the United States, that the same may be laid before their respective Houses.
[Ratified 29th day of January, 1849.]

RESOLUTIONS
1848-49. A Resolution to suspend the collection of Cherokee bonds, until the laying off the Turnpike road from the Georgia line to Salisbury. (Page 229).

Chapter Four
North Carolina Laws

Resolved by the General Assembly of the State of North Carolina, That Jacob Siler, the agent of the State for the collection of Cherokee bonds, be instructed, and he is hereby instructed, to suspend the further collection of debts due on Cherokee bonds, until the Turnpike road authorized by the present General Assembly, to be laid out and constructed from Salisbury, West, to the Georgia line, is laid off and the contracts let out; provided the same be properly secured.
[Ratified 29th day of January, 1849.]

RESOLUTIONS
Resolutions of A Private Nature.
1848-49. Resolution in favor of William Angel. (Page 465).
Resolved, That William Angel, purchaser of section No. 163, in district No. 15, Cherokee land sales of 1836, be released from the payment of the sum of thirty dollars, with interest from the date of his bonds given for the same: and that the Treasurer be allowed the same in the settlement of his accounts.
[Ratified 27th day of January, 1849.]

RESOLUTIONS
Resolutions of A Private Nature.
1848-49. Resolution in favor of Isaiah Cook and others. (Pages 468-469).
Resolved, That the Secretary of State be, and he is hereby requested to issue a grant to Isaiah Cook of Macon county, for section No. 3, in district No. 11, purchased by John Poteat at the Cherokee land sales of 1836; also to Nancy Fulton for section No. 18, in district No. 12, purchased by Robert and Jesse Fulton, at Cherokee land sales of 1820; also to David Guyer, for section No. 60, in district No. 17, purchased by David Ballew, at Cherokee land sales of 1838; also Ezekiel Dowdle, for section No. 49, in district No. 13, purchased by James Rodgers, at Cherokee land sales of 1836.
[Ratified 29th day of January, 1849.]

REPORT OF THE PUBLIC TREASURER
1848-49. Cherokee Bonds.
July 1847 Cash received of Jacob Siler, agent, am't collected of Cherokee bonds   2,000.00

Chapter Four
North Carolina Laws

Oct 1847 Jacob Siler, agent amount Collected on Cherokee bonds
3,958.00

Dec 1847 Jacob Siler, agent, money collected on Cherokee bonds
1,205.89

Apl. 1848 J. Siler, agent amount collected on Cherokee bonds
3,513.61

June 1848 J. Siler, agent, money on Cherokee Bonds   3,821.00

Oct. 1848 Jacob Siler, agent, amount collected on Cherokee Bonds
638.85
Oct. 1848 Cash received Jacob Siler, as advanced payment on lands sold by Act of Legislature   602.15

Jan. 1847 By Cash paid Jacob Siler for travelling to and from Raleigh to make returns   53.00

****

LAWS OF THE STATE OF NORTH CAROLINA PASSED BY THE GENERAL ASSEMBLY AT THE SESSION OF 1850-51.
RALEIGH: T.J. LEMAY, STATE PRINTER, 1851.

CHAPTER XXII. CHEROKEE LANDS.
1850-51. An Act to provide that copies of certain papers on file in the office of Secretary of State, relating to Cherokee lands, shall be evidence in certain cases. (Pages 60-61).
Sec. 1. Be it enacted by the General Assembly of the State of North Carolina, and it is hereby enacted by the authority of the same, That the list made and transmitted to the Governor, in pursuance of the first section of an act, ratified on the 7th day of January, A.D., 1845, entitled " An Act more effectually to secure the debts due for Cherokee lands, and to facilitate the collection of the same, by the commissioners appointed under the provisions of said act," and all the reports and certificates made to the Governor, by Jacob Siler, the agent for the State, in pursuance of any statute relating to his office or prescribing the duties thereof; and all deeds or written evidences of the surrender of Cherokee lands, by the purchasers thereof, their heirs, devisees, assignees or securities, executed in pursuance

Chapter Four
North Carolina Laws

of the act aforesaid, or an act entitled an act to amend an act, passed at the last session of the General Assembly, entitled an act more effectually to secure the debts due for Cherokee lands and to facilitate the collection of the same, shall deemed and held to be records; and any part of the list aforesaid, certified to be such by the Secretary of State, and countersigned by the Governor, or copy of any such deed or written evidence of surrender, report or certificate certified by the Secretary of State and countersigned by the Governor in like manner, shall be received in evidence by all courts in this State without further proof.

Sec. 2. Be it further enacted, That this act shall take effect from and after its ratification.
[Ratified 29th January, 1851.]

CHAPTER XXIII. CHEROKEE LANDS.
1850-51. An Act authorizing the transfer of books, bonds, &c., from the Treasurer's office to the Agent of the State, for the collection of Cherokee Land Bonds. (Pages 61-62).

Sec. 1. Be it enacted by the General Assembly of the State of North Carolina, and it is hereby enacted by the authority of the same, That whenever the agent of the State for the collection of Cherokee Bonds, shall have executed his bond to the State of North Carolina, in the sum of one hundred thousand dollars, with good and sufficient security, to be approved of by the Governor and Public Treasurer, it shall be lawful for the Public Treasurer and Comptroller to transfer such books, papers and bonds in their respective offices, as may be necessary to the settlement of the Cherokee land debts to the office of the said agent.

Sec. 2. Be it further enacted, That the said agent shall, on or before the first day of January, in each and every year, make a statement to the Governor, setting forth the amount he has received for Cherokee lands, and whether the same has been in money or in work on the Western Turnpike Road; and also what amount of money has been paid on orders given by the commissioner to superintend the building of the aforesaid road, together with the amount remaining in his possession.

Sec. 3. Be it further enacted, That, hereafter, the receipts of the aforesaid agent of the State for the collection of Cherokee Bonds, showing that full payment has been made for any tract of land in the county of Haywood, Macon or Cherokee, together with the proper certificate of sale, Transfer, deed or warrant and certificate of survey, shall be sufficient evidence on which the Secretary of State may issue a grant to the purchaser or enterer of said tract of land.

Chapter Four
North Carolina Laws

Sec. 4. Be it further enacted, That so much of an act of the General Assembly, passed in 1840-41, as requires the agent of the State, in the collection of Cherokee Bonds, to make remittance of moneys collected by him, and report to the Treasurer's office, together with all laws and clauses of laws, coming in conflict with this act, be, and they are hereby repealed.
[Ratified 27th January, 1851.]

CHAPTER XXIV. CHEROKEE LANDS.
1850-51. An Act to provide relief for the purchasers of Cherokee Lands, secure debts due to the State, and authorize the sale of lands surrendered to the State under the acts of 1844-5 and 1846-7. (Pages 63-67).

Whereas, by acts of the General Assembly, passed at the sessions of 1844-5 and 1846-7, all persons who purchased lands at the sale of 1838, and who were unable to pay for them, were authorized to surrender said lands to the State; and whereas a large number of tracts were surrendered under the provisions of said act; and whereas, by the subsequent act of 1846-7, those lands were assessed by agents appointed under said act, and the purchasers were, upon giving new bonds with approved security, permitted to take up the lands surrendered at the price fixed upon them by the agents of the State; ; and whereas it is but just and right that all purchasers should have the same measure of relief extended to them:

Sec. 1. Be it therefore enacted by the General Assembly of the State of North Carolina, and it is hereby enacted by the authority of the same, That the Governor of the State shall appoint three persons, not residents of Cherokee county who shall constitute a board of valuation, whose duty it shall be to value all the lands surrendered to the State and have not been taken up, also the lands of insolvent purchasers which have not been surrendered, as well as the lands of solvent purchasers (if desired to do so by such solvent purchasers) at a fair valuation: Provided, that no money shall be paid to any claimant, on account of any loss or damage which he or they may have sustained previous to the passage of this act.

Sec. 2. Be it further enacted, That in order to guard the interest of the State, the said board of commissioners shall have no power to reduce the price of any lands valued by them, below the valuation placed thereon by the Commissioners appointed to superintend their survey under the act of 1836, under which act the first quality was valued at four dollars per acre, the second quality at two dollars per acre, and the third quality at one dollar per acre, the fourth quality at fifty cents per acre, and the fifth

Chapter Four
North Carolina Laws

quality at twenty cents per acre. Provided further, That the said board of commissioners, in valuing the land of solvent purchasers, under this act, shall have no power to reduce the price of any tract below one half of what it was sold for in 1838. And it shall be the duty of the board of valuation to make out duplicate lists of such valuation as soon as may be. One copy of which shall be filed in the office of the clerk of the county court of Cherokee county, and the other they shall transmit to the Governor of the State, to be filed in his office, and the same shall form a part of the records of said offices.

Sec. 3. Be it further enacted, That the commissioners hereby authorized to be appointed, shall, within sixty days after the acceptance of their appointment, meet at the town of Murphy, in the county of Cherokee, for the purpose of proceeding in the execution of their duties; that the commissioners appointed by the county court of Cherokee county shall advertise for thirty days previously, at the Court House and three other public places in said county, and also in both the newspapers published at Asheville, the time and place of meeting of the said commissioners. And all persons desirous of taking the benefit of this act shall, within ten days next preceding the day appointed for the meeting of the commissioners aforesaid, apply either in person or by agent to the commissioner appointed by the county court of Cherokee county, whose duty it shall be to attend for that purpose, and render unto him a list containing the number of the tracts of land, the district in which they lie, and the number of sections of all the lands they desire to be valued under the provisions of this act. And the said commissioner shall enter the same in regular order, in a book prepared for that purpose, so that the board of valuation may, when met, proceed in the performance of their duty as herein required.

Sec. 4. Be it further enacted, That the commissioners aforesaid shall take and subscribe an oath, before some justice of the peace of Cherokee county, that they will, in accordance with the provisions of this act, and to the best of their judgments, value the land aforesaid fairly and impartially as between the purchasers or those entitled to their privileges and the State, and that they will endeavor to do equal and impartial justice between the purchasers themselves; and the said board shall give to each of the purchasers, or the persons entitled to their privileges, whose lands they may value, a certificate setting forth the district and valuation of each tract valued by them as aforesaid.

Sec. 5. Be it further enacted, That the comptroller of public accounts shall furnish, as soon as may be, after the passage of this act, to the agent of the State, who may be entrusted by law with the collection of

Chapter Four
North Carolina Laws

Cherokee bonds, a full and complete statement, containing the names of all the purchasers of Cherokee lands at the sale of 1838, who were returned solvent under the act of 1844; also the names of all the purchasers whose lands have been surrendered to the State; which statement shall exhibit the amount of the bonds given for the original purchase of each tract of land, together with the date of the same and the several payments made thereon, together with the date of each payment. And upon the receipt of the said statement, the agent shall proceed upon application of the purchasers aforesaid; and upon their producing the certificate of the board of valuation, showing the amount of the valuation of each tract, to deduct the payments which have been made to the State on each tract, from the valuation thereof, and for the balance due, if any, he shall take from the purchasers, or such other person or persons as may be entitled to the privileges of the original purchaser, bonds with good and sufficient security, payable in four annual instalments.

Sec. 6. Be it further enacted, That upon the settlement provided for in the last preceding section being made, and new bonds with good and sufficient security, to be approved by the agent of the State, being given, the said agent is hereby authorized to cancel and surrender up to said purchasers, their heirs, devisees or assignees all the bonds given to the State for said lands: Provided, nevertheless, that in case more than one tract shall be included in the same bonds and only a part of the tracts valued, then and in that case the agent shall not deliver up the bonds to the purchaser, but credit them for the tracts valued upon new bonds being given for such tracts, as in other cases where separate bonds had been given for each tract.

Sec. 7. Be it further enacted, That as a full compensation for the performance by them of the duties herein required, the said board shall be allowed the sum of three dollars each, for every day they may be necessarily engaged in the discharge of the duties herein required, and three dollars for every thirty miles in travelling to and from Murphy, to be paid by the agent of the Cherokee lands out of any monies in his hands, upon the affidavits of the members of the board, setting forth the number of days each may have served; and their receipts shall be received by the Public Treasurer from the said agent of Cherokee lands as cash, in any future settlement with him; and the said agent shall be allowed such compensation, for the additional services required of him by this act, as the Governor, Treasurer and Comptroller may allow, on satisfactory proof being made to them, of the number of days which the said agent may have

Chapter Four
North Carolina Laws

served, or such other evidence of the amount of service performed by him under this act.

Sec. 8. Be it further enacted, That none of the commissioners herein allowed and authorized to be appointed shall be purchasers of the Cherokee lands or liable on the Cherokee bonds or in any way interested in either.

[Ratified 27th January, 1851.]

CHAPTER XXV. CHEROKEE LANDS.
1850-51. An Act to authorize the sale of Refused Lands owned by the State in the Counties of Cherokee and Macon. (Pages 67-72).

Whereas, in the 4th section of the act of 1836, which authorized the survey and sale of lands acquired of the Cherokee Indians, it is provided, "and the principal surveyor, under the direction of the commissioners, shall cause to be surveyed as much of the said Cherokee lands as in their" opinion will command the sum of twenty cents per acre, and the residue of said land shall remain subject to the disposition of the Legislature, and when the surveyed lands are exposed to public sale, the land of the first quality shall not be sold for less than four dollars per acre; and land of the second quality, not less than two dollars per acre; and lands of the third quality, not less than one dollar per acre;and lands of the fourth quality, not less than fifty cents per acre; and lands of the fifth quality, not less than twenty five cents per acre; and whereas a small proportion of the tracts which were surveyed and offered for sale under the above recited act, did not command the minimum price, and consequently yet remain unsold, which it is the interest of the State should be disposed of:

Sec. 1. Be it therefore enacted by the General assembly of the State of North Carolina, and it is hereby enacted by the authority of the same, That it shall be the duty of the Board of Commissioners, who may be appointed under an act "for the relief of the purchasers of Cherokee lands and to secure debts due to the State," in addition to valuing the lands, as therein provided for, to value all the lands which surveyed under the act of 1836, and which were not sold by the State in 1838; and in fixing a valuation upon said lands, as well as those aforementioned, it shall be the duty of the said Board of Commissioners to take into consideration the localities of said lands, and the facilities which the purchasers may have in the transportation of their produce to market, and all other circumstances which tend to increase or diminish the value of those lands, except the improvements, which are not to be included in the valuation.

Chapter Four
North Carolina Laws

Sec. 2. Be it further enacted, That whereas many poor persons, being destitute of homes, have settled on said lands, who have made improvements thereon, with the intention of becoming purchaser; when they were disposed of, in order to furnish all such persons an opportunity of becoming purchasers, who desire to do so, after said valuation is made, it shall be the duty of said commissioners to furnish each occupant with a certificate, setting forth the district and number of the tract by him or her occupied, and also to furnish the agent of Cherokee bonds with a list of all such tracts valued, setting forth the value of each, and the name of each person entitled, in their opinion, to the pre-emption privilege under this act.

Sec. 3. Be it further enacted, That all persons who reside on any of the tracts of land to be valued under the 2nd section of this act, or have made or own improvements thereon, which add value to the land, shall have a pre-emption right to purchase the lands they or either of them have occupied or improved, at the valuation placed thereon by said board; and upon such person or persons presenting to the agent the certificate of the commissioners, to be issued under the 2nd section of this act, and entering into bonds, with two or more securities, to be approved by the agent, payable to the State in four annual instalments for the said valuation, it shall be the duty of said agent, upon receiving the said certificates and bonds, to issue a certificate to the purchaser, setting forth the tract by him or her purchased.

Sec. 4. Be it further enacted, That the provisions of the 3rd section of this act shall extend to the surveyed tracts, if any, in the county of Macon, and shall entitle the persons who may reside thereon, or own improvements on said tracts of land, to pre-emption rights to purchase said lands at the minimum price thereof; and, upon giving bonds as required in the 3rd section, shall be entitled to receive of the agents certificates of purchase as therein provided for.

Sec. 5. Be it further enacted, That the rights of pre-emption, provided for in the foregoing sections of this act, shall extend to all settlers upon vacant lands, in the county of Macon, which have not been subject to entry under the act of 1836; and upon such person or persons making satisfactory proof to the entry taker, that he or she reside on or have improved any of the vacant lands aforesaid, it shall be his duty to issue a warrant to the surveyor of the county to survey such person one hundred acres, to include his or her improvements; and upon the payment to the State of the sum required to be paid for other vacant lands in said county, the grants shall issue as in other cases of entries upon the land which have

Chapter Four
North Carolina Laws

been subject to entry; and the same fees shall be paid to the entry taker, surveyor and Secretary of State.

Sec. 6. Be it further enacted, That the persons entitled to pre-emption privilege, under the 5th section of this act, shall make their locations and pay the money to the State therefor against the first day of August next; after which time all of the said lands that shall remain vacant or not paid for, shall be liable to be entered as other vacant lands are now entered in the county of Macon, to be paid for at the same price, within six months from the time the location is made; otherwise the same shall be void.

Sec. 7. And Whereas many poor persons, being destitute of homes, have also settled upon the unsurveyed lands in the County of Cherokee, which lands were not surveyed under the act of 1836, because they were not considered worth twenty cents per acre; Be it therefore further enacted, That all persons who, prior to the first day of January, 1851, resided on any of said lands, or had made any improvements thereon which add value to the land, shall be entitled to a pre-emption privilege to one hundred acres, to include their improvements, at twenty cents per acre; and upon making satisfactory proof to the agent of Cherokee bonds that he or she is entitled to the pre-emption privilege within the meaning of this section of the act, it shall be his duty to issue a certificate to such person claiming the pre-emption privilege, setting forth the location of the hundred acres claimed; and upon such certificate, it shall be competent for the persons entitled to the pre-emption privilege to have the said lands surveyed, at his or her own expense, in a square or oblong square, to include his or her improvements; and duplicate copies of such survey shall be made, one to be forwarded to the Secretary of State, and the other to be presented, with the original certificate of occupancy, to the agent; and upon payment being made to him, one fourth of the price of said land, and upon entering into bonds with two or more securities, to be approved by the agent, payable to the State, in three annual instalments, for the remaining three fourths, to issue to said purchasers certificates of purchase, setting forth the number of the tract, the district in which situated, the number of acres and the price sold for.

Sec. 8. Be it further enacted, That the certificates issued to the purchasers under this act, shall entitle them to all rights and privileges the holders of certificates were entitled to under the said act of 1836.

Sec. 9. Be it further enacted, That all persons who make advance payments under this act, shall be entitled to the same discount as provided

Chapter Four
North Carolina Laws

for under the 12th section of the act of 1836, prescribing the mode of selling Cherokee lands.

Sec. 10. Be it further enacted, That in all cases where two occupants occupy the same lands, or live near each other, unless otherwise agreed upon between themselves, the line shall be run so as to divide the distance equally between their dwelling houses; and in case two persons claim the same improvements and the occupant right thereto, the person having the prior right, unless he has conveyed his claim to the subsequent settler, shall have the right of pre-emption.

Sec. 11. Be it further enacted, That the rights of pre-emption hereby granted to persons residing on, or who own improvements on the surveyed lands of Macon and Cherokee, and also upon the vacant lands in the last named county, provided for in this act, shall have until the first day of October next to avail themselves of the pre-emption privilege and to give lands [bonds?] as required by this act.

Sec. 12. Be it further enacted, That in case the act for the relief of purchasers of Cherokee lands, and this act granting pre-emption rights, shall pass, all lands held under certificates, in the county of Cherokee, shall be liable to the same taxes, both State and county, as other lands in this State.

[Ratified 28th January, 1851.]

RESOLUTIONS.
1850-51. Resolution for the relief of certain purchasers of Cherokee lands, residing in Macon county. (Page 508).

Resolved, That the benefits of an act of the present session of the General Assembly, to provide relief for certain purchasers of Cherokee lands, shall be extended as well to those purchasers in Macon county who bought in 1836, as those who bought in 1838.

[Ratified 28th January, 1851.]

RESOLUTIONS.
1850-51. Resolution granting land for a church. (page 508).

Resolved, that ten acres of the unsurveyed land, in the county of Cherokee, belonging to the State, be, and is hereby given to the Baptist Denomination in the vicinity of Fort Hembree, for the purpose of building a church thereon,

Resolved further, That the Secretary of State be authorized to issue a grant for the same, after it shall have been surveyed and its

Chapter Four
North Carolina Laws

boundaries described, on condition that ten cents per acre be paid to the agent of the State, and his receipt forwarded to the Secretary.
[Ratified 28th January, 1851.]

RESOLUTIONS.
1850-51. Resolution authorizing Jacob Siler agent of the State to correct a mistake in the sale of a tract of land to Isaac Moody. (Page 514).
Resolved, That Jacob Siler, agent of the State be, and he is hereby authorized to correct a mistake made in the sale of a tract of land to Isaac Moody, which tract appears on the certificate to be No. 141, which should have been No. 140, and that the money paid to said agent and bonds taken shall be made to apply to the tract No. 140 instead of No. 141.
[Ratified 28th January, 1851.]

RESOLUTIONS.
1850-51. Resolution in favor of Jacob Siler. (Page 822-823).
Whereas, Jacob Siler, agent of the State for the collection of Cherokee bonds, collected on a bond due to the State from John Painter and his securities, and paid over the same to the Treasurer, five dollars and five cents money that was due the State, after decucting a credit which was not perceived at the time of settlement, and whereas said agent, after discovering the mistake, paid back to the said Painter the sum of five dollars and five cents which he had over-paid:
Be it therefore resolved, That the Public Treasurer pay to the said Jacob Siler or place to his credit five dollars and five cents, the sum paid into the Treasury by mistake, if on examination he deems him entitled thereto.
[Ratified 22nd January, 1851.]

RESOLUTIONS.
1850-51. Resolution in favor of Jason Sherrill. (Page 823).
Whereas, at the sale of Cherokee Lands in 1820, Henry Wikle became the purchaser of a tract of land in the county of Haywood, in District No. 2, Section No. 12, containing one hundred and forty seven and three quarter acres, and subsequently conveyed it to Jesse C. Corkerham, who transferred his interest therein to Jason Sherrill, the present occupant; but in consequence of said deed of conveyance having been lost or mislaid, and the said Jesse Corkerham having removed from the State, said Sherrill

Chapter Four
North Carolina Laws

is unable to obtain a grant for said land, notwithstanding the State has received payment in full therefor:

Be it therefore resolved, That the Secretary of State be authorized to issue a grant to said Jason Sherrill, his heirs or assigns, for said tract of land, upon satisfactory proof being made that he is the present owner thereof, and that payment has been made in full to the State.
[Ratified 27th January, 1851.]

****

PUBLIC LAWS OF THE STATE OF NORTH CAROLINA PASSED BY THE GENERAL ASSEMBLY AT ITS SESSION OF 1854 - 55: TOGETHER WITH THE COMPTROLLER'S STATEMENT OF PUBLIC REVENUE AND EXPENDITURE
RALEIGH: HOLDEN & WILSON, PRINTERS TO THE STATE, 1855

COMPTROLLER.
Statements of the Comptroller of Public Accounts, for the two Fiscal Years ending October 31st 1853 and 1854. (Page 183).
Comptroller's Statement.
Public Fund-Receipts
Cherokee bonds $1,631.00

****

PRIVATE LAWS OF THE STATE OF NORTH CAROLINA PASSED BY THE GENERAL ASSEMBLY AT ITS SESSION OF 1854-55
RALEIGH, HOLDEN & WILSON, PRINTERS TO THE STATE, 1855

CHAP. 318. CHEROKEE LANDS.
1854-55. An Act for the relief of Solomon Newton. (Pages 445-446).

Sec. 1. Be it enacted by the General Assembly of the State of North Carolina, and it is hereby enacted by the authority of the same, That Solomon Newton shall have a right to purchase section No. 2 of Willnotas' reservation in Jackson county, at a price to be fixed by Jacob Siler and Mark Coleman, who are hereby appointed commissioners for that purpose; and on the value of the lands being ascertained as aforesaid, he may file his bonds, payable to the State in one and two years, in legal instalments with

Chapter Four
North Carolina Laws

good security, to be judged of by the agent of the State for the collection of Cherokee bonds; and when it is certified to the secretary of State by said agent, that said bonds are fully paid, he shall issue a grant to said Newton of all such rights that the State has in said lands.

Sec. 2. Be it further enacted, That this act shall take effect and be in force from and after its ratification.
[Ratified the 15th day of February, 1855.]

****

PUBLIC LAWS OF THE STATE OF NORTH CAROLINA PASSED BY THE GENERAL ASSEMBLY AT ITS SESSION OF 1856-57
RALEIGH: HOLDEN & WILSON, PRINTERS TO THE STATE, 1857

COMPTROLLER'S STATEMENT
1856-57. (Page 108).
Jacob Siler, agent for collecting Cherokee bonds,   200.00.

COMPTROLLER'S STATEMENT
1856-57. (Page 155).
Jacob Siler, agent for collection of Cherokee bonds,   640.00.

COMPTROLLER'S STATEMENT
1856-57. (Page 157).
Jacob Siler, agent for collection of Cherokee bonds,   260.00.

Index

1

13 United States, 199

A

Abram
  A Cherokee Indian from Chilhowey., 206
Allen
  Colonel, 178
  James, 33
  James, a Tuscarora, 33, 35
  James, a Tuscarora., 37, 38
An Nu Chah
  A Cherokee Indian from Tuskuga., 206
Anee chah
  Chief of Tuskega, 256
Anna ke hu jah, or the Girl of Tuskega, 249

Annee chah of Tuskega, 249
Arrington
  Mr., 67, 70
Ashley
  Thos., 20
Atta Kulla Kulla
  A Cherokee Indian from Notchey Creek., 206
Atta kulula' kulla, or the little Carpenter of Natchey Creek., 249
Attakullakulla
  a Cherokee Indian, 204
Attus ah, or the Norward Warrior of the mouth of Tellico River, 248
Averit
  Henry, 54
Avery
  Mr, his speech., 224
  Mr., 209, 219
  Mr., his Interrogation of the Indians., 219
  Mr., His speech, 250

  Mr., His speech., 236
  Mr., Speech of., 209
  Waightstill, 194, 197, 247, 253, 254, 257
  Waightstill, a Commissioner, 194
  Waightstill, a Commissioner., 206
Awo Yah, or the Pidgeon of Natchey Creek, 248

B

Banner
  H.L., 65
Baptist Denomination, 291
Barnwell
  Collo., 14, 15
Baron
  de Graffenried, 9
Basket
  Billie, a Tuscarora, 33, 34

Index

Billie, a
  Tuscarora., 41
Billy, a
  Tuscarora., 37, 38, 42
Thomas, a
  Tuscarora, 34
Thomas, a
  Tuscarora., 37, 38
Baskett
  Billy, a
    Tuscarora., 41
Baskit
  Billy, a
    Tuscarora., 42
Baskitt
  William, a
    Tuscarora., 45
Bate
  Hum., 31
  James, a
    Tuscarora, 34
Bates
  Henry, 43
  Humphrey,
    Petition of., 29
Beloved Man
  the Indians also referred to their great men as "beloved man, 202
Beloved Man of Virginia
  The Indians referred to the Governor of Virginia as a "beloved man.", 202
Belt
  A symbolic belt whereby the Indians hold fast to one end, and the whites hold fast to the other end., 214
Bentley
  James, 54
Bethlehem in the Forcks of Delaware, 187
Big Bullet, a Cherokee killed by a white man, 196
Big Bullett
  a Cherokee Indian murdered by a white man., 203
Big Fellow
  A Creek Indian., 211
Big White Owl
  A Cherokee Indian from Notchey Creek., 206
Big Wolf
  (Governor Tryon.), 236
  The name given to Governor by the Cherokee Indians., 224
Binford
  Jno M, 64
  Jno. M., 86
  John M., 84, 86
  Mr., 61
Black Smith
  to dress the Indian's guns., 193
Bledsoe
  Isaac, 247
Blount
Billie Junr., a
  Tuscarora., 41
Billie Senr., a
  Tuscarora., 41
Billie, a
  Tuscarora, 33, 34
Billy, a
  Tuscarora, 34
Billy, a
  Tuscarora., 37, 38
Capt. George, a
  Tuscarora, 34
George, a
  Tuscarora, 33
George, a
  Tuscarora., 37, 38
Governor, 170, 177
James, 29
Lightaea, 22
Thomas, a
  Tuscarora, 33, 34
Thomas, a
  Tuscarora., 37, 38
William, 164
William, a
  Tuscarora., 52
William, Esqr., 164
Wm., Agent for North Carolina., 164
Blountt
  Mr. Tho., 4
Blunt
  Billie Junr., a
    Tuscarora., 41, 42
  Billie Senr., a
    Tuscarora., 42

Index

Billy Junr., a
    Tuscarora., 42
Billy Senr., a
    Tuscarora., 41, 42
Wm., a
    Tuscarora., 53
Bogar
    Wm., 191
Bostick
    Absalom, 180
Boundary Line, 208
Boundary line run by Donelson, 192
Bradley
    John, 184
Brandon
    Christopher, 191
    Geo., 191
    Jas., 191
Brice
    Capt., 11
    Mr., 4
    William, 4
Bridgers
    Saml, a
        Tuscarora, 35
    Saml., a
        Tuscarora, 33
    Saml., a
        Tuscarora., 41
    Samuel, a
        Tuscarora, 33, 41
    Samuel, a
        Tuscarora., 37, 38, 42
Bridges
    Bonner, 26
    Cashy, 26
British Parliament, 186
Britt
    Wm., 4
Brittain
    Wm., 177, 178
Brooks
    Cash, 202
Brown
    Bartley, 191
    James, 189
    Jas., 190
    Jno., 191
Bryan
    Col. Needham, 40
    Jonathan, a Commissioner for Georgia, 214
Bullock
    Leo Hen., 220
    Leo. Hen., 221
Burch
    David, 191
Burges
    L., 84
Burnsides
    Jno., 191

C

Cabarrus
    S, 64
    S., 61, 66
Cain
    Billie, a
        Tuscarora, 33, 35
    Billy, a
        Tuscarora., 37, 38, 42
    John, a Tuscarora, 33, 34
    John, a
        Tuscarora., 37, 38
Cameron
    a British Agent, 196, 198

Alexr., 199
British Agent, 222
D., 65
D., Chairman., 71
Dun., 64
Mr., 61, 199
Canada, 57, 200
Canaliskeeticowee
    A Cherokee Indian., 214
Cane
    William, a
        Tuscarora, 44
Capes
    Look-Out, 18
Capt. White Eyes, 202
Carey
    Mr., 8
Carney
    Mr., 61
Carolina, 215
Carson
    Jna., 184
Carter
    Col., 194
    Colo., 219
Carters Valey, 242, 246
Carters Valley, 232
Cary
    Miles, 8
Castellaw
    James:, 19
Caswell
    R., 46
    Rd., 195
    Richard, Esqr., 195
    Richard, Governor., 44
Cearney
    S.W., 64
Ceasar's Islands, 85
Cetico

Index

A Cherokee
  Indian Town.,
  206
Cettico
  An Indian Town,
  219
Chain of Friendship,
  233
  During Treaty
    negotiations,
    the Chain of
    Friendship is
    mentioned
    often as a link
    that bound the
    two parties
    together in
    friendship., 204
Charles
  Wineoak, a
    Tuscarora, 33,
    34
  Wineoak, a
    Tuscarora., 37,
    38
Charles Town, 210
Charlestown, 211
Charlton
  George, 30
  William, 29, 30
Cheeweyeh
  An Indian town in
    the Valley
    Settlements.,
    255
  His speech, 255
Cherokee Indian,
  Called the Big
  Bullet, 197
Cherokee Indians,
  183
Cherokee Lands, 292
Cherokee Nation,
  211
Cherokees, 193

Lower Towns.,
  210
Middle Valley
  Towns., 210
Sell land to
  Richard
  Henderson.,
  220
Willnotas'
  reservation.,
  293
Chesnut
  A Cherokee
    Indian from
    Tellicho and a
    new town at its
    mouth., 206
Chilhoway
  an Indian town,
  200
Chilhowey
  An Indian Town.,
  206, 219
Chinistiska
  A Cherokee
  Indian, 214
Choctaw Traders,
  194
Choownatee
  A Cherokee
  Indian, 214
Chota
  A Cherokee
    Indian town.,
    242
  a Cherokee Town,
    204
  An Indian Town,
    206
  An Indian town.,
    236, 241
Chote
  A Cherokee
    Indian town,
    236

A Cherokee
  Indian town.,
  211, 223, 228,
  233, 253
a Cherokee town,
  200
A Cherokee
  Town., 215
An American
  Agent to reside
  in., 236
an Indian town,
  200
An indian Town.,
  217
An Indian town.,
  230, 237, 244,
  252, 254
An Indian Town.,
  210
Indian town., 193
Chow, We, Hah
  A Cherokee
    messenger.,
    207
Christian
  Col., 194, 207,
    214, 250
  Col. william, 193
  Col., his speech.,
    232, 235
  Col., His speech.,
    243
  Col., Speech of.,
    218
  Col., Virginia
    Commissioner,
    192
  Colo., 218, 235
  Colo., his speech
    to the
    Commissioners
    ., 231
  Colo., his speech.,
    222

300

Index

Colo., speech of., 228
William, 254
A Commissioner, 205
Wm., 197
Churton
  Mr. William, 18
  W.C., 18
Cities and Towns
  Knoxville, 177
  Newbern, North Carolina, 177
  Rawleigh, North Carolina, 178
City of Washington, 86
Clana nah
  A Chief of Cowee, 254
Clayton
  L., 184
Clenton
  Edwd., 191
Cleronakee
  A Cherokee Indian, 214
Clifton
  Peter, 54
Cloooketa
  A Cherokee Indian, 214
Cochran
  Jonathan, a Commissioner for Georgia, 214
Cockerell
  Edwd., 21
Coleman
  Mark, 293
Commissioners Speech, 203

Commonwealth of Virginia, 242
Coope
  John, 21
Corkerham
  Jesse, 292
  Jesse C., 292
Cornelious
  Billie, a Tuscarora, 33, 35
  Charles, a Tuscarora, 33, 36, 37
  Isaac, a Tuscarora., 41, 42
Cornelius
  Billy, a Tuscarora., 37, 38
  Charles, a Tuscarora., 38
  Isaac, a Tuscarora., 41
Council Fire, 207
County of Franklin, 164
Coward
  Wm., 20
Cowee
  A Cherokee town in the Middle Settlements., 254
Creek
  Camp, 239
  Deep, 32
Creek Indians, 210, 211
Creek Killer
  A Cherokee Indian from Tellicho and a

new town at its mouth., 206
Creek Nation, 193, 230
Creek Town
  a council for War against Georgia, 193
Creeks
  An Indian Tribe, 210
  Bare, 16
  Camp, 239, 246
  Catashny, 16
  Clouds, 239, 242, 246
  Contentnea, 17
  Deep, 37, 48, 64, 77
  Mckamies, 226
  McKamies or McNamies, 239
  McNamies, 246
  Muddy, 181
  Notchy, 203
Cumberland Gap, 192, 202, 222, 226, 234

D

Davidson
  Benjm., 184
  James, 184
Davie
  William R., 64
  William R., Commissioner., 56
  William Richardson, 62, 64, 75, 76, 77, 81

301

Index

Wm. R., 59
Wm. R.,
  Commissioner.
  , 60
de Graffenried
  Hon. Baron,
  Landgrave., 13
Dearborn
  H, 59
  H., 58, 60
Dearbourn
  H., 56
Declaration of
  Independence,
  199
Denis
  Billie, a
  Tuscarora, 33,
  34
Dennis
  Billy, a
  Tuscarora., 37,
  38
Dereham
  Tho., 4
Dewits Corner, 213
  Treaty signed
  between the
  State of South
  Carolina, and
  the Cherokee
  Indians., 211
Dickinson
  Wm., 191
Dinsmoor
  Mr., 184
Dobbs
  Arthur Esqr., 29
  Arthur, Governor,
  187
Dobbs Parish, 187
Donaldsons Line,
  242
Donelson
  Col., 242

Colo., 220, 232
Donelsons Line, 220
Donovin
  Hugh, 191
Dragging Canoe, a
  Cherokee, 198
Draging Canoe
  A Cherokee
  Indian., 209,
  252
  Absent from the
  Treaty
  negotiations.,
  209
Drayton
  William Henry, a
  Commissioner
  for South
  Carolina, 214
Dudley
  Christopher, 23,
  24, 25
  Mr., 22, 23
Dugan
  Robt., 191

E

Earle of Granville,
  40
Eden
  Charles, 18
  Charles, Esqr,
  Governor, 18
Egerton
  Wm., 21
Elder Brother of
  Virginia
  That is, the
  Governor of
  Virginia., 203
Elder Brothers
  The Indians
  referred to the

White
  Commissioners
  and other
  important
  White men as
  their Elder
  Brothers, 200
Eliss
  John, an Indian
  trader., 188
  John, warns
  settlers to
  leave., 188
England, 14
English Agents, 194

F

Falling Run, 37, 48,
  77
Falls of Ohio, 201
Farrel
  Thos, 191
Feast of Saint
  Michael the Arch
  Angel, 33
Floid
  Mat, 191
Florida, 200
Florida towns
  Pensacola, 194
Forks of Ohio, 201
Forster
  Andw., 191
  Arthur, 191
  Henry, 191
Fort Patrick Henry,
  192, 193, 256
Fort Rutledge, 212,
  213
Fort Seneca, 211
Forts
  Erection of a fort.,
  191

Index

Fort Hembree, 291
Fort to be erected at Warlicks Mill, 187
Henry, 241, 245, 253
Robisons, 234
Rutledge, 212
Seneca, 211
Freeman
Wm., 54
Frontier Inhabitants Interests of, 192
Frunteers of Anson County, 190
Fry
William, 26, 28
Willm., 28
Frys
William, Deposition of., 26

G

Gaither
Mr., 60
Gale
Christopher, 9, 11, 12, 13, 19
Christopher, Esqr., 20
Christopher, Esqr., Chief Justice., 24
Major Christopher, 10
Rev. Miles, Rector of Keighley in Yorkshire, 9
Galphins
Mr., 211
Mr., at Cowpen at Oguchy., 211
Gardiner
John, 23, 25
John, Deposition of., 22
Mr., 24
Gardner
John, 22
Garisons
To prevent mischiefs., 12
Gatlin
Edward, 4
Gazette from Charlestown, 211
General Washington, 206, 227
George
Billie, a Tuscarora, 33, 35
Billy, a Tuscarora., 37, 38
Snip Nose George, a Tuscarora, 33
Snip Nose, a Tuscarora., 37, 38
Snipnose, a Tuscarora, 33, 35
Georgia, 163, 164, 193, 210, 211, 212, 213, 251
Gibs
Robert, Esq, Gov., 12
Gibson
Walter, 42
Walter, a Tuscarora., 41, 42, 46, 52
Walter, a Tuscarora.., 42
Gilkey
Saml., 191
Gist
Col., 193, 198, 199, 207, 217, 227
Col. Nathaniel, 206
Colo., 210, 229, 230, 239, 240, 247, 250
Mr., 211
Nathaniel, 247
Glascock
William, a Commissioner for Georgia., 214
Glasgow
James, Sec., 195
Governor of Virginia, 235
Great Being
God, as referred to by the Indians and the Commissioners., 203
Great Britain, 192
Great Brittain, 15
Great Chain of Friendship, 204
Great Limestone, 246
Great Warrior of America, 240
The Indians when they referred to General Washington., 239
Green
Capt. Wm, 191

Index

Jeremy, 191
Reverend Doctor, 184
Greene
   Doctor, 185
Grier
   Mr. Andw., Commisary for Washington District., 256
Grymes
   Saml, 34

H

Haley, 199
Hammond
   Leroy, a Commissioner for South Carolina, 213
Hardy
   Jos., 26
   Jos., Coroner, 27, 28
   Joseph, Coroner, 28
Harland
   Ellis, an Indian trader., 230
Harnett
   Mr. Cornelius, 31
Harris
   E., 64
   Mr. Edward, 61
Harry
   a Tuscarora., 37, 38
Harry, a Tuscarora, 33
Hart
   David, 220, 221
   Geo., 198
   Nathaniel, 220

Natl., 221
   Thomas, 220, 221
Harvey
   John Esq., 9
Hawking
   William, 86
Hawkins
   Mr., 86, 170
   William, Commissioner., 86
Hawks
   F.L., 9
Haywood
   J, 178, 179, 180
Henderson
   Colo., 250
   Colo. Richard, Memorial of., 220
   David, 19
   Richard, 182, 220, 221
   Richard, purchased land from the Indians., 220
Henly
   Peter, Esqr., Cheif Justice., 27
Henry
   Fort, 247
   Joseph, 184
   P., 193
Herndon
   Colo., 178
Herring
   John, 19
Hicks
   David, 19
   Mr Robert, 18
Highwasaw
   An Indian Town., 206
Highwassee

An Indian Town, 205
Hill
   Wm., 65
Hix
   James T., a Tuscarora.., 43
   John, 42
   John, a Tuscarora., 41, 42
Hogg
   James, 220, 221
Holbrook
   John, 19
Holston River, 193
Hooker
   Mr., 70
Hookes
   Mr., 67
Hopewell, 182
Horry
   D., a Commissioner for South Carolina, 214
House
   James, 54
Howcott
   Edwd., 20
Howet
   Thos, a Tuscarora, 35
Howett
   Thomas, a Tuscarora, 33
   Thomas, a Tuscarora., 38
Howitt
   Thomas, a Tuscarora., 37
Hugh
   Wm., 191
Hughy
   Jas., 191

Index

Hunt
  J, 178, 179, 180
  J, CHC, 61, 66, 67, 70, 182
  J., 66, 67, 70, 82
  J., CHC, 70
  J.,CHC, 71
Hunter
  Coll., 7
Huntington
  Commodore, 5
Hyde
  Madam, 11
  Mr., 8
Hyman
  Hugh, 54

I

In He Ke Hiyah
  A Cherokee from Tuskuga., 206
India Towns
  Hocomawananck towns, 17
Indian
  John Cope, an Indian, Tryal of., 19
  John Cope, an Indian., 19
  Sighacka, an Indian., 24
  Thomas Blount, an Indian, 4
Indian Commission, 53
Indian Head Line, 48
Indian Nation
  Pamptico, 18
Indian Nations
  Bare River, 16
  Catashny, 16

Connamocksock, 18
Coranine, 18
Core, 16
  Machapunga, 18
  Neusiok, 18
  Nuse, 16
  Pamptico, 16
  Tuscarora Indians., 32
  Tuscaroras, 32
  Tuskarora, 29
Indian Scouts
  Scouters, 187
Indian Town
  Haruta, 17
  Tosneoc, 17
Indian Towns
  Anna Ooka, 17
  Canookehee, 16, 17
  Catashny, 17
  Chatooka, 18
  Chunaneets, 17
  Conauh-Kare Harooka., 17
  Contah-nah, 17
  Eno, 17
  Eukuskuerent, 16
  Juninits, 16, 17
  Kenta, 16, 17
  Kentah, 16
  Naur-he-ne, 17
  Oonossoora, 17
  Rarookahee, 16
  Rauroota, 16, 17
  There were three Indian Towns, 201
  Taherooka, 17
  Tarharota, 16
  Tarhunta, 17
  Tarhuntah, 16
  Toherooka, 16
  Tostehant, 16

Tostehaut, 16, 17
Indian Traders, 193
  John Eliss, 188
Indian Woods, 85
Indians, 186
  An Act for the Tuscaroras, 47
  Assaults & robberies against settlers, 190
  Assaults by., 187
  Bare River, 3
  Big Bullet, a Cherokee, 195
  Billie Basket, an Indian., 31, 32
  Billie Blount, an Indian., 32
  Billie Cain, an Indian, 31
  Billie Cain, an Indian., 32
  Billie Cornelious, an Indian., 31, 32
  Billie George, an Indian., 31, 32
  Billie Mitchell, an Indian., 32
  Billie Netop, an Indian., 32
  Billie Owin, an Indian., 31
  Billie Owins, an Indian., 32
  Billie Roberts, an Indian., 32
  Billie Sockey, an Indian., 31, 32
  Billy Blount, an Indian., 32
  Billy Denis, an Indian., 32

Index

Billy Roberts, an Indian., 32
Burning and threatening to take lives., 190
Calabas, 189
Cannuesk, an Indian, 17
Canuneskguoshkene, an Indian, 17
Capt. Joe, an Indian., 32
Catabas, 189
Catauba, 190
Charles Cornelious, an Indian, 31
Charles Cornelious, an Indian., 32
Cherekee, 190
Cherokee, 170, 294
Cherokee Bonds., 294
Cherokees, Boundary line., 194
Cherokees, Trade with, 181
Cheuntharoonthoo, an Indian, 17
Chowan Indians, Petition complaining of encroachments, 189
Colsera, called Henry., 17
Commissioners appointed., 68
Committing a crime., 26
Complain of encroachment, 216
Complain of encroachments on the Watauga., 219
Corees, 12
Coresniena, called Barber., 17
Creeks, 170
Disposition of, 177
Ehehosguos, called Lawson., 17
Enslaved, 11
Enugnerehau, an Indian, 17
Eruntanhyne, an Indian., 17
Ettacullacula or Carpenter, 181
George Blount, an Indian., 31, 32
Harry, an Indian., 31, 32
Heunthanotineh, a Tuscarora., 15
Heuntha-not-neh, an Indian., 17
Intoxicated, 44
Isaac Miller, an Indian, 31
Isaac Miller, an Indian., 32
James Allen, an Indian, 31
James Allen, an Indian., 32
James Mitchell, an Indian., 32
James Strawberry, an Indian., 27
James, an Indian., 18
John Cain, an Indian., 32
John Cope, a Christian Indian., 20, 21
John Cope, an Indian, 20
John Cope, an Indian., 21
John Litewood, an Indian., 32
John Rogers, an Indian., 31, 32
John Senicar, an Indian., 31, 32
John Walker, an Indian, 32
John Walker, an Indian., 32
John Wiggins, an Indian, 31
John Wiggins, an Indian., 32
Justice to, 192
Killing their Calves, 4
King Blount, 21, 24
King Blount, an Indian., 20
King Thomas Blount, Chief of Tuscaroras., 29
Lewis Tufdick, an Indian., 31, 32
Longboard, a Tuscarora Chief., 68
Longboard, a Tuscarora., 69
Lysle Ounskininenee,

Index

called Squarehookis., 17
Massacre By Indians, 12
Massacre by Indians., 14
Matchepungo Indians, 16
Meherrin, Encroachment against., 8
Mingoes, an Indian Tribe whose members were from different Nations, 200
Mohawk Nation, 57
Mohocks, 36
Nawoontootsere, a Tuscarora, 15
Neneuhguotkan, called John Pagett., 17
Newoonttootsery, an Indian., 17
Oconostota, a Cherokee, 194, 195
Old Indian, by name of Sighacka., 23
Owins, an Indian., 32
Petition of Whitmell Tufdick., 51
Prisoners, 11
provisions for., 192
Purchasing land from, 181
Saccorusa, a Tuscarora Chief., 68
Saccorusa, a Tuscarora., 69
Sacorusa, a Tuscarora., 68
Samuel Bridgers, an Indian., 31, 32
Samuel Smith, a Tuscarora., 69
Saponies, 6
Saroonha Herunttocken, an Indian., 17
Saroonha, an Indian., 17
Saroonha, Tuscarora, 15
Scalping of, 178
Senekoes, 13
Shanaws, Sinakers and Cherekees or a Mixter, 190
Shawanaws, Mingoes, Sinakers, & Cherekees, 187
Sighacka, an Indian, 23
Sinnicars (Senecas), 189
Snip Nose George, an Indian, 31
Snip Nose George, an Indian., 32
South Carolina Indians, 14
Telicesky, 181
Thomas Basket, an Indian., 32
Thomas Blount, an Indian., 31, 32
Thomas Howett, an Indian., 31
Thomas Howits, an Indian., 32
Thomas Senicar, an Indian., 31, 32
Tom Blount, 15
Tom Blount, an Indian., 17
Tom Jack, an Indian., 32
Tories & Indians, 181
Touginanah, an Indian, 17
Treaty formerly laid out to Tuscaroras., 30
Treaty with the Tuscaroras., 70
Tuscarora, 6, 8, 12, 15
Tuscarora Chiefs, 60
Tuscarora Indians, 33
Tuscarora lands leased., 51
Tuscarora Nation, 24, 67
Tuscaroras, 31, 36, 38, 39, 40, 48, 56, 58, 60, 71
Tuscaroras addicted to drinking., 48
Tuscaroras Attack Settlers., 9
Tuscaroras complaint., 49

307

Index

Tuscaroras
  Lands., 51
Tuscaroras, Bill
  with., 68
Tuscaroras,
  Petition of., 29
Tuscaroras, unfair
  dealings with.,
  49
Tuscaroras., 38
Tuscaroroe, 1, 2
Tuscaroroes,
  Great Men of,
  3
Tuscorodos, 3
Tuskarooroe, 18
Tuskarora, 29
Tuskarora Indian,
  maiming of.,
  25
Tuskaroras, 13
Tusks
  (Tuscaroras),
  189
Villany
  committed by.,
  12
William Pugh, an
  Indian., 32
William Taylor,
  an Indian., 32
Wineoak Charles,
  an Indian., 31,
  32
Wm. Pugh, an
  Indian., 32
Wooach or Little
  Pidgeon, 181
Young Tyler, an
  Indian., 17
Indians Complain of
  encroachments on
  the Nonachuckey,
  219
Indians on the Island
Refers to the
  Indians
  attending the
  Treaty
  negotiations.,
  202
Indians Vs. Wm.
  King, 53
Irvine
  Capt. Callender,
  58

J

Jack
  Thomas, a
    Tuscarora, 33
  Thos, a
    Tuscarora, 34
  Tom, a Tuscarora,
    34
  Tom, a
    Tuscarora., 37,
    38
Jefferson
  Thomas, 81
Jenings
  E., 8
Joe
  Capt., a
    Tuscarora, 33,
    34, 35
  Captain, a
    Tuscarora., 37,
    38
Johnson
  Sir William, 36
Johnston
  Alexr., 191
  Gabriel,
    Governor, 188
  John., 43
  Mr., 170
  Samuel Junr., 55

Samuel, Junr., 54
William, 220, 221
Jolly
  Jos, 191
Jones
  Allen, 39, 40
  Capt., 178
  John, 20
  Jos., 191
  Robert, 32, 33,
    34, 37, 38, 39,
    49, 61, 68, 69,
    71, 72
  Robert Junr., 32,
    51
  Robert, a
    Tuscarora, 37
  Thos., 21
  Willie, 39, 40, 41,
    42, 43, 50
Judge Friend
  A Cherokee
    Indian, 252

K

Kay eta ch or the
  Old Tassel of
  Toquoe, 247
Kearns
  John, 247
Kelse
  Jno, 191
  Joseph, 191
Kelsey
  Jno, 191
Kenedy
  George, 191
Kennedy
  Wm., 191
Kentuckie, 192, 201,
  220, 232, 234,
  235

308

Index

A country bought from the Norward Indians., 222
Settlements on., 242
Kimsey
  Thos., 28
King
  William, 41, 44
  Wm., 40, 54
King of Great Britain, 31, 199
King of Great Brittain, 27
Knott
  Elizabeth, 26, 27, 28
  Elizabeth, Murder of., 28
  Mrs., 26

L

Lanier
  Robert, 194, 197, 247, 253, 254, 256
  Robert, a Commissioner, 194, 206
Latta
  Jno., 191
Lawson
  Hugh, 191
  Mr., 10, 13
  Mr., Barbarously Murdered., 10
Legge
  Hum:, 4
Leigh
  J, 179
Lenoir
  Wm., 177

Letter of the Secretary of War, 57
Lewis
  Mr., 81
  Wm., 177
Lewis & Wood, 181
Lewton
  Constant, 21
  Thomas, 21
Lightwood
  John, a Tuscarora., 37, 38
Liscomb
  John, 26, 27, 28
  John, Deposition of., 26
Litewood
  John, a Tuscarora, 33, 34, 35
Little Tallassa
  a Cherokee town., 199
Loesch
  Jacob, 187
  Mr. Jacob, 186
Lokert
  Alexr., 191
Long Board, a Tuscarora., 65
Long Island, 203, 218
  on Holston River, 220
Long Island on Holston, 194, 241
Long Island on Holston not to be included in land ceded by the Indians., 239
Long Island on Holston River, 192

Lovick
  J., 21
  John, 21
Lowry
  George, an Indian trader in Toquo., 230
Lunt
  Ezra, 65
  Ezra, Acct., 86
Luton
  Tho., Foreman, 21
Luttrell
  John, 220, 221
Lying Fish
  A Cherokee Indian, 209, 252

M

Mackilwean
  Jas., 189
  Mr. Francis, Deputy Surveyoy, 188
Maddison
  Mr., 192
Mague
  Lawrence, 19
Mankiller
  A Cherokee Indian from Highwasaw., 206
Mankiller of Great Highwassee a Cherokee Indian, 205
  Speech of., 205
Martin
  Alex, SS, 51
  Alex., 170
  Brice, 247

309

Index

Capt. Jo., 230
Maye
  Jas, 191
McCaughrey
  Cormick, 191
McCluer
  Arthur, 191
McDonald
  Mr., 199
McDowel
  Colo. Charles, 256
McEwain
  Jas., 191
McMillan
  Alexr., 191
  Jno., 191
Means
  Jas., 191
Middle Settlements, 226, 239
Milburn
  Saml., 54
Miller
  David, 184
  Isaac, a
    Tuscarora, 33, 35
  Isaac, a
    Tuscarora., 37, 38
  James, 191
  Nathl, 191
  Robt., 191
  Robt., Junr., 191
Mingoes, 202
Minshew
  Rd., 189
Mitchel
  Billy, a
    Tuscarora., 43
  David, 191
  James, a
    Tuscarora., 41, 42

  Jas., 191
  Thos., 191
Mitchell
  Billie, a
    Tuscarora, 33, 35
  Billy, a
    Tuscarora., 37, 38
  James, a
    Tuscarora, 33, 34, 35
  James, a
    Tuscarora., 37, 38, 41, 42, 45, 52
Mobile, 198
Moody
  Isaac, 292
Moore
  Thomas, 184
  William, Senr., 184
Mountain
  Cumberland, 219
Mountains
  Cumberland, 232, 235, 242
  High Rock or Chimney Top, 239
  High Rock or Chimney Top., 246
  Occonnee, 212
  Powels, 220
  Unacay, 211, 217
Murder
  of a white woman by Indians, 189
Murphy
  Charles, Interpreter., 207
  Wm., 184

N

NC Counties
  Albemarle, 18, 20, 23
  Albemarle, Provost Marshall., 19
  Anson, 180, 181, 188
  Anson, Petition for Patrol Company, 190
  Anson, Petition of Inhabitants, 188
  Anson, Petition of the Inhabitants, 187
  Bath, 24
  Beaufort, 22, 23, 24
  Bertie, 27, 28, 29, 32, 47, 71, 76
  Buncombe, 178, 179, 182
  Cherokee, 291
  Chowan, 4, 20, 27
  County of Franklin, 164
  Currituck, 27
  Green, 177
  Haywood, 292
  Hyde, 22
  Jackson, 293
  Macon, 289, 291
  Pasquotank, 27
  Perquimans, 27
  Rowan, Petition of the Inhabitants, 187
  Tyrell, 27
NC Towns

Index

Bathe Town, 10
Edenton, 19, 27, 28, 29, 70, 73
Fayetteville, 164, 165
Halifax, 70, 73, 80
Murphy, 287
New Bern, 18, 39, 44, 46
Newbern, 51, 69, 72, 80, 189
Raleigh, 57, 64, 77, 80, 82
Netop
  Billie, a Tuscarora, 33, 36
  Billy, a Tuscarora., 37, 38
Nevill
  Mr., 11
Newbern, 210, 237, 244
Newel
  Saml., 234
Newton
  Solomon, 293
Niagara, 201
Nicholson
  Nathan, 191
Nikson
  Richard, 25
Nixon
  Richard, 23
  Richard, Deposition of., 23
  Richd., 23
Nixson
  Richd., 24
No. Hampton, 84
Nolachuckey
  Inhabitants of., 226
Nolachucky
  Waters of., 225
Nonachuckie
  Settlements on., 219
Nonachucky, 239
North Carolina, 192, 196, 213
  Commissioners of, 192
Northern Tribes
  Raids against Kentuckie, 201
Northern Tribes of Indians, 252
Norward Indians, 200, 208
Notawagoes
  Sent out raiding parties., 201
Notchey Creek
  An Indian Town., 206
Nottawagoes
  Agreed to go to War with the Delawares against the white people., 201
Nottowagoes
  One of the Northern Tibes suffering from encroachment., 201

O

Oconostota
  a Cherokee Indian, 204
Oconostoto
  A Cherokee Indian, 214, 219
  A Cherokee Indian from Chota., 206
  A Cherokee Indian., 229
Oconostoto of Chote, 247
Odle
  Benjamin, 184
  G., 184
Ogg
  Geo, 163
  Geo., 164, 165
  George, 164
  George, Deposition of., 164
Old Raven
  A Cherokee Indian., 214
  His speech., 223
  Speech of., 214
Old Tasel
  a Cherokee Indian, 202
  Speech of, 202
Old Tassel
  A Cherokee Indian, 214
Old Tassell
  a Cherokee, 200
  A Cherokee Indian, 250
  a speech by, 200
  His speech, 227, 228
  His speech., 226, 239, 251
  Speech of., 217
Oliver
  Andrew, 54

311

Index

Oo koo ne kah, or
the White Owl of
Natchey Creek,
249
Oos ku' ah, or
Abram of
Chilhowey, 248
Ooskuah
a Cherokee
Indian, 214
Oostosse' the, or the
Mankiller of
Highwassa, 249
Ootossetch of
Highwassa, 248
Orkney
Lord, 14
Orr
Robt., 184
Oterson
Jas, 191
Oustassittee
A Cherokee
Indian, 214
Outlaw
Mr., 60
Over Hill Cherokees,
256
Over hill Towns,
252
Over Hill Towns,
239, 241
Overhill Cherokee
Indians, 192
Overhill Cherokees,
236, 246
Overhill Country,
253
Overhill Indians,
241, 245
Overhill Settlements,
231
Overhill Towns,
226, 245
Owen

Billy, a
Tuscarora., 37,
38
Owens
a Tuscarora., 37,
38
Owin
John, a
Tuscarora., 41,
42, 43
Owins
Billie, a
Tusacrora, 33
Billie, a
Tuscarora, 33,
34
John, a
Tuscarora., 41,
42
Owins, a Tuscarora,
33, 34

P

Painter
John, 292
Pamlico, 3
Park
Anthony, 191
Parks
David, 191
Patton
Jas., 191
John, 184
Robt., 184
Wm., 191
Pensacola, 211, 251
Troops at, 193
Philadelphia, 229
Pickens
General, 183
Pickering
Timothy, Letter
of, 184

Pidgeon
A Cherokee
Indian, 229
A Cherokee
Indian from
Notchey
Creek., 206
Chief of Notchy
Creek, 203
Pipe of Friendship
Known in Indian
lore as the
Peace Pipe.,
204
Pollock
Colonel Thomas,
17
Colonel Thomas,
Esqr., 20
Cullen,
Deposition of.,
19
Honorable
Thomas, Esq.,
16
Tho, 20
Thomas, 20
Thomas Junr.,
Esqr., 21
Thomas,
Deposition of.,
20
Thos. Junr., 21
Porter
Joshua, 23, 24, 25
Joshua, Esqr., 22
Mr., 8
Pot Clay
A Cherokee
Indian from
Chilhowey.,
206
Potclay
a Cherokee
Indian, 204

312

Index

Chief of
  Chilhowey, 203
  Speech of., 204
Powell
  Wm., 4
Precincts
  Beaufort, 12
President of the United States, 82
Preston
  Col. William, 193
  Colo., called Elk by the Cherokee., 228
  William, 254
  William, a Commissioner., 206
  Wm., 194, 197
Prestons
  Colo., 210
Price
  Thomas, Agent, 181
  William, 188
  William, Petition of, 188
Privateers
  Trade against, 5
Prout
  Joshua, 180, 182
Prouts
  Joshua, Petition of, 180
Pugh
  Billey, a Tuscarora., 52
  Billie, a Tuscarora., 41, 42
  Billy, 43
  Billy, a Tuscarora., 41, 42
  John, 43
  John, a Tuscarora., 52
  Molley, a Tuscarora., 46
  Thomas, 32, 33, 34, 37, 38, 39, 40, 41, 42, 43, 48, 49, 50, 51, 54
  Thos, Commissioner., 54
  Thos., 32
  William, 43
  William, a Tuscarora, 33, 34, 35
  William, a Tuscarora., 37, 38
  Wm., a Tuscarora., 45

Q

Quaker Meadows, 256
Quakers, 7
Quebeck
  Citizens from Quebec may have advised the Nottowagoes about white encroachment., 201
Queens Revenue, 6
Queluca
  A Cherokee Indian from Highwasaw., 206
Quitsney's Meadow, 29
Quu lu kah of Highwassa, 249

R

Raleigh
  N.C., 15
Randel
  John, a Tuscarora., 45
Randolph
  John, a Tuscarora., 52
Raven
  a Cherokee Indian, 202
  A Cherokee Indian, 219, 228
  a Cherokee Indian from Tellicho and a new town at its mouth., 206
  A Cherokee Indian., 230
Reading
  Lyonell, 4
  Mr., 4
Redd
  John, 247
Reed
  John, 247
Reeding
  Mr., Garrison, 17
Renfrew
  Christ. Thos., 187
  Christ. Ths., 186
Rhodes
  Elisha, 54

Index

Richard Henderson
and Company,
220
Richardson
Dan, 20
Riddick
Jo, 60, 66
Jo, SS, 61
River
Enoree, 191
Roanoke, 32
Rivers
Bare, 18
Bear, 18
Capefare, 13
Catabo, 188
Catauba, 187
Catauba, South
Fork of., 187
Catawba, 225
Chatooka, 16
Cumberland, 221
French Broad,
183
French Broad,
181, 183, 225
Holston, 192, 211,
220, 226, 231,
239, 242, 245,
246
Kentuckie or
Louisa, 221
Louisa, 220
Marrattuck, 40
Morattock, 64
Morattock, 77
Morattuck, 2
Neuse, 17
Nolachuckey, 226
Nolachuckie, 202,
239
Nonachuckey,
219
Nonachuckie, 246
Nuse, 12, 16

Ohio, 220, 221
Pamplaco, 12
Pamptico, 16
Pungo, 18
Watauga, 202
Roanoke, 32, 37,
48, 56, 59, 64,
77
Susquehannah, 37
Swannanoah, 181
Tugalo, 164
Watauga, 219
Weatuck, 13
York, 5
Roberts
Billie, 41
Billie, a
Tuscarora, 33,
34, 35
Billie, a
Tuscarora., 41,
42
Billy, a
Tuscarora., 37,
38, 42
Molley, a
Tuscarora., 45
Thomas, a
Tuscarora, 33
Thomas, a
Tuscarora., 45
Tom Roberts
Junr, a
Tuscarora., 42
William, a
Tuscarora., 45,
52
Robinson
Charles, 189
Robison
Captain James,
temporary
Agent., 252
James, 247
Rodgers

John, a
Tuscarora., 41
Roge
Jno., 20
Rogers
John, 42
John Rogers, a
Tuscarora., 37
John, a Tuscarora,
33
John, a
Tuscarora., 38,
41, 42
Rogers, a
Tuscarora, 34
Roggers
John, a
Tuscarora., 52
Rowan
Matt., 31
Rowan County, 256
Runaway Negroes,
241
Rutherford
Genl., 193, 194,
210
Jas., 184

S

Saccorusa, a
Tuscarora, 65
Savanukeh or the
Raven of Chote,
248
SC Towns
Charles Town, 12
Scotsmen, 198
Scott
Jas., 184
Seneca
In South
Carolina., 230

Index

John, a Tuscarora
or Seneca., 38
John, a
Tuscarora., 37
Thomas, a
Tuscarora., 37,
38
Senecar
John, a Tuscarora,
35
Tho., a Tuscarora,
35
Senicar
John, a Tuscarora,
33
Thos., a
Tuscarora, 33
Tom, a Tuscarora,
33
Sexton
William, 184
Sharp
Mr., His speech.,
240
William, 194,
247, 253
William, a
Commissioner,
206
Wm., 191
Sharpe
William, 194,
254, 256
William, a
Commissioner,
194
William, house
of., 257
Wm., 197, 257
Shelby
Capt. Isaac, 256
Col., 210
Col. Evan, 193
Colo., 218
Evan, 254

Mr., 192
Shelbys
Colo., 219
Sherrill
Jason, 292
Ships
Garland, 5
Merchant Ship, 5
Privateer Sloop, 5
Shute
Gyles, 22, 23, 24,
25
Siler
Jacob, 292, 293,
294
Sitgreaves
Jno., CS, 51
Ske' aktu kah of
Cetico, 249
Skeyuca
A Cherokee
Indian from the
Island Town &
Cetico., 206
Skia Tu Ka
A Cherokee
Indian from the
Island Town &
Cetico., 206
Skullaluska
A Cherokee
Indian, 214
Slade
J., 86
Jere., 82
Jeremiah, 86, 87
Slavery
Stealing of, 170
Smith
Benj, a
Tuscarora., 52
Billy, a
Tuscarora., 43
Henry, 54
Jno., Clk, 31

John, a
Tuscarora., 41,
42, 45
Major Daniel,
Clerk., 207
Richard, 4
Samuel, 85
Samuel, a
Tuscarora
Chief., 68
Samuel, a
Tuscarora., 65
Society Parish, 27,
28
Socket
Billy, a
Tuscarora., 38
Sockey
Billie, a
Tuscarora, 33,
35
Billy, a
Tuscarora., 37
Sope
Michl., 191
South Carolina, 194,
210, 213, 251
Spies on the frontier,
179
Spotswood
A., 15
Gov. Spotswood
of Virginia., 14
St. Michael, 38
Standley
David, 34
States
Georgia, 164, 181
Georgia,
campaign
against, 194
Maryland, 14
North Carolina,
180, 182

Index

South Carolina, 77, 179
Virginia, 9, 26
Stevenson
   Jno, 191
Stewart
   a British Agent, 198
   British Agent, 222
   Capt., 5
Still
   Isaac, 19
Stith
   B.H., 65
Stokes
   M, 67
   M, Clk, 66
   M, Clk, 60, 61, 70
   M., 66
   M., Clk, 67, 70
   M.,Clk, 70
Stone
   David, 86
   Mr., 86
   Zed, Commissioner. , 54
   Zedekiah, 50, 54
Storey
   Geo., 191
Stuart
   a British Agent, 196
   British Agent, Emmisary of., 211
   Mr., 36
Sun ne waut of Big Island Town, 250
Sunnuah
   A Cherokee Indian from the Island Town & Cetico., 206
Swain

Geo., 184
Swamps
   Chyahick, 29
   Quitsna, 41
   Quitsnoy, 64, 77
   Raquis, 64
   Roquis, 77
   Tacon, 41
   Unacawick, 41
Swann
   Sam, 31
Swiss and Palatines, 9

T

Tallassa
   a Creek Town, 193
Tarapine
   A Cherokee Indian from Highwasaw., 206
Tarleton
   Capt., of Liverpole, 5
Tassell
   His speech., 229
   Objected against giving up the Great Island on Holston River., 247
Tate
   Robt., 191
Taylor
   William, a Tuscarora, 33, 34
   William, a Tuscarora., 37, 38

Wm., a Tuscarora, 33
Tellicho
   An Indian Town, 206
Tha ta qulla, or the Potclay of Chilhowey, 250
Thalhoona Koo
   An Indian messenger., 255
The Great Chain, 207
The Island Town
   A Cherokee Indian Town., 206
The Lords Commissioners For Trade., 14
The Old Tassel
   A Cherokee Indian from Toguse., 206
The Raven
   A Cherokee Indian, 247
   A Cherokee Indian from Chota., 206
   His speech, 240
   His speech., 233
   His speech., 235
   Speech of, 218
Tholloweh, or the Raven from the mouth of Tellico River, 248
Thomas
   Thomas, a Tuscarora., 52
   Tom, a Tuscarora., 41, 42

Index

Thompson
  Lewis, 46
Tille' hau' ch, or the
  Chesnut of
  Tellico, 249
Toguse
  An Indian Town.,
  206
Tom, 191
Toos tooh, from the
  mouth of Tellico
  River, 248
Toqua
  An Indian Town.,
  217
Travis
  Edwd, 25
Travise
  Edwd., 24
Treaties
  Treaty with the
  Indians, 181
Treaty, 1
  Tuscaroras with
  the U.S., 62
  With Overhill
  Cherokees, 192
Truewhitt
  Levi, 4
Tufdick
  Lewis, a
  Tuscarora, 33,
  34
  Lewis, a
  Tuscarora., 41,
  42, 43, 45, 52
  West, a
  Tuscarora, 41
  West, a
  Tuscarora., 41,
  42, 52
  Whitmel, a
  Tuscarora., 42

Whitmel,
  Tuscarora
  Chief., 41
Whitmell, a
  Tuscarora., 41,
  42, 45, 52
Tuffdick
  Lewis, a
  Tuscarora., 37,
  38
Whitmill, a
  Tuscarora., 46
Withmell, a
  Tuscarora., 47
Turner
  James Esqr., 85
  Mr., 60
  Simon, 50, 54
  Sn,
  Commissioner.
  , 54
Tus ka sah, or the
  Tarapine of chiles
  tooch, 250
Tuscarora
  Nation of., 85
Tuscarora Nation,
  44
Tuscarora Indian
  Lease, 43
Tuscaroras
  Commissioners
  appointed., 72
  Land reverts to
  the State in
  1916., 76
  Lands reverted to
  the State in
  1916., 69
  Longboard, Chief,
  78
  Longboard,
  Chief., 71, 72,
  79, 83, 86

Sacarusa, Chief,
  71, 72, 79, 86
Sacarusa, Chief.,
  71, 78
Sam Smith, 83
Samuel Smith,
  Chief., 71, 72,
  78, 79
Saquaresa, Chief.,
  83
Treaty, 75
Treaty Ratified.,
  82
Tuscarora War.,
  44
Tuskarora Nation
  Commissioners
  for., 54
Tuskaroras
  Indian Nation., 41
Tuskiga old Towns
  Cherokee Indian
  towns., 219
Tuskuga
  A Cherokee
  Indian Town.,
  206
Twightwes
  One of the
  Northern
  Tribes., 201
  Sent out raids on
  white people
  above the Falls
  of Ohio, 201
Tylor
  Nicholas, 4

U

Unacas[?]
  Plantations, 183
United States
  Interests of, 192

Index

Utaseh or Norward Warrior A Cherokee Indian from Tellicho and a new Town at its mouth., 206

V

Validity of private purchases from the Cherokees., 220
Vance
  D., 179, 184
  David, 178, 179
  David, Petition of, 179
Vann
  Joseph, 230
  Joseph, Interpreter., 207
  Joseph. a half Indian, 199
  Mr. Joseph, 199
Virginia, 194, 196, 204, 213, 215

W

Wachovia, 186, 187
Wade
  Colo., 181
  Thomas Junr, 181
  Thomas Junr., 181, 182
  Thomas, Indian Trader, 180
Waetton
  Philip, Constable, 19

Walker
  John, a Tuscarora, 33, 35
  John, a Tuscarora., 37, 38
Walston
  Jno., 54
War with England, 207
Ward
  Bryan, an Indian Trader., 164
  Mr., 163
  Mr. Bryan, 163
Warlicks Mill, 187
Warriors Ford, 232, 242, 246
Washington
  County of., 242
  Genl., 229
  George, President, 170
Washington County Troops in, 193
Watauga, 238
  County of., 241
  Inhabitants of., 226
  Settlements on., 219, 224
  Waters of., 225
  White settlements on., 219
Watauga & Nolachuckie, 238
Watauga and Nolachuckie Inhabitants of., 238
Watson
  William, 54
Wattaugah Line, 181
Webster
  Moses, 184

Welsh
  Wm., 184
West
  Capt., 24
  Collo. Robert, 19
Whealer
  Hary, a Tuscarora, 35
Whiskey Delivered, 199
Whitaker
  Nat. C., 65
White
  Jno. Junr., 21
  Wesley, 17
White Hall, 210
  An early trading center in southeast Bladen County., 210
Whitmel
  West, a Tuscarora., 43
Whitmell
  W., a Tuscarora., 45
Wiggins
  James, 41
  John, a Tuscarora, 33, 35, 37
  John, a Tuscarora., 38
Wikle
  Henry, 292
Wilkinson
  Mr., at Keowee, 237
Willanawaw of Toquoe, 248
Willanawaw or To Tac Ka Ch A Cherokee Indian from Toguse., 206

Index

Willenewau
  a Cherokee
    Indian, 202
Willey
  Chief of Tuskega, 256
William
  Williams, 32
  Williams, 32
  Williams Junr., 43
Williams
  B., 57
  Benjamin, 59, 60
  J., CC, 165
  John, 19, 220, 221
  Samuel, 41
  William, 32, 33, 34, 37, 38, 39, 40, 41, 42, 43, 48, 49, 50, 51, 54, 55
  William., 42
  Williams, 33, 37, 42
Williamsburgh, 244
  in Virginia, 194
Williamson
  A., 211
  Andrew, 213
  Andrew, a Commissioner for South Carolina, 213
  Col., 194, 217
  Col., letter from., 210
Williamsons
  Colo., 210
Wilson
  James, 184
  Jas., 191
  Richd., 20
  W., 184
  Wm., 86
Wine Oak
  Charles Junr., a Tuscarora., 41, 42, 43
  Charles Senr., a Tuscarora., 41, 42
  Charles T., a Tuscarora., 43
Wineoak
  Charles Junr., 41
  Charles Junr., a Tuscarora., 41
  Charles Senr., 41
  Charles Senr., a Tuscarora., 41, 42
Wineoak Charles, a Tuscarora., 45
Wingate
  Edward, 22
Winget
  Edwd., 20
Winston
  Joseph, 194, 197, 206, 247, 253, 254, 256
  Joseph, a Commissioner, 194
Withro
  Jno., 191
Wms. Burgh
  in Virginia, 195
Wms.burgh, 207
Womack
  Jacob, 247
  Major, 256
Wright
  Sir James, of Georgia, 181
Wyatt
  John, 26

Y

Young
  Mr. Saml., Deputy Surveyor, 188
  Thos., 191
Young Tassel
  A Cherokee Indian, 209

ABOUT THE AUTHOR

WILLIAM L. BYRD, III has been involved in genealogical and historical research for more than thirty years. His primary areas of interest are Native Americans, African Americans, West Indians, East Indians and Moors in Virginia, North Carolina, and South Carolina.

He has been published by the *North Carolina Genealogical Society Journal*, the *Magazine of Virginia Genealogy*, *The Rowan County Register*, and *The South Carolina Magazine of Ancestral Research*. He has also co-authored articles with Sheila Stover in the *North Carolina Genealogical Society Journal*, *The Augustan Society Omnibus*, the *Pan-American Indian Association News*, and the *Eagle: New England's American Indian Journal*. He has received an "Award of Special Recognition" from The North Carolina Society of Historians in the category of "The History Article Award" for preserving North Carolina history.

He is a U.S. Army Veteran from the Vietnam era, and served with the U.S. Armed Forces Overseas. He is currently retired, and resides with his family in Hickory, North Carolina.

CB ЕО

Other Heritage Books by William L. Byrd, III:

Against the Peace and Dignity of the State: North Carolina Laws Regarding Slaves, Free Persons of Color, and Indians

Bladen County, North Carolina Tax Lists: 1768 through 1774, Volume I

Bladen County, North Carolina Tax Lists: 1775 through 1789, Volume II

For So Long as the Sun and Moon Endure: Indian Records from the North Carolina General Assembly Sessions, & Other Sources

In Full Force and Virtue: North Carolina Emancipation Records, 1713-1860

North Carolina General Assembly Sessions Records: Slaves and Free Persons of Color, 1709-1789

North Carolina Slaves and Free Persons of Color: Chowan County, Volume One

North Carolina Slaves and Free Persons of Color: Chowan County, Volume Two

North Carolina Slaves and Free Persons of Color: Pasquotank County

North Carolina Slaves and Free Persons of Color: Perquimans County

Villainy Often Goes Unpunished: Indian Records from the North Carolina General Assembly Sessions, 1675-1789

Other Heritage Books by William L. Byrd, III and John H. Smith:

North Carolina Slaves and Free Persons of Color: Burke, Lincoln, and Rowan Counties

North Carolina Slaves and Free Persons of Color: Hyde and Beaufort Counties

North Carolina Slaves and Free Persons of Color: Iredell County

North Carolina Slaves and Free Persons of Color: Mecklenburg, Gaston, and Union Counties

North Carolina Slaves and Free Persons of Color: McDowell County

North Carolina Slaves and Free Persons of Color: Stokes and Yadkin Counties

www.ingramcontent.com/pod-product-compliance
Lightning Source LLC
Chambersburg PA
CBHW071955220426
43662CB00009B/1143